The
Best Years
of
YOUR LIFE

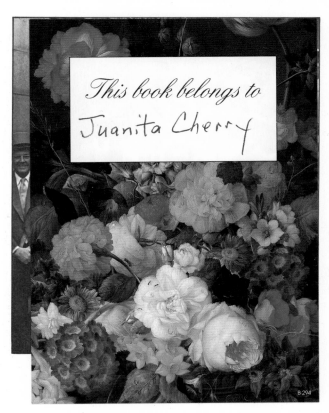

This book belongs to
Juanita Cherry

B 294

The Best Years of YOUR LIFE

Dr. Miriam Stoppard

Special photography by Camilla Jessel

Ballantine Books · New York

For my Mother and Father, Bobbie and Ken,
and all their friends

Library of Congress Catalog Card Number: 85-90874

ISBN: 0-345-30763-1
This edition published by arrangement with Villard Books

Cover design by Georgia Morrissey

Manufactured in the United States of America

First Ballantine Books Trade Edition: April 1986

10   9   8   7   6   5   4   3   2

Preface

Up until recent times very little attention was paid to our special needs as we grew older. Our mature years were quite commonly regarded as a time of increasing decrepitude and frustration. Today, however, we certainly expect to live longer and we are in a position to benefit from modern scientific discoveries with regard to prolonging good health and the current re-thinking of life choices. As a result, for most of us this period is the most important in our lives. It has become increasingly necessary, therefore, to provide products and philosophies that will sustain people throughout this very important period – a fact borne out by the increasing attention paid to this age group by all areas of society. It is my hope that this book, with its practical, positive outlook and wealth of useful information should add years to a reader's life, or at the least, make it a healthier and happy one.

Contents

Retirement 185

This is the time in our lives when we are required to make abrupt changes in our standards of living, daily activities and social contacts. Here, the sociological, ethnic, psychological and financial issues of retirement are discussed as well as pre-retirement plans and preparation.

Specialist help 199

It can be useful to consider help from various other health specialists as long as you bear in mind that you can't necessarily expect outstanding results. Your doctor will advise you of the benefits or disadvantages.

Special medical problems 211

The special conditions that show as we get older occur because our bodies' machinery is shifting down a gear and this alters the way they work. This chapter considers the warning signs that may represent something dangerous so that you are aware of them and can seek appropriate medical help in good time without feeling alarm.

Living with long-term ailments 265

Fifty onward is a significant stage in our lives when we may not be as fit and healthy as we would like, or we may have a partner or parent who needs our special attention. Here are suggestions for various aids to overcome any lack of full mobility or any other long-term ailment.

Adapting your environment 297

This chapter illustrates the best methods to "age-proof" the house in order to make it more comfortable and safe, and it introduces some of the numerous labor-saving devices available.

Growing through life

Today, we expect to live a good deal longer than our ancestors did. At age sixty-five the average life expectancy of men is seventy-nine and women eighty-three. This means that the majority of us live one third of our lives beyond fifty. It is not surprising then that there is a clamor for products and philosophies to enable us to get the most out of this important period in our lives.

Research has shown, irrespective of gender, that people with the greatest feeling of well-being are the older ones – at last we have arrived. Our satisfaction with life, however, depends on success in the spheres of work and social relations. Through these we may find mature love, true friendship, the freedom to make independent choices, self-respect, and a fulfilling lifestyle.

Throughout our mature years we constantly search for some meaning in life and by middle age we are in a better position to confront this question. Now is the time for us to step back from the rat race and consider those dormant skills that hitherto we have not had the time and courage to develop. The tendency is to think that we have stopped growing. The truth is that growth in the latter one-third of life can bring ultimate happiness.

Fifty plus

It's time to have confidence and pride in celebrating our fiftieth, sixtieth and seventieth birthdays. No longer need we worry so much about what other people think or say, and we needn't be as concerned with saying the right thing at the right time to the right people.

Women and middle age

Many women find their greatest happiness in middle age. They have passed the menopause, their grown-up children have left home and they are friends with them, but not confined by them; they have a firm feeling of their own identities for the first time. They feel less lonely, less bored and more in tune with their inner needs and the outside world.

Women in middle age are more likely to report no major fears for the future. Generally, women thirty-five to fifty feel better about themselves than they did when they were younger, and they may even reach a new level of sexual pleasure. This is a very different view of the life-cycle from that held by younger women. For many, a sense of accomplishment influences how smoothly they enter middle age. For most, a satisfactory job can help this transition as the mothering role diminishes. Paid employment seems to contribute most to self-esteem.

Adjustment can be difficult for women who have interrupted their careers for family life. Such women were obviously independent and achievers with many intellectual interests when they were younger. During the long years of marriage they suppressed their ambition to become conscientious wives and mothers. As they enter middle life many of these women report that their energy levels seem to be going down, their weights going up and their spirits, especially as the youngest child leaves home, are sinking into despondency.

The intelligent "doers" manage to pull out of this as they disengage from their mothering roles and are stimulated to revive their more assertive goal-oriented skills.

Many women feel excited as they move into their fifties. They start to be themselves, they no longer repress their anger or carry on trying to be perfect in order to make everyone love them. It could even be the time when women realize they could be better off without the men who have kept them in unsatisfactory, bad marriages.

Some studies show that there are women who find life increasingly satisfying in their fifties and even more rewarding as they get older.

Men and middle age

The picture is not quite the same for men at this age. They are likely to feel distinctly dissatisfied at fifty: worried about health, career and missed opportunities and aging. However, research has proven that satisfaction follows the same path as with women—satisfaction rises.

Men, like women, quite mistakenly feel that getting older is synonymous with things getting worse. The pattern of milestones within a man's life is more volatile than a woman's, men's ups and downs occur more frequently and usually at different times from women's. Nonetheless, it seems probable that older men are happier and more satisfied with life than younger men.

Men who are more satisfied with life and happiest are those who have expanded their interests well beyond those provided by their careers. By the age of fifty if not before, they are involved in art, music, gardening, dancing, cooking and community service – all things that lead to self-esteem and the discovery of leadership qualities they didn't know they had. They walk or jog, play strenuous sports and get involved in outdoor activities with their children and friends. They feel more relaxed, laugh more, and get more aesthetic enjoyment out of their environment! Many men in their fifties and sixties

SATISFACTION WITH LIFE

Gail Sheehy in her book *Pathfinders* describes a questionnaire relating to members of the American Bar Association. Those lawyers who were judged to be happiest and most contented were almost all older than forty-seven. Those who were older than fifty-five thought life was wonderful and were loving it, but the most contented age group of all consisted of lawyers over the age of sixty-five.

Ages 37 to 45
"Not enough time for anything but work."
"Obsessed with money and material success."
"Feel this is my last chance to pull away from the pack."
"Worry about becoming trapped by others finding out I am not as good as they thought I was. About messing up my personal life."
"Uncertain about my objectives. Ambivalent about my values."
"Envy the spirituality of others."

Ages 46 to 55
"Finally feel I have it all together."
"Secure enough to stop running or struggling."
"Easy to relax, open myself to new feelings, take vacations."
"Not so concerned about what others think of me."
"More willing to help others, not so competitive and compulsive."
"Feel that time is running out."
"Suddenly notice my friends are looking old and unhealthy."
"Was over-monitoring my own health."

Ages 56 to 65
"Delighted to see vigor of life is continuing."
"Pay more attention to my body and I am in better physical condition than I was five years ago."
"Sex is still important."
"Feel a new tolerance. Formed companionship with my mate."
"More focus on the spiritual dimension."
"Vacations are essential."
"Less concerned with money, more concerned with comfort."

feel an opening up of their expressive, artistic and intuitive lives, the "feminine" sides of their characters, which they repressed as part of their younger "macho" image.

Opportunities for the future

One of the most reassuring thoughts of all is that we have special strengths and new potentials in middle age that we don't have at any other time of life and that usually find their expression between forty-five and sixty. Here are some of them:

- Relaxation of stereotyped roles.
- Greater assertiveness in women.
- Greater expressiveness in men.
- Being free to say what we think.
- Being free to pick up past interests.
- More time and money for ourselves.
- More tolerance toward others.
- Greater opportunities for companionship with our partners.

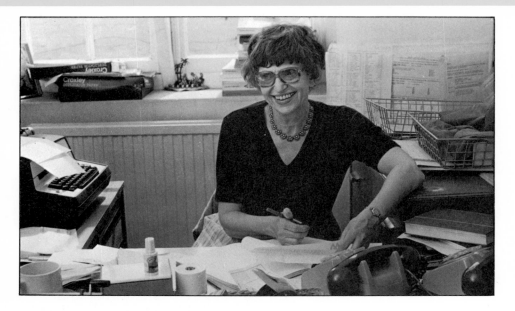

- A chance to make new friendships with our children.
- The possibility of contributing to the community, and having time for hobbies.

By the time we are in middle and later age we know ourselves better than at any other stage in our lives. We know who we are, what we need, and how to get it. All we have to do now is make the effort in the best way we know how.

One of the mistakes that all of us make at every age is believing we'll be doing the same things, having the same interests, same aims, same friends, the same preoccupations. If we imagine having a brisk game of tennis now and imagine trying to do that in twenty years' time, of course it's depressing. But chances are we won't be doing that or wanting to. If we're still playing tennis, the game will depend more on finesse than speed, and be just as pleasurable for that. But luckily tennis could be replaced by leisurely and sociable lawn bowling, golf and other relaxing sports that open up new interests and friends for us.

Most of us are quite rightly stubborn about resisting any pressures that may be put on us to reduce our daily commitments because removal of anything prominent in our lives may, we think, lead to a vacuum. This need not necessarily be so. Research has shown conclusively that release from demanding, lengthy work means more enjoyable leisure time, closer family ties and better physical health. Our fifty plus years are increasingly being considered a normal and expected phase of the life path we look forward to, prepare for, and enjoy.

What we forget is that each age has its own pleasures and its own excitements. No one I've talked to who is contented with life as he or she grows older will admit that life is any less thrilling or less challenging. This is because our view of life and what makes it satisfying and fulfilling changes, if we let it and don't fight against it. It's as though the prescription for our eyeglasses changes as we get older so that we see the same things in a different way. Different enough so that what we wish and what we can achieve are not disparate. And this is as you'd expect. We'd be a sadly adapted race if we hadn't learned how to make each of our ages successful and happy. The truth about our mature years is that we've learned most of the lessons and consolidated them, so if we allow ourselves to grow we stand a greater chance of achieving happiness than at any other time in our lives.

The rewards are marvelous to enjoy. Remember those words by Ezra Pound: "One of the pleasures of middle age is to find out that one *was* right and that one was much righter than one knew at say seventeen or twenty-three."

Society and the older generation

Why should the number of years we have lived be considered so important? Physical, mental and social ages are far more important than chronological age. We have to resist the relationship that society tries to create between chronological age and human value. Ten years older does not mean ten years worse. It means ten years more valuable. Many of us overlook the important fact that society *needs* us as we get older. Of course, society has need for "junior" and "senior" people but there is no need to press people into premature responsibility or premature retirement or, for that matter, to hold them back from opportunities they wish to pursue regardless of age. We would all be helped if we bore in mind the difference between aging and being old. As aging is a continuous process over the years, it should be looked on more as a dynamic change or set of changes, rather than a cliff we jump off at a certain time.

Turning the clock back

We will probably see "old age" rolled back for quite a time to come. Very recently, statisticians would define "old" as sixty-five. More and more, this definition is moving toward seventy-five. This makes more sense in terms of life span and the activity older people can enjoy if they are encouraged to. In the USA the mandatory retirement age is now in the process of being moved back to the age of seventy – a sign that a government recognized the retirement age of sixty-five was an increasingly inappropriate one. Renaldo Madure, the anthropologist, found a colony of artists in northern India in which the oldest members were encouraged to be at their most creative and to advance themselves and their art on into old age. In the West, people reach an early peak and then face years of doing little. At last this is changing.

There is a move to stop pushing older people aside. More of us are realizing that people and society take leave of each other whenever they want to with mutual consent. There is a lessening in the extent to which society steers people to the sideline. Of course, there is a natural tendency for older people to remove themselves from the mainstream of society. What we have to guard against is discrimination and segregation of the older members of society as a matter of political expedience.

Most of us nowadays accept that we are older; this is "successful aging" (see *Keeping a tranquil mind*), which means that we have the inner calmness, confidence, experience and maturity to be of great benefit to society for many years to come. Of course, in order to be able to do this we must keep as physically active as we possibly can.

In the past, old and young alike worked together as best they could on whatever tasks had to be done to keep the family and the community in a healthy state. Older people worked as long as they were able and the young worked as early as they were able. It was the way a person functioned that determined when he or she entered and departed from the work force.

In today's world the young and old are increasingly excluded from this role. The basis for this is not biological, because children and older people are generally healthier and stronger than their ancestors; it is cultural. People are defined as too young or too old for much longer periods of their lives than they ever were before. We have to guard against this sociological type-casting. We must begin to see aging as it was seen not so very long ago, as a ritualistic progression from having one's worth measured in terms of productivity through experience to wisdom and seniority.

Keeping physically fit

Good health is not the prerogative of the young. Researchers in the USA have recorded that many people remain active and fit until well after their late seventies. However, as our bodies begin to age from our early twenties onward, they require special attention if we are to keep them as fit as possible. This chapter therefore concentrates on the initiation and maintenance of good health habits at as early an age as possible, and the adaptation of routines to meet changing lifestyles. Feeling physically well, rather than just being not ill, involves adjusting our health habits to accommodate natural changes.

Knowing what and why changes occur as we get older means that we can make sensible decisions about changes in diet, exercise programs, skin care, smoking and drinking habits, choice of clothing, sleeping patterns, even about where we live and work. Most important, we can put these changes into practice early enough to offset some of the undesirable aspects of aging.

Nutrition, diet and aging

"We are what we eat," is a well-accepted adage. "How we eat is how we age," also has a good deal of truth in it. There are several theories that relate aging to dietary intake. Some researchers believe that cell death and regeneration have a dietary component, and most people accept that diet plays an important part in the development of some of the diseases that accompany aging.

In the UK at least, the medical world is convinced that adequate dietary intake of fiber can prevent such conditions as diverticulosis, cancer of the large bowel and possible heart disease. Too much sodium in the diet can aggravate high blood pressure, congestive heart disease, cirrhosis of the liver and fluid retention. Arterial disease seems to be related to the amount of fat and cholesterol in our diet. Refined sugars have been implicated by some researchers as major components in the development of heart disease, besides playing a role in dental caries and diabetes (see *Special medical problems*).

Changing calorie needs

Although the number of calories we need to take each day almost certainly decreases with age, there is no evidence to show that we need less nutrition. The quality of the food, if anything, should be higher than when we were younger.

Minimal requirements will keep away actual disease but they are not satisfactory; older people living at minimum nutritional levels may not have the reserves to get through a period of increased stress such as injury, surgery or infection.

The great bulk, at least 58 percent, of our daily calorie needs should come from *carbohydrates*. Those that are not used are converted to fat. Refined carbohydrates should account for no more than 10 percent of our total calories. Natural, unrefined, whole food (complex) carbohydrates such as fruit, vegetables, grains and cereals should comprise at least 48 percent of our daily diet, providing energy plus minerals, vitamins and roughage.

Naturally, our calorie needs depend very much on our age and the amount and type of activity we undertake and this should be reflected in our daily diet. Below, I have set out a

SAMPLE BALANCED DIET

Our bodies need energy to perform two functions: first, to keep all our basic body functions in good order; second, to provide the extra energy that is burned up when we do active exercise. Some of us are *fast burners* and manage to use up more energy than we consume, thus staying slim no matter how much we eat, while others are *sleepers*, using fewer calories than they take in and getting fat. As we get older our metabolisms do slow down gradually so we need to adjust our daily calorie requirement accordingly. In order to maintain our ideal weight we need to balance the calories we take in against those we expend each day.

Breakfast
tea or coffee (6)
2 fl oz (57ml) milk (36)
½ oz (14g) sugar (56)
2 oz (55g) muesli (210)
2 oz (55g) slice of whole grain
  toast (136)
½ oz (14g) butter (105)
2 oz (55g) boiled egg (80)

Lunch
6 fl oz (168) tomato soup (120)
2 oz (55g) cheddar cheese (190)
1 oz (28g) lettuce (30)
1½ oz (42g) beets (18)
2½ oz (69g) tomato (10)
1 tbs french dressing (60)
2 oz (55g) slice of whole grain
  bread (136)
½ oz (14g) butter (105)
5 fl oz (124g) fruit yogurt (110)
coffee or tea (0); 2 fl oz (57ml)
milk (36); ¼ oz (7g) sugar (28)

Dinner
¼ melon (30)
4 oz (112g) roast beef (320)
4 oz (112g) green beans (8)
4 oz (112g) roast potatoes (120)
4 oz (112g) stewed apples (76)
1 glass red wine (22)

complete diet which, with added snacks and drinks throughout the day, will provide approximately 2000 calories daily.

Protein needs   These should provide 12 percent of total daily calories. There is no great change in our protein needs as we get older. There is some evidence to show, however, that if we are stressed by infection, gastro-intestinal problems, surgery and other illnesses, we lose more protein from our bodies than we did when we were younger, and this leads to a relative increase in our protein needs during illness. This is particularly important information for those of us taking a marginal protein diet. A low protein intake is often the result of the high cost of protein-rich foods or the inability to chew properly.

Fat needs   These should provide no more than 30 percent of total daily calories. Our bodies' need for fat doesn't change with age at all. The American Heart Association recommends reducing the level of saturated fatty acids to less than 10 percent of our total calories. The remaining 20 percent should be evenly divided between mono- and polyunsaturated fats.

Mineral needs   Iron, calcium and potassium are the three minerals that may present problems as we get older. Iron deficiency is fairly common at any age, but it is a difficult mineral to absorb. The tendency to develop an iron deficiency anemia is worsened as we get older because of poor diet and because blood may be lost from the gastro-intestinal tract through such things as a peptic ulcer, hiatus hernia or diverticular disease (see *Special medical problems*). An interesting study in Scandinavia has shown that the hemoglobin level of a person − a good measure of iron deficiency − is often associated with the inability to chew foods rich in iron.

Meat improves the absorption of iron from other foods, and if we are unable to chew meat as we get older we may develop iron deficiency anemia. Potassium deficiency is often caused by bouts of diarrhea or treatment with diuretic agents, though physicians are usually careful in the latter case to give potassium supplements. There is no evidence to suggest that our calcium needs increase as we get older, but the use of calcium by the body is certainly related to sex hormones, to a sufficient amount of vitamin D in the diet and to the exposure to sunlight required for the Vitamin D to promote calcium absorption. Over the age of sixty-five calcium supplements may be necessary to counteract osteoporosis (see page 232).

Vitamin needs

Vitamin C

Our vitamin needs do not alter as we get older. Foods rich in vitamin C may not only be expensive but also heavy to carry and this makes them difficult to handle. A relatively cheap source of vitamin C, the potato, is often mistakenly eliminated from diets in attempts to lose or maintain weight. It is important for us as we get older to take some foods containing vitamin C every day, as it is believed that our ability to retain vitamin C in our bodies decreases.

Vitamin B

Although the incidence of vitamin B deficiency seems to become more common as we get older it is not always related to an insufficiency in our diets. Our gastro-intestinal tracts may become less able to absorb vitamin B12 as we get older and so injections may be required to correct the deficiency.

Deficiencies of the vitamin *riboflavin* are rare; soreness at the corner of the mouth, or greasy skin around the curve of the nostril, suggest a problem. Green vegetables, eggs, milk and liver are good sources of riboflavin. This vitamin is resistant to heat but not sunlight – so milk should not be left in the sun.

Vitamin A

This is found in all dairy products, liver, fish and green, yellow and red vegetables. As we grow older we may become faddy about milk, butter and cheese and we may find vegetables hard to chew and digest, leading in some cases to a vitamin A deficiency. However, this is not very common. Recent research suggests that vitamin A may be protective against the development of certain cancers.

Vitamin D

As we get older we tend not to go outdoors as often and therefore we have less opportunity to expose our skin to the sun. If this happens, lack of vitamin D, necessary for calcium absorption, may occasionally become a problem, especially if we have reduced our intake of milk. Milk is not always very popular because it can lead to digestive problems; the best sources of vitamin D are fortified milk and fish liver oils.

Unbalanced diet

One of the effects of not eating the right vitamins is that our diet becomes unbalanced, even though our intake of calories may be adequate. This results in obesity. We may selectively reject the most nutritious foods, along with meat, and balance our calories by taking in foods containing hardly any nutrients at all, for example, refined flour, refined sugar, fat

FACTORS AFFECTING WHAT WE EAT

At all ages we are affected by psychological, social and domestic factors that determine the sort of food we eat and its quality and quantity. So too is food influenced by our lifestyles. Some studies have shown that as we get older we attach more importance to the social reasons for eating foods than to nutrition. Other factors can contribute:

Teeth

If we have lost teeth or have problems with our dentures, then we are likely to avoid foods that are hard, sticky and difficult to chew, opting for those that are softer and easier to chew. This can lead to a lessening in the amount of fiber in the diet, with bowel complications. Chewing problems are all too real.

If we wear dentures we have to chew food four times as long as a person who has teeth to masticate our food. The more teeth we lose, the less efficient we become at chewing. Any chewing problem is made worse by our producing less saliva and having dry mouths. This makes mastication difficult and swallowing hard.

Smell and taste

As we get older our senses of smell and taste become less acute. This doesn't just make food less savory; it may also actually suppress our appetites, so that we tend to eat less good food as we get older. As our sense of taste goes we may begin to overseason foods. This can irritate our mouths and other sensitive parts of our digestive tracts. Adding too much salt can contribute to high blood pressure, heart disease and malfunction of our kidneys.

Certain medical conditions such as a stroke or Parkinson's disease, arthritis and certain sight disorders can mean that we suffer a decline in the very fine co-ordination needed for cutting food, lifting it to our mouths and chewing. All our fine co-ordination declines to a certain degree as we get older, but difficulties with handling utensils, appliances and foods make eating less pleasant.

Habit

Many of us claim to feel discomfort after eating certain foods. This becomes more and more common as we get older. What's more we tend to become somewhat entrenched in these attitudes and feel recalcitrant about changing dietary habits to the extent that they become fads. This kind of inflexibility can sometimes lead to dietary deficiency and certainly to an unbalanced diet.

Income

If our incomes become reduced, we have to buy smaller quantities of food. Sales or quantity discounts are no longer available, and many of the packaging and marketing ideas in stores are geared toward younger, wealthier consumers.

Psychological reasons

For all of us food is a comforter. As we get older we may seek solace in eating to help us over the loss of a loved one. It is not uncommon for the loss of a mate or a friend to cause great dietary upset. The loss of companionship can affect our desire to shop, cook, eat and our ability to remain interested in food. Widowers in particular suffer. Having been taken care of most of their lives by loving spouses, they find themselves unable to make the same effort when they are alone. The worst nutritional problems occur among elderly widowers. Women, however, when they find themselves bereft of a partner, may very well retain their ability to look after themselves, but will often no longer have the financial resources to do so.

and alcohol. An excessive intake of empty calories, along with the rejection of high-quality foods, results in obesity.

Obesity is prevalent as we get older and it is considered to be the most important one of medical problems today. There are many statistics to show that obesity shortens life and increases the severity of certain diseases.

However, as we get older, a bad diet has an ever-increasing negative effect on how we cope with life. It reduces our potential to become rehabilitated after having any disease and it means that recovery from major fractures and strokes is more difficult. There are absolutely no physical benefits to being overweight. Over-eating, over-drinking, and over-smoking are never good, but as we get older they not only can ruin our enjoyment of life, they increase aging and may make serious illness fatal.

Dietary fat and health

There is an association between diets rich in saturated fats and coronary heart disease. This may mean that the more saturated fats we eat, the more likely we are to die of heart attacks. In Europe, the Scandinavians are the people who eat the most animal fat and they also suffer the most heart attacks. The Italians, who eat the least animal fat, though a lot of vegetable fat, suffer least from heart attacks. In certain primitive cultures, with diets of mainly corn and beans and very little meat or eggs, heart disease is virtually unknown. There is a tribe living in northern Mexico whose members are not known to have suffered from cardiac or circulatory disease. These people are thin and small and weigh on average less than 133 pounds (60 kg). Their daily calorie intake is well below the level recommended by nutritional experts in developed countries who say that these tribesmen are undernourished. However, these people can run races lasting a continuous 48 hours, maintaining a steady pace of 6 miles an hour for over 150 miles. They can chase a deer until the animal has dropped from exhaustion! Could it be that the Western nutritionists are wrong; that these Mexicans are ideally undernourished and we are overnourished?

Almost all animal fats are saturated, and almost all vegetable fats are unsaturated. Saturated fats are "saturated" with hydrogen atoms and this gives them a high melting point. They are, therefore, solid at room temperature – like lard, for instance. Unsaturated fats have empty spaces in their molecules instead of hydrogen atoms, and this lowers their melting point; thus they are liquid at room temperatures – like vegetable oil. It is thought that very unsaturated fats (polyunsaturated) may even remove some of the fatty deposits from the coronary arteries, though this is still a controversial point.

Most authorities would agree that it's a good rule to keep the amount of fat in your diet low, be it animal or vegetable – no more than one ounce (28g) per day. It is better to substitute vegetable oil for lard, and soft margarine for butter.

Foods vary in the amount of saturated and unsaturated fats they contain, though their calorific values are identical. We still do not know how cholesterol causes heart disease, but a statistical association between high blood cholesterol and heart disease has been proven. It is, therefore, a wise step if we avoid foods that contain large quantities of cholesterol. The yolks of eggs and shrimp are particular rich, so as a preventive measure we should eat these foods sparingly and indeed avoid them altogether if we have heart trouble.

A number of studies have shown that the incidence of heart disease is lower in areas where the drinking water is hard. So if you are going to install a water softener in your domestic water supply, make sure it leaves the drinking water untouched.

Dietary guidelines from the American Heart Association will promote a healthy heart. Though you may have to change your lifestyle to follow them, you may well live a little longer.

TIPS FOR A HEALTHY HEART

To control your intake of cholesterol-rich foods:
- Eat no more than three egg yolks a week, including eggs used in cooking.
- Limit your use of shrimp and organ meats.

To control the amount and type of fat you eat:
- Use fish, chicken, turkey, and veal in most of your meat meals for the week; use moderate-sized portions of beef, lamb, pork, and ham less frequently.
- Choose lean cuts of meat, trim visible fat, and discard the fat that cooks out of the meat.

- Avoid deep fat frying; use cooking methods that help to remove fat – baking, boiling, broiling, roasting, stewing.
- Restrict your use of fatty "luncheon" and "variety" meats like sausage and salami.
- Instead of butter and other cooking fats that are solid or completely hydrogenated, use liquid vegetable oils and margarines that are rich in polyunsaturated fats.
- Instead of whole milk and cheeses made from whole milk and cream, use skimmed milk and skimmed milk cheeses.

The American Heart Association recommends a fat-controlled, low cholesterol daily meal plan to reduce the risk of heart attack. It includes 2 servings (6-8 ounces total) of cooked meat or fish (3-4 ounces, not including fat or bone) or nuts, dried beans and peas (3-4 ounces); at least 4 servings of vegetables and fruit (including at least 1 serving of a vitamin C source and 1 of a vitamin A source); 4 servings of whole grain bread and cereals; 2 or more cups of low fat milk products (skim milk, buttermilk, skimmed milk yogurt and cheeses); 2-4 tablespoons polyunsaturated fats and oils (margarine, salad dressing, shortening); the intake of cakes, pastries, ice cream, etc., should be restricted severely.

In Britain vegetarian diets are often prescribed for people who have suffered from heart disease. Doctors usually prescribe diets for heart patients on an individualized basis.

A balanced diet The rational approach to good nutrition as we get older is exactly the same as when we were younger. We need to aim at an intake of natural foods in the amounts needed to provide the essential nutrients, including high quality protein – to at least a minimal level, and to take in only sufficient calories for

CORE FOOD LIST

Food Group		Amount to Use Daily	Approx. Kilocalories	Approx. No. of *A.D.A. Exchanges
Breads (4 servings per day):	Bread or toast (whole grain or enriched)	2 slices	140	2
Cereal (whole grain or enriched)	Cooked OR Ready-to-eat	1/2 cup 3/4 cup	70	1
Potatoes or substitute (white)	Baked or boiled OR Mashed potato OR Rice, pasta	1 medium 1/2 cup 1/2 cup	90	1
Fruits (2 servings per day):	Citrus juice or juice of other fruits	3/4 cup	80	11/2
	Whole fresh fruit (peach, apple, etc.) OR Cut or sliced fruit, berries, grapes, etc.	1 medium 1/2 cup	70	1
Meat and meat substitutes (6 ounces (170g) per day):	Lean meat, fish, fowl (flesh only) (1 egg or 2 tablespoons peanut butter may be substituted for 1 ounce (28g) meat)	6 ounces	300	6
Milk and milk substitutes (2 cups per day):	2% Low fat milk (1 cup yogurt, 1 ounce cheese or 1/2 cup cottage cheese may be substituted for each cup of milk)	2 cups	300	2
Vegetable (1 serving per day):	"A" Vegetable (spinach, snap beans, cabbage, tomatoes, summer squashes, cucumber) OR "B" Vegetable (peas, lima beans, winter squash, carrots)	1 cup 1/2 cup	50	1
			*A.D.A. = American Dietary Association	
TOTAL CALORIFIC VALUE (per day)			1100	

maintaining our desirable weight. To meet this aim, the table of core foods (below) can be used as a general guideline for our minimal requirements. In general, the core food plan allows a variation of items within each basic food group. It doesn't allow changes in the food groups that provide the minimal amounts we need. Because there are differences in the amounts of nutrition we get from different foods, no one food group can be substituted for another – though calorie value seems the same. The core food list alone is hardly palatable as an everyday diet. It lacks those certain items that make food tasty (butter and other fats, and sugar) and 1100 calories a day is quite often not sufficient to maintain or approach a desirable weight. Most of us will want and require more than 1100 calories a day, and it is

ESTIMATING MEAT PORTIONS

All portions of fish, poultry and meat are two to three ounces (60-80g) cooked weight without bone, skin and visible fat

2-3 Ounces (60-80g) of Fish
1/3 cup canned tuna or salmon
1/2 cup cooked lobster, crab
5 medium clams, oysters
3 medium scallops
8 medium sardines
1 medium fish fillet

2-3 Ounces (60-80g) of Poultry
1 medium chicken leg
1 medium chicken thigh
1 slice chicken, turkey
1/2 medium chicken breast

2-3 Ounces (60-80g) of Meat or Substitutes
2 slices beef, veal, lamb, pork
1 x 3 inch (7.5cm) diameter beef patty
1 lamb or pork chop
1 slice Canadian bacon
4 tablespoons peanut butter

OPTIONAL FOODS

	Amount	Approx. Kilocalories
Fats:		
Butter or margarine	1 teaspoonful	34
Coffee cream	1 tablespoonful	32
Whipping cream	1 tablespoonful	55
Salad Dressing, French or Italian	1 tablespoonful	72
Mayonnaise	1 tablespoonful	93
Thousand Island Dressing	1 tablespoonful	90
Cooking or salad oil	1 tablespoonful	124
Sweets		
Sugar, granulated	1 teaspoonful	15
Jelly, jam	1 tablespoonful	55
Candy bar, plain chocolate	1 ounce	148
Desserts		
Apple pie	1/8 of 9-inch (22cm) pie	302
Cupcake, chocolate, iced	1 medium	203
Ice cream, vanilla	1/2 cup	147
Snacks		
Nuts, mixed	1/2 cup	438
Peanuts, shelled	1/2 cup	421
Popcorn	1 cup	64
Potato chips	1 cup	91
Pretzel	Medium size	78
Corn chips	1/2 cup	112
Cheese tidbits, nips	1/2 cup	110
Alcoholic Beverages		
Whiskey – bourbon, Irish, rye	1 ounce (28g) fluid	83
Scotch whiskey, gin, rum	1 ounce (28g) fluid	75
Wine	1 ounce (28g) fluid	33
Beer	12 ounces (340g) fluid	151

Standard measuring spoons are to be used and are to be filled level, not heaped.

important that we should know which additional foods can be allowed. It might be argued that as long as we are approaching, or are at our desirable weights, we can eat anything else that we want, such as butter, margarine, sugar, sweets, pastries, fried foods of any kind, and alcohol, but it is better to pursue a middle course. It is better for us if we try to eat larger amounts of natural foods, but you may find some of the optional foods listed on the previous page useful.

It is never easy to change the habits of a lifetime, and changing our eating habits is notoriously difficult. Shifts are no less difficult as we get older, but here are a few hints that might help you to change your thinking and your lifestyle with regard to what you eat, and on page 27 are some myths exploded.

TIPS TO ACHIEVE A BALANCED AND HEALTHY DIET

- Some of the most basic factors have to be tackled first. It is important that you face up to the fact that you may have some kind of chronic ailment that requires a special diet, that there may be social problems, that you may have difficulty in chewing, or that money might be short. If these difficulties are ignored, nothing else can be put right. So you should seek help from your doctor, social worker and therapists to help you to correct these factors as far as you possibly can.

- Go for as simple a diet as you possibly can. One that hasn't unneccessary restrictions, which caters to your likes and dislikes as much as possible, and one which allows you good food to look forward to with at least one or two treats a day. You are going to have to impose some kind of discipline on yourself, so decide that you are going to have yourself regularly weighed so that you can report your progress to your family and doctor.

- No goal can be achieved quickly, and you have all the time in the world, so set yourself realistic goals that can be reached in months or perhaps even a year. By this time, you will have achieved the additional goal of modifying your inadequate diet into a balanced and healthy one.

Our attitudes to food

The majority of people go into middle age eating an unhealthy diet, and most continue to eat the same diet until they die. Such a diet consists of many highly refined processed foods from which much of the goodness has been removed, where the flavor is artificially boosted with too much salt, too much sugar and, often, saturated fats. Snack foods are readily available and fast food restaurants encourage fast, often stressful, eating of junk foods.

Many of us are misinformed about our diets, and in the belief that we are following sensible guidelines we may be doing the opposite by eating too much protein and too many dairy products. We are conditioned to consume far more fat, sugar, calories and cholesterol than we need. If we haven't done so

The new foods I'm supposed to eat will be too expensive
In the first place you could cut your meat bills in half. Fresh food is much cheaper than processed food.

I enjoy my food a lot and don't want to give it up
You've learned your food preferences. It's not too difficult to unlearn them and learn new, possibly more enjoyable ones and you don't have to give up any food altogether.

I don't think I could change my eating habits, it would be difficult for me
It's easier if you make gradual changes. Tell your family what you're doing and they will support you.

I think I'm healthy as I am
If you're eating a typical Western diet you could be still healthier if you cut down on salt and sugar and become more vigilant about the amount of fat you eat for the long term.

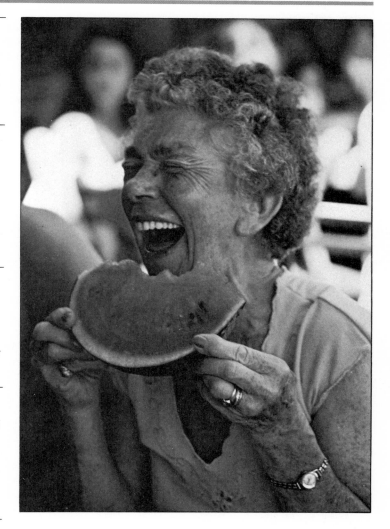

before, now is the time to call a halt. It's one of the simplest and most important ways we can help shape our futures for good health. This entails making adjustments to our diets, not sweeping changes but fine tuning, and none of the changes need mean deprivation. However, we can't expect to make many changes in life-long habits without feeling a certain amount of resistance. It is important that we take things easy at first, recognizing those areas that may act as stumbling blocks to our efforts.

Sticking to a chosen diet

Most people who reach middle age with a weight problem have tried, perhaps several times, to lose weight. Some people may have tried every diet available and still have not been able to lose as much as they would like. Others may have been able to take off weight only to put it back on, and so have had difficulty in maintaining a good weight. It's not the aim of this book to lay out examples of the many diets that have been popularized in the past; their plethora suggests that none has the answer.

The answer lies within ourselves. In our willpower and our determination to reach a good weight and stay there. The way to achieve this is not through intermittent dieting, certainly not through crash dieting (not advisable at any age but it does become more dangerous as we grow older) but through changing our eating patterns. We may feel demoralized at the prospect of having to try again to do something we've failed to do earlier in life. It is my hope that some of the following suggestions on *how* to change your eating habits will help you more successfully than those diet sheets and books that told you *what* to change.

One of the reasons why you stand a better chance of success this time is that any changes you make in your food patterns will affect your life, and its length, more than any change you tried to make previously. Losing weight will lower your blood pressure, your blood cholesterol, and so lower your risk of a heart attack. Just by losing weight you will feel more physically active. Your heart risk will drop again as you abandon your inactive lifestyle. Some of the relaxation techniques that are used for weight control will help you counteract stress in

IMAGERY TRAINING

Researchers at Stanford University believe that overcoming a craving can be helped by this drill — conjuring up images that make the craved-for food seem less attractive. Let's say that what you crave most is a nice, big fat steak and French fries. Get a basin of dripping or a block of lard from the refrigerator and look at it. Spoon some of it on to a plate. Feel it with your fingers. Now you are ready to start the drill.

1. Find a quiet place and sit or lie down.
2. Get as physically and as mentally relaxed as you can.
3. Think of your steak and French fries, the look, the smell, the overall picture.
4. Now think of the appearance and texture of the dripping that comes from the steak and French fries.
5. Imagine that this thick fat is slowly working through your arteries.
6. Link the image of the food with the sludge in your arteries.
7. Now think of a less fatty but delicious food — turkey.
8. Link this image with clean, healthy arteries throughout your body.

HOW TO CHANGE TO A HEALTHY DIET

CONTROL FAT AND CHOLESTEROL INTAKE

Reduce weekly servings of whole milk, cheese (other than low-fat cottage cheese), fatty meats (beef, lamb, bacon, spareribs, sausages, and luncheon meats) and ice cream by one-half. (Do not eat chicken skin.)

Change from ice cream to ice milk and from whole milk to non-fat milk

Reduce meat fat by trimming and by broiling or roasting instead of frying

Eliminate, except for rare use, intake of organ meats such as liver, sweetbreads and brains

Change from butter or hard margarine to soft margarine

Change from lard or shortening to unhydrogenated vegetable oil including olive oil if desired. Avoid use of large amounts of vegetable oils as you want to lower your total fat intake

Reduce consumption of egg yolk to no more than four a week. Use egg whites liberally

Reduce consumption of fast foods, processed and convenience foods

LOWER THE SALT IN YOUR DIET

Eliminate, except for rare use, high-salt items such as bacon, ham, sausage, frankfurters, luncheon meats, salted nuts, sauerkraut, pickles, canned soups, canned vegetables, potato chips and other salted snack foods

Switch from regular table salt to a light salt (one-half sodium chloride, one-half potassium chloride)

Gradually decrease salt use in cooking to about one-third previous levels; simultaneously decrease, and eventually eliminate salt use at the table

Explore the use of other flavors in your cooking – spices, herbs, lemon, wine, vinegar, are all tasty substitutes

WATCH THE AMOUNT OF SUGAR YOU EAT

Reduce comsumption of soft drinks by half. Limit intake to to two or three a week or switch to diet versions.
Gradually eliminate use of sugar in coffee or tea and on fruit

Substitute fruit for pastry, cake, pie, or other sweets in one-third of all desserts

ADD FIBER TO YOUR FOOD

Increase intake of complex-carbohydrate foods – including legumes (e.g. beans, peas, lentils), starchy root vegetables such as potatoes, as well as other vegetables and fruits

Gradually introduce lightly milled or whole-grained cereals into your food plan (e.g. whole-wheat bread and flour, bulgur, couscous, cracked wheat, rolled oats, brown rice, etc.)

Increase intake of whole fruits (fruit juices lack much of the fiber contained in whole fruits)

Increase intake of whole vegetables (vegetable juices lack much of the fiber contained in whole vegetables and often contain significant amounts of added salts)

LIMIT THE EMPTY HIGH-CALORIE FOODS

Reduce intake by one-third

Partially or fully replace such foods with complex carbohydrates

Because alcohol may add to weight control problems and may displace valuable nutrients, limit alcohol consumption so that no more than 10 percent of your total calorie intake is derived from alcohol, e.g. approximately two bottles of beer or three glasses of wine or two cocktails per day

"Don't foods"
It is very important that we avoid as many rich foods and their sources as we possibly can. There is a great deal of cholesterol in eggs, meat and milk and hidden salt in cake mixes and savory snacks.

everyday life, and unburden your cardiovascular system accordingly. You may have been through all this before and feel that you can't try it again. However, it's never too late to start again. It has been shown many times that small attentions to our lifestyle will benefit us immediately.

Coping with problem foods

Nearly all of us can manage to give up most of the high-calorie foods, but there are always one or two favorites that cause us problems. We may be convinced intellectually that we shouldn't eat these foods, but unfortunately this doesn't automatically cancel out our craving. Imagery training helps.

Conquering the urge to eat

Sometimes our eating urges can be almost too difficult for us to control. Don't wait for them to overtake you out of the blue. Instead practice a suppression drill that has been devised by behavioral scientists to prepare us for coping with the urge when it strikes. It can be made equally useful when trying to give up smoking.

SUPPRESSION DRILL

Try to practice the drill every day for a couple of weeks or so. It's different from the usual method of dealing with cravings because it makes you face the craving. It can be practiced at any time of the day or night.

1. Sit or lie down in a quiet room.
2. Think of the food you really want.
3. Concentrate on the food until you really want to eat it.
4. Imagine an unpleasant sensation connected with food — a bitter taste — and if this doesn't reduce your desire for the food go on to think of feeling sick, being fat, having dirt mixed with your food.
5. When the urge to eat is under control, relax as deeply as you can.
6. Reward yourself (not with food).

Maintaining our ideal weight

For all of us up to now, the major difficulty in our lives has been maintaining control of our weight, and we all need help against relapsing. Some of the major pitfalls to be on the lookout for are considered on page 31.

Eating socially

We mustn't fall into the trap of feeling that we owe it to our host or hostess, or ourselves, to reciprocate his or her hospitality by eating heartily. If the choice is open to us we must avoid rich, high, empty calorie foods. However, there's no need to reject them altogether if we don't have this choice; we might emulate one famous film star who dines out a great deal — she leaves half of everything on her plate, even if she likes it. I have a mental list of my favorite, healthy foods that are real treats and I choose these whenever I see them on the menu.

WEIGHT IN PROPORTION TO HEIGHT

Following are 1983 Metropolitan Life Insurance Company weight tables by height and size of frame, for people aged 25 to 59, in shoes and wearing five pounds of indoor clothing for men, three pounds for women.

MEN				WOMEN			
Height	Small	Medium	Large	Height	Small	Medium	Large
5'2"	128-134	131-141	138-150	4'10"	102-111	109-121	118-131
5'3"	130-136	133-143	140-153	4'11"	103-113	111-123	120-134
5'4"	132-138	135-145	142-156	5'0"	104-115	113-126	122-137
5'5"	134-140	137-148	144-160	5'1"	106-118	115-129	125-140
5'6"	136-142	139-151	146-164	5'2"	106-121	118-132	128-143
5'7"	138-145	142-154	149-168	5'3"	111-124	121-135	131-147
5'8"	140-148	145-157	152-172	5'4"	114-127	124-138	134-151
5'9"	142-151	148-160	155-176	5'5"	117-130	127-141	137-155
5'10"	144-154	151-163	158-180	5'6"	120-133	130-144	140-159
5'11"	146-157	154-166	161-184	5'7"	123-136	133-147	143-163
6'0"	149-160	157-170	164-188	5'8"	126-139	136-150	146-167
6'1"	152-164	160-174	168-192	5'9"	129-142	139-153	149-170
6'2"	155-168	164-178	172-197	5'10"	132-145	142-156	152-173
6'3"	158-172	167-182	176-202	5'11"	135-148	145-159	155-176
6'4"	162-176	171-187	181-207	6'0"	136-151	148-162	158-179

Losing enthusiasm

As with any "contract" made with our families and friends to help us make a change of habit, their enthusiasm starts to wear off after a while. Envy at our success may even creep in. We must attempt to keep them interested by making new goals.

Changing our personal lives

Our enthusiasm and morale may flag if our lives are abruptly interrupted by accident, illness, domestic problems, difficulties at work, extensive travel, etc. One of the best ways to protect ourselves against relapse is to be flexible, resetting our goals more realistically in the face of upset.

Sudden cues to eat

Just seeing a box of chocolates or smelling the aroma of cooking will stimulate our desire to eat. We can either decide it's not time for a treat and overcome our urge with suppression drill or, as long as we're realistic and truthful with ourselves, we can allow ourselves a treat.

Rewarding our achievements

Most of us are stingy with ourselves over rewards. If we're attempting to change our basic habits we should reward ourselves for every step of progress we make, with positive, encouraging statements, pleasurable activities, symbolic rewards and material rewards. They are important. They increase morale and renew enthusiasm.

HEALTH HAZARDS OF THE WESTERN DIET

Substance	Protein	Calcium & milk	Sugar
Average consumption	12% of total calories consumed	For many children 4 glasses a day. For many adults 2 glasses a day	128lbs of sugar per year per person and 24% of total calories are derived from sugar
Hazard to health	Animal protein contains animal fat, e.g. an untrimmed sirloin steak is 70% fat in terms of the number of calories it provides. Trimmed, it is still 45%. A near vegetarian diet provides more than an adequate amount of protein. All the rest we eat is possibly hazardous	It's important to reduce the amount of butterfat we eat (70% of the calories in cheese is from butterfat); see hazards to health of saturated fat	It may promote heart disease by increasing the levels of certain lipoproteins that are associated with atherosclerosis; it contributes to tooth decay
Food	All animal proteins, but especially red meat and dairy products	Full-fat milk, butter, cheese, dairy products from full-fat milk	All commercially-baked foods, cake mixes, ice cream, canned fruit, puddings, sweets, chocolate, biscuits, pickles, sauces, canned beans, liquor, sodas
Alternative food where possible	White meats, fish, low fat dairy products, vegetable proteins like legumes, nuts, the skins of fruit and vegetables (jacket potatoes)	Skimmed milk and skimmed milk products. Low-fat cheese	Fresh fruit and vegetables, whole grain rice, potatoes, legumes (beans, peas and lentils), cereals, low calorie drinks, natural sugars like fructose and dextrose
Action	Reduce protein intake to 8-10% of total calories consumed. Not all of this need be in the form of meat, or even animal protein. Start to take meat as a condiment	Reduce your daily intake of milk	Alter ratio of refined to unrefined carbohydrates so that emphasis is on unrefined food. Cut down on intake of sugar as a whole
Benefits & comments	Fewer problems with obesity. The benefits are the same as those when restricting cholesterol and saturated fats	Whole milk can be harmful. We would be not less well getting the calcium we need from vegetable sources; broccoli, artichokes, and greens are all high in calcium; so is non-fat milk, low-fat cheese	There is no biological need for sugar as such. Sugar tends to be linked to the rest of the carbohydrates, including the complex ones, have fallen into disrepute because of "low carbohydrate diets"

Salt	Cholesterol & saturated fats
10-20/day (1g/day is ample for health)	15% of total calories eaten
It leads to elevated blood pressure. Some races consume 1g/day or less and their blood pressure is much lower and doesn't rise with age. Solomon Islanders who cook their food in sea water have high blood pressure	Animal fats in general are saturated. Vegetable fats except palm oil and coconut oil are unsaturated. The animal fat in shellfish, poultry and wild game is less saturated than in red meat. Cholesterol levels are closely associated with saturated fat intake and they influence the incidence of heart attacks and strokes
Hidden salt in bacon, cake mixes, cheese, peanut butter, crackers, chips, salted nuts, canned fish, soups, canned vegetables & vegetable juice, frozen vegetables, pickles, French fries, cookies, bread, sausages, corn flakes	There are large amounts of cholesterol in egg yolks, shellfish, organ meats such as liver and kidney. There are significant amounts of cholesterol in all meats. Nearly all animal foods have some cholesterol as do cakes
Wholegrain bread and cereals, fresh vegetables, fruit, fish, meat, untreated nuts, puffed rice, shredded wheat	Cholesterol is absent from all vegetable foods. Low fat milk, cheese, yogurt, egg whites, chicken without skin, turkey, soft margarine
Gradually reduce intake to wean your palate back to being salt sensitive	The American Heart Association suggests that less than 10% of total calories should be derived from saturated fat
Elevated blood pressure level drops. There is no biological need for a high salt intake. Salt tastes are learned, so they can be unlearned. Heavy salt users can tolerate loss of salt	Low cholesterol levels and low saturated fat diets can slow down and sometimes halt the development of atherosclerosis. There is no proof yet that they will prevent heart attacks (they have many causative agents) nor is there any to suggest they do any harm. My own opinion is that we should lower our intake of cholesterol

33

Hazards of the Western diet

Research has shown quite conclusively that the majority of people living in Western countries are eating an unhealthy diet. In addition to eating too much fat, we also eat too much sugar and too little fiber. In the chart on pages 32-33 I have outlined those hazards in diet that we should attempt to avoid, where they occur, how best to go about avoiding them and the benefits that will follow.

Exercise

A decrease in physical activity is directly related to aging. Exercise greatly helps the metabolism of food by the body, and it will relieve tension and promote mental well-being as well. If for any reason our vigor decreases, our desire and ability to take part in physical activity is affected. Mental stress from depression and anxiety can further dampen our desire to participate in any kind of physical activity. A chronic cycle of less activity and more stress, withdrawal and depression may follow, with results that are very worrying.

Inactivity— stress syndrome

The inactivity-stress syndrome becomes more common as we grow older. It adversely affects our energy and motivation no matter what we attempt to do. It is infectious, it pervades all aspects of our everyday living and it follows that we get less out of life. We are able to participate less, enjoy ourselves less, and we become less and less happy – no further argument is needed in favor of retaining our physical activity.

As we get older, however, we can no longer rely on having mobile joints, supple muscles and strong bones. Our insurance policy is exercise. Exercise promotes an agile, healthy body that will respond quickly. We need to have strong muscles that can maintain effort and give us stamina. Just as important, we need to have healthy minds that are eager to encourage our bodies. None of this will happen if we neglect our bodies. They have to be put through their paces regularly to bring them up to the level of physical fitness that must be maintained. Exercise will keep us young.

How exercise keeps us young

Heart benefits
It may decrease the risk of a heart attack. Much medical research has shown that there is a relationship between inactivity and coronary heart disease. There is also research that shows a connection between exercise and lowered risk of heart disease. It has been shown that high levels of high density lipoproteins (HDLs) are associated with a lower incidence of

heart attacks. Later studies have shown runners to have elevated HDL levels, possibly putting them at lower risk of heart attacks.

Exercise is also important in the rehabilitation of heart attack patients, who usually undergo graded exercise programs to get them back to full and active lives. It makes the heart stronger by widening the arteries, making a complete blockage, by, for instance, a blood clot, less likely.

Psychological benefits

Anyone who has exercised will tell you about the sense of euphoria felt after completing an exercise program. This is not just due to the satisfaction of having done something well, it is a hormonal effect. If we exercise we will release many beneficial hormones throughout our bodies. One of them affects our state of mind. It counteracts depression and makes us feel tranquil and generally content with life.

Muscle and joint benefits

There is no doubt that if we exercise regularly we will have healthier muscles, joints and tendons, resulting in fewer aches and pains such as fibrositis, lumbago, sciatica and even arthritis. The health of our joints and bones depends largely on the strength of our muscles, ligaments and tendons because these support and protect them. All of these are improved by exercise. Stiffening of the joints and limitation in the range of joint movement, unyielding muscles, inelastic ligaments, poor posture and softening of the bone can all be legacies of an inactive life and are not easily put right.

Lung benefits

Through exercise the efficiency of our hearts and lungs is improved to the point where they can take care of any emergency. Their health is such that they can spring to action and cope with the demands of our bodies. We can walk, run and play for longer. In other words our bodies become more tolerant of exercise, and our physical working capacities increase. Our body metabolisms improve. If we exercise regularly, our bodies become lean and our muscle-to-fat ratios improve. These are the bodies that the best athletes have. During exercise cholesterol and triglyceride, both of which are associated with heart disease, drop markedly. Appetite is suppressed by exercise, and carbohydrate metabolism and ability to cope with sugar is significantly better in those of us who exercise, no matter how moderately. One of the most significant benefits which will come as a result of exercise is that we will not feel so breathless.

We look better, younger

There is hardly one aspect of body function that is not affected by exercise, but most important, particularly as we get older, is posture. We cannot hold our bodies properly without strong back muscles; these keep our spines erect. In this respect, posture is not only important if we are to look better as we grow older, it is also a protection against developing backache. The bones of the spine tend to soften as we get older, particularly in women. We may lose height because the vertebral bones tend to become thinner.

However, with good, strong back muscles, even slight softening of the spine can be mitigated, preventing rounded shoulders and an aging hump from developing. Just as important, an erect spine holds the chest at maximum capacity so that our lungs can work efficiently. Not only are our chests helped, so are our hearts and the muscles of our chests that help our breathing. Our digestion is helped by an erect spine. Strength and mobility exercises help to prevent a hesitant, shuffling walking pattern; joints remain supple, the tendons don't tighten and weaken. This strength gives us confidence so that there is less likelihood of our falling and fracturing bones.

Guarding against back pain

Our spines take a tremendous amount of wear and tear in our everyday lives. The amount of movement that occurs in the neck as we move our heads from side to side and up and down causes a great deal of strain.

Because of its crucial position in the body, the spine is subjected to strain all day and most of the night, too, if we don't sleep on a mattress that supports the back. Think of the stresses on the lower part of the back from all the bending, stooping, twisting and turning that we do in the course of a normal day. An artificial joint would wear out in a very short time given this amount of stress, so that it is not surprising that the spinal joints tend to wear out, too. If we stand or sit, lift or bend wrongly, walk incorrectly, or drive in a bumpy car, we are overworking our spines and their muscles and ligaments. Even if we do not injure them we overtire them, and this can lead to backache and pain.

Because the lower back is pivotal in all the movements of the body, once it has been injured it rarely returns to normal. No matter how much care is taken to make sure that the injury has healed, there is always a certain weakness left. It is, therefore, very important to learn how to use your back properly, in order to strain it as little as possible to prevent injury from ever recurring. As a result of good posture, the spine is rested and the ligaments and muscles in the back do not suffer from any strain and the nerves are not compressed by the bones.

Good posture   There are proper ways to stand, sit, bend, lift and walk that throw the strain of all these movements on to much stronger muscles and joints than the spine. These joints are more stable and less likely to be injured. The intervertebral discs between the spinal bones can be injured so very easily. They take so long to heal that it is worth protecting them; it makes common sense to use the stronger muscles and joints that do the work of the spine in order to protect it from being overstrained.

Standing
To assume good posture when you are standing, hold your shoulders firmly but not rigidly backward and downward with your head up and your stomach pulled in. There is nothing "sergeant-major-like" about it. If you fix your arms to your sides and your shoulders back too rigidly, you will find that your breathing is restricted. Just taking up this posture helps to accentuate the curvature of the spine and to keep it well supported by the muscles of the back and shoulders.

Good posture

Bad posture

The most stable position for the spine (a pile of 24 tiny bricks stacked one on top of the other) occurs when it is supported by the muscles of the back. This is maintained by holding shoulders straight and down, and chin slightly at a right angle to the neck.

Bad posture flattens out the natural curves, putting pressure on muscles, joints and ligaments. The result will be aches and pains.

TIPS FOR POSTURE

- Practice walking along in a straight line, so that you correct any tendency to walk with your feet too far apart or with your toes pointing out.

- When you walk, try to balance your head and upper and lower torso in line.
- Try to center your body over the balls of your feet.
- Also, lead with your thigh, not your foot.

Sitting

At work and at home we spend much or our time sitting, so we should make sure that we use well-designed chairs. A chair that is good for posture is one that keeps the angle of the spine to the hip at about 120 degrees, ensuring maximum comfort and minimum strain on spinal joints and spinal muscles. In addition, a well-designed chair should be convex where the back joins the seat so that the lower part of the spine is well supported. Look out for this feature when you are buying a new chair and when you are buying a car.

Sit back on the seat of the chair and make sure that you are comfortable and upright with your shoulders and head balanced over your hips. Whenever you reach forward from this position don't reach forward from the arms but bend from your hips. You can practice sitting correctly and stretching forward in the proper way so that it feels natural and comfortable.

Driving

We spend a great deal of our time driving, and it is essential for both driving comfort and safety that our car seats be designed to support the lower part of the spine. If you have a car in which the seats do not provide enough support, most car accessory shops can provide you with a cushion that can fit into the lower part of your seat to provide you with support.

Sleeping

Considering that we spend approximately one-third of our lives asleep, it is worth paying some attention to the sort of mattress we sleep on. While most of us love fluffy, downy, soft mattresses, they are extremely bad for our backs since they allow our spines to curve outward. A firm mattress is much better than a soft one. Old-fashioned beds with a box that provides an inflexible base are better than those without. Most of us know someone who, having injured his or her back, has been told by a doctor that the best way of curing back pain is to put an old door underneath the mattress to support the back during the night. What is good when we are in pain is even better when we are not. It prevents an overworked spine from being strained more than is absolutely necessary.

Avoiding back injuries

Many back injuries occur when we attempt simple, everyday tasks in the wrong way or when we are doing something very strenuous when unfit. There are right and wrong ways for us to use our backs.

LIFTING, BENDING AND PUSHING

It's important to maintain good posture when lifting or carrying heavy weights or bending. Not only does it make life easier, it also save unnecessary wear and tear on muscles and joints. Here are some tips to help every day.

Kneel right down when doing a job at floor level, such as cutting a dress or weeding. Stooping is very tiring and a strain on the back.

To shift a big weight, such as a wardrobe, push with the back not your hands. It's always best to ask for help.

To lift a large or heavy object, bend down from the knees, not the waist. Carry a heavy package close to the body, not out in front. Again, bend when putting it down.

How fit are we?

Before we can aim for the right level of fitness for our ages we must know how unfit we really are. This can be assessed in a simple way by examining the response of our hearts to exercise. Strenuous exercise is that which increases the oxygen requirements of the body above normal. Incidentally, our hearts and lungs are only exercised when we increase our oxygen requirements above normal. This happens when exercise involves large muscle groups such as those of the legs, the hips, the pelvis, the arms and the shoulders, as it does in jogging, swimming, cycling and rowing. We measure the response of our hearts by taking our pulses.

If we have unfit hearts they will start to beat very fast when we exercise strenuously because this is the only way they can pump more blood around our bodies to keep up with our increased demand for oxygen.

A fit heart, however, will not beat as fast because it can pump out more blood with each beat than an unfit heart. Anyone who has been told by a doctor that he or she has had heart trouble, should not undertake any heart or lung exercises. Even if you have no symptoms, consult your doctor before undertaking any aerobic exercise program.

TAKING YOUR PULSE RATE

Age	Pulse rate
50-54	117
55-59	113
60-64	109

To get an idea of how fit you are, run on the spot for 30 seconds, then take your pulse (count beats for 15 seconds and then multiply by 4). This is your pulse rate for mild exertion. Consult a health professional to learn the proper method if you have any trouble.

When you exercise, your pulse rate should not go any higher than the rate you have just calculated. The aim of heart and lung exercise is to keep up this pulse rate for about 15 to 20 minutes. The pulse rate you should be aiming for is shown.

"Whole-body" exercises

The aim of "whole-body" exercises is to maintain a pulse rate for a period of ten minutes of continuous exercising. As a margin of safety, your pulse rate must go no higher than the personal pulse rating that you have calculated. If, after running on the spot for 30 seconds, you find your pulse rate is at your personal pulse rating, you can continue taking your pulse every minute or so to make sure that your heart is not being overstrained. If, after 30 seconds, your pulse rate is higher than your personal rating, then you must wait and and rest until it falls. You should continue to do this every half minute or so if the exercise increases your pulse rate beyond your personal rating. When you are very unfit you must stop your exercises frequently for rest periods. It is very important to do so to make certain that you do not overstrain your heart.

As we improve our fitness we will be able to go for longer periods without raising our pulse rates above our own personal ratings, and we will have to rest less often. We will achieve our goal when we are able to exercise continuously for ten minutes without our pulse rate going above our personal rating. To do these exercises properly we are going to have to become very familiar with taking our own pulses.

Clothing We must pay some attention to our clothing and make sure that it looks and feels just as we want it: loose; comfortable; absorbent. Shoes should be light with plenty of room for our toes to move about and good support over the arches of our feet, say with laces. Track shoes are ideal.

Warm-up exercises We should always start off with some warming-up movements to get our joints and muscles working. The following are ideal: arm circling, done standing with feet wide apart and arms hanging loosely; side bends standing with feet wide apart and hands on hips; and trunk and hip bends, standing about 18 inches (0.5m) behind the back of a chair with hands and arms outstretched, and alternate ankle reaching, standing with feet wide apart with both palms resting against the front of the upper left thigh (see page 42).

These warm-up exercises improve the mobility and flexibility of our bodies ensuring that they stay as supple as possible. They help to promote agility and good posture. When we are exercising we should start off with the warm-up exercises or mobility exercises. We should then go on to the strengthening exercises, which help to increase our muscle power so that we can go through our daily tasks easily and prevent undue wear and tear and injury. Last of all come the heart and lung exercises, which give us endurance and the stamina to make a sustained effort. These are sometimes called aerobic exercises and they have become very popular recently.

Mobility exercises These are designed to take all our major muscles and joints through a complete range of movement. Once we have achieved mobility fitness we will be able to move, stretch, twist and turn in all direction with freedom and without feeling any discomfort or pain in our muscles or joints.

Strengthening exercises These are designed to enable our bodies to cope with the extra effort we are sometimes called upon to make in special circumstances, so we build in a safety margin of extra strength over and above the normal requirements. It is important that we have this reserve because when it is not there, making a sudden and extreme effort can result in damaged muscles, ligaments and tendons and even a slipped disc. To build up those extra resources we need to increase the duration and force of the exercise we take, a little at a time.

Strength will not suddenly arrive when we start exercising, it will develop as we start doing things we know we are capable of on a regular basis. Walking up a nearby hill to the store is better than going to the store at the other end of the street.

WARM-UP AND MOBILITY EXERCISES

Arm swings and shoulder rolls (5 times)
Stand with your feet slightly apart and swing forward with your right arm, then backward. Repeat with your left arm. Now slowly roll each shoulder forward and then backward in a full circle.

Body bends (3-5 times)
Stand with your feet slightly apart and place your hands on your hips. Bend slowly forward as far as you can manage and then backward. Take this exercise gently at first.

Body turns and side stretches (5 times)
Again stand with your feet apart. Now turn your body to the right and back and then to the left and back. Next, place your left hand on your left hip and extend your right arm over your head. Now change hands.

TIPS FOR EXERCISE

- Always find out how fit you are before you start on an exercise program, and if you are in any doubt about your fitness, check with your doctor.
- Always choose activities and exercises that you enjoy, or you will never stick to your exercise program.
- Exercises shouldn't be a chore. If they are, you are doing the wrong ones.
- Exercises should never be physically punishing. If they are, you are pushing yourself too hard.
- The best form of exercise is one that fits in with your daily life, like taking the dog for a walk, cycling to work or to the store, climbing stairs rather than taking the elevator, and doing the odd bit of exercise while you are working at the sink.

- There is no need to spend a lot of money on expensive equipment. You can do all your exercises effectively without buying anything.
- Never exercise on a full stomach. Always wait at least an hour. Spend a few minutes loosening up before beginning your strenuous exercises.
- Never be overzealous about increasing the length of your exercises too rapidly. Slowly and surely should be the motto. Always check your pulse rate so that you reach the level of fitness suitable for your age over a period of weeks, and this should never be less than six weeks.
- Once you have reached your level of fitness try to exercise at least three or four times a week to maintain it.

NECK, SHOULDER AND ARM EXERCISES

Arm circling (3 times)
Stand erect with your feet slightly apart and your arms by your side. Bring one arm forward, upward and backward to make a large circle. Next reverse the direction of the swing.

Shoulder swings (10 times)
Lean forward with your feet apart to as close to 90° as you can comfortably manage and swing each arm from side to side across your body. Next, swing both arms together.

Neck rolls (3-5 times)
Let your head fall forwards, then slowly pull it up. Let it fall to the side then pull it up again.

Arm lifts (3-5 times)
This is quite a vigorous exercise so do take it easy at first. It's not necessary to hold weights, in this case books, to gain strength and mobility. Stand with your feet apart, your knuckles facing away from your body (far left). Now raise your arms horizontally, slowly turning your hands so that your palms face the ceiling (center). Finally, raise your arms to meet above your head (left). Slowly reverse to the starting position.

BACK, HIP AND LEG EXERCISES

Single knee pull (5 times)
Lie on your back on the floor and grasp one leg with both arms so that you can pull it back onto your chest. Then hold for the count of 5 before repeating with your other leg.

Leg lifts (5-10 times)
Lie on your side and raise your leg as near to 45° as you can manage and hold for the count of 2. Then lower. Try to keep your leg straight.

Ankle circling
Sit down and cross your legs. Now, slowly trace a circle with your toe. Repeat this motion with your other foot.

Reaching and bending (3-5 times)
Stand erect with your feet slightly apart and one hand in the air. Breathe in and stretch upward as far as possible still keeping your feet flat on the ground. Now, breathe out slowly, bend over and touch the ground between your feet. Do bend your knees if you feel the need because this is quite a difficult exercise to master. Repeat the exercise with your other arm.

Groin stretch (3 times)
Stand with your feet as wide apart as possible and your back straight. Bend knee forward and count 5. Then rise onto your toes for the count of 3.

Calf stretch (3 times)
Stand facing a wall. Lean against it and let your hips hang forward for the count of 5. Then rise onto your legs for the count of 3.

Thigh stretch (3 times)
Stand at a right angle to the wall, for support. With your free hand pull your ankle up toward your bottom and hold for the count of 5.

Fitness playing sports

Playing sport of any kind is a valuable way of looking after our health, keeping our bodies supple and agile. It also involves getting out of the house and a change of surroundings. Through sport we manage to meet other people and keep our social lives active and varied.

Many sports are played outdoors, which is a good deal better and more interesting for us than remaining indoors all day. Whether we win or lose they bring a great deal of physical and emotional satisfaction, because they involve perfecting quite complex, physical movements, which can bring the joy of achievement. If we play team games, team spirit can do wonders for our morale, and simply being a member of the team gives us a sense of being needed and a feeling of security in belonging to a group. The social aspects of sport also make a great plus.

Renewing our interest

If we gave up sports completely when we were young, or were never interested in them, it may be worth thinking about trying one again. We may always have had a desire to take up a particular sport but never had the time. Well now we do and we mustn't be put off by the fact that we are getting older. Many sports can be taken up for the first time quite successfully in our fifties and sixties. I know of a newspaper editor who took up skiing at the age of fifty-three, and now, as he approaches sixty, he manages the moguls also like a young man. I have seen old couples on ski slopes. Not, of course, racing downhill, but taking things easily and gracefully on safer, shorter skis. As long as we prepare ourselves for skiing with several weeks of mobility and strengthening exercises before we go away, this is a wonderful sport to take up.

Knowing our limits

We mustn't rely on playing a sport to keep us fit. We may be fit enough to play most sports without being really physically fit. This is because most sports don't require use of the large muscles of legs, arms, pelvis and shoulder girdle for any length of time. They don't exercise the whole body to the point where the heart and lungs are being fully stretched. The only sports that do this are running or jogging, swimming, cycling and, possibly, tennis. To really exercise the body well at any of these sports, however, we need to do them briskly.

There is absolutely no need for us to play a sport flat out, either to enjoy it or to keep ourselves healthy. We should participate at our own speed, with people who want to play it at about the same speed and with the same force and enthusiasm.

45

Swimming

This is for almost all of us the perfect sport. Once we are immersed the water takes the weight off our bodies, so that our limbs become weightless and our joints are relieved of strain. Just floating in water is a treatment in itself for our muscles, joints and bones. The water supports all our movements through the full extensions of our joints and limbs, so that we can exercise with very little discomfort. As a result, our joints can gain in flexibility and our muscles can gain in movement and elasticity with us hardly being aware of it.

Swimming is good for the whole body, exercising all our muscles. If we do it for pleasure, even once a week, we can do much to keep our bodies flexible and strong. It is extremely good for relaxation and rehabilitation after an illness, especially for our backs and legs. Swimming can also be used as a method for keeping fit, though it would involve swimming fairly hard for twenty to thirty minutes at least four times a week.

Tennis

This is an enjoyable, sociable sport that we can play at any age. It is particularly good for keeping our shoulders, arms, and legs supple and strong, and helping our co-ordination. Tennis is also very good for our posture and for keeping our youthful stride, and it can be played at any pace.

It's a sport that enables us to socialize before and after playing. It's important to play tennis at a steady pace at first, with partners of similar ability.

Golf

Although golf is not a sport that will keep us fit, it's very good for improving our strength, flexibility and muscular co-ordination. Because golf is mainly walking, and slow walking at that, the calorie expenditure is quite low – about 1000 calories for eighteen holes. So it really can't be used as a means of shedding weight. The amount of energy that we expend during golf depends a great deal on whether or not we carry our golf clubs, or drive ourselves around in a golf buggy.

Obviously we will be fitter if we do the former, but as we get older it's very nice to take things more easily and slowly, with less strain and fuss. Carrying our clubs will certainly exercise our bodies and our hearts more than traveling around in a buggy. It has been shown that the heart rate will rise to an average of about 113 beats per minute if we carry our clubs, whereas it stays at a fairly steady 80 if we drive around in a cart. Thus we are asking our hearts and lungs to work about 50 percent faster if we opt for carrying our clubs. Remember that having a drink at the 19th hole may gain us more calories than we used in playing the game.

Cycling

Here is an excellent way to exercise as it involves the whole body, and again it is one of those sports that we can regulate according to how much we want to work our bodies. If we cycle steadily and energetically for twenty minutes or more, it's an extremely good way of increasing the strength and endurance of the whole body, including our hearts and lungs.

It is one of those sports that can make us physically fit in tip-top condition as it's very good for strengthening the large muscles in our bodies and it is also efficient at strengthening our knees, ankles and hip joints.

It is also very good for the shoulders, though we don't often notice that we are using them. Because some roads are now very busy it might be worth considering an exercise bicycle – to practice on at any time, day or night.

Lawn bowling

This is a game that is growing in popularity in almost all parts of the world. It is not a sport that will help to make us fit, but it does help to ensure that our leg muscles are strong and also that our shoulders and arms are flexible and mobile with good co-ordination. One of the real benefits of this game, and others like it that involve social involvement, is that through its formalized activity of game rules, certain courtesies of playing, the stimulus of competition, the protocol of dress and the opportunity for renewing old friendships and possibly making new ones, there is help in maintaining personal esteem, good spirits and self-confidence.

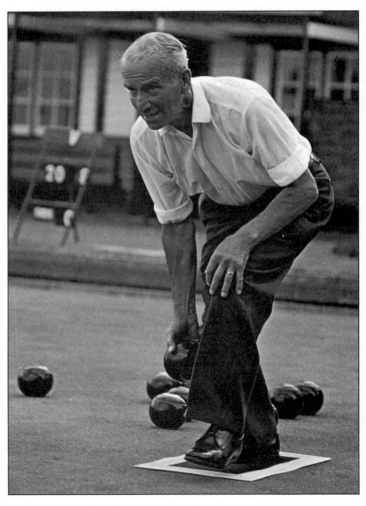

Dancing

According to the sort of dancing we choose to do, we can exercise our bodies gently or very actively. Many couples take up ballroom dancing, which aside from its social pleasures, will help to keep the body and joints flexible and co-ordinated. Other types of dancing that involve running, jumping, stretching and swinging exercise our bodies as much as bicycle riding or running. We can get out of breath in a very short time and so the heart and lungs are fully exercised, too. This kind of dancing is called aerobic dancing. We should never continue aerobic dancing if we get very out of breath, if any part of the body feels painful or if we develop a pain anywhere. We don't have to dance this hard in order to gain benefit from it, and this is particularly the case as we get older.

We can use aerobic dancing to become physically fit, as long as we approach the program very gradually, increasing the amount of effort we make over a period of about six weeks. Remember that very vigorous aerobic dancing can equal the amount of energy that basketball players or top tennis players use when they are at full stretch.

Walking and jogging

We can walk for pleasure or we can walk to keep fit. Brisk, vigorous walking so that we sweat and pant for about 20 minutes, three or four times a week, is an excellent way of staying fit. It exercises all the muscles in our bodies and it also exercises our hearts and lungs. If we haven't been walking to keep fit before, however, it would be foolhardy to start taking long vigorous walks out of the blue. We need to make sure that we get ourselves fit first over several weeks.

TIPS FOR WALKING

- Always do your flexibility exercises before you go out to walk.
- To start with, walk on level ground and avoid hills.
- Always walk "within your breath." This will mean that your heart is beating at about 60 percent of its maximum rate.
- The level of intensity of exercise that you should be aiming at is one that allows you to have a limited conversation while you are moderately out of breath.
- Never push yourself further than you feel you want to go. Never try to strain.

- Don't try to increase the speed at which you walk. Try to increase the distance or the time you spend walking.
- At the beginning never walk into the wind. This will increase your workload by quite a lot. If you suffer with heart disease you should work out your walking program with your doctor first.
- Work at your walking until you can walk continuously for about three miles without stopping in about 45 to 55 minutes.

Walking is an enjoyable, relaxing exercise, but remember not to walk too far without taking a break.

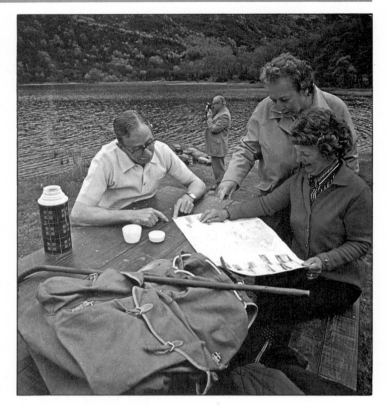

Once we have reached this level of walking, we are ready to go into the jogging/walking program. We need to start by doing mobility exercises (page 42), and then walking briskly for a while and jogging until we feel we need a rest, then back to walking until we feel ready to run again. We can repeat these cycles for 20 minutes or so. We should do this at least every other day but not more than five days a week. Once we can manage this quite comfortably we can start trying to jog at our own pace with a friend or alone.

You can perform a test to see whether or not you are healthy enough to start jogging right away. Try and walk three miles in 45 minutes. If you can, you can probably start jogging without any risks, but if you cannot, you must stick to the brisk walking exercises already described until you can progress to jogging. Remember, do the mobility exercises before you start and, if possible, after you finish. Do check with your doctor before you take up jogging; he or she will tell you whether there is any danger in exerting yourself. It is most important to take things easy at first.

TIPS FOR JOGGING

- Jog at a comfortable rate for about 50 yards (45m) to start off.
- Slow down and walk 100 yards (90m).
- Keep repeating this cycle until you have been going for about 20 minutes.
- Never exercise to the point where you feel that you are completely out of breath, dizzy or sick.
- Never extend the time limit over 20 minutes until you can jog for the whole of the 20 minutes.
- Very gradually increase your jogging up to half an hour.
- There is no particular benefit in extending your time beyond half an hour unless you are really seriously involved in exercising.

Make jogging comfortable

Most people jog for fitness and it is important that you try to develop a comfortable and economical style. Here are a few suggestions that may help.
- Run with your arms bent at the elbows and your wrists and fingers held loosely. The forearm should be about parallel to the ground. Your hands should just about scratch your abdomen when you run.
- Try to run tall and upright but avoid leaning forward. Keep your back as straight as you can and your head up. Look about 15 to 20 feet (5-6m) in front of you, and try not to look at your feet.
- Keep your stride fairly short; don't force the pace by reaching out.
- If you are feeling a bit stiff, shake out your arms to ease your shoulders.
- As you land take your weight on the heel of the foot and then roll forward onto the ball before taking off again. If this is a bit difficult just run flat footed until you develop the heel-toe technique.
- Don't try to run on your toes as this will strain your calf muscles.
- Breathe fairly deeply and help yourself by pushing your abdomen outward as you breathe in. It doesn't matter how much noise you make, in fact making quite a bit of noise often helps.

Jogging is somewhat different from other sports. Only ten years ago it was uncommon to see people jogging in the streets. Nowadays it is fairly common to see track-suited, middle-aged people jogging. Jogging has almost become a national addiction. To a jogger the reasons for this are pretty plain. Some people may start jogging for the fun of it, some do it to lose weight or to reduce tension, and others do it just to tone up their muscles. Some people do it for self-discipline.

For many people jogging is truly addictive but unlike other addictions it is helpful rather than harmful. Very often it helps to control other personal habits that are undesirable, like smoking. People who start to run find it easier to reduce their consumption of cigarettes and may stop altogether. Jogging, of course, has all the benefits that regular exercise has on the whole of the body. It helps the body to use up oxygen; it lowers the heart rate, thereby saving us between ten and twenty thousand heartbeats a day; it increases the efficiency of the heart and lungs; it lowers the blood pressure and it helps to burn up extra weight.

Medical check-ups

Doctors and patients can become dangerously polarized in their views about medical check-ups. Doctors sometimes tend to fear that too much knowledge can be dangerous. Patients, on the other hand, feel a desire to know — they even feel the right to know — every single bit of medical information about themselves and will take advantage of all the medical check-ups that are available. In my opinion both are wrong. I feel it is possible for everyone who wants to have information about how his or her body functions and maintains itself to have it without becoming a hypochondriac in the process. The

Your doctor will be quite willing to explain why he or she is performing various tests.

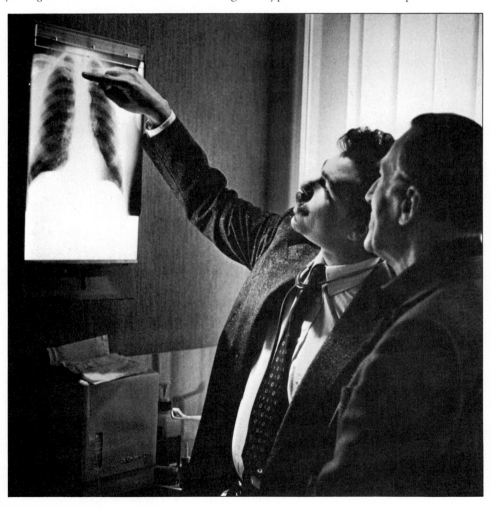

obsessive patient who gathers medical data about his or her own body at every opportunity and becomes overworried if the slightest thing goes wrong is at fault and is in more danger from this than from any ailment he or she may have.

The most important aim of medical check-ups is to prevent disease in the long term, and most of us should see the long term as stretching throughout our lives. Ideally we should start looking after our bodies at an early age — during our teens would be my recommendation — but certainly in our twenties and thirties. If we haven't started earlier, there is nothing to be lost in starting to look after our bodies now. We can make the greatest changes if we start early, but we can still make substantial changes if we start late, and it is never too late to make small changes.

Your doctor will give you sound advice as to how often your medical check-up should be done, but you should use your own initiative when you feel the need. As a reminder, you can keep a medical check-up chart at home and show it to your doctor to get him or her involved. An understanding physician will reciprocate.

Whenever you are going to have a medical check-up you should ask your doctor if the tests will be useful, how they will be done, what they will examine, what results he or she expects and how these results will be interpreted. You should also ask how you will be given the results of what the test has shown, and what you should do.

As we get older, some of the medical tests that were important when we were young become less relevant and others achieve greater importance. There are certain tests that become increasingly important as we grow older; their purpose, when they are recommended and where they are carried out, is explained in the chart on pages 54-55.

I should like to give you one piece of advice about the results of medical check-ups. Even though you think you know how often you need check-ups and how results should be interpreted, make sure that you heed the advice of your doctor. In all probability some of the tests will come back not quite normal, but let your doctor assess the importance of this. By all means question your doctor as to what steps you might take to improve the situation, but if your doctor reassures you that nothing further need be done try and take his or her advice. If it is impossible to do this ask for a referral to a specialist for a second opinion.

MEDICAL CHECK-UPS

Name of test and purpose	When recommended	Frequency of follow-up
Chest X-ray To detect recent, current, and sometimes past, disease of the lungs	To check that the lungs are clear after a chest infection; if you spit blood; if you have chest pains. *Not* recommended on a regular basis.	Not applicable
Blood pressure To check on the state of the heart and arteries	Regularly for everyone, but especially if you have a family history of high blood pressure, heart or kidney disease, stroke or diabetes; if you are overweight	Annually
Complete physical examination To check on the general health of heart, lungs, brain, ears and major internal organs	At periodic intervals or after a serious illness or surgery; if you are worried by a non-specific symptom	Annually or as scheduled by you and your doctor
Internal examination To examine the pelvic floor, perineum and pelvic organs. This is less important after the menopause	At periodic intervals or if you have a persistent complaint of the pelvis, vagina or perineum; if you have *any* bleeding after menopause	According to your doctor or gynecologist
Pap smear To detect pre-malignant changes in the cervical cells.	At periodic intervals or if you have a positive family history of risk factors	As your doctor advises
Mammography To detect small breast lumps	At periodic intervals after 40 or if you fall into a high risk group, or a positive family history	Annually or as your doctor advises if you are in a high risk group
Eye tests To detect defects in vision and glaucoma	At periodic intervals or if you have a pain in the eye and it is red	As your doctor advises
Dental check-ups To check on the general health of teeth and gums; to detect caries, and incorrect alignment	At periodic intervals, and especially if your parents have poor teeth; if you have a rare dental disorder, like soft teeth	Annually
Rectal examination To check on size and consistency of prostate, for presence of hemorrhoids, for blood in stool and for rectal cancer	If any bowel or urinary symptoms appear	Annually unless symptoms develop
Stool test To check for presence of microscopic amounts of blood in stool	At periodic intervals or if any bowel symptoms appear	Annually

Who will arrange test and where	What the results will show	Who can interpret the results
Your doctor or a surgeon in a hospital X-ray department	Most diseases of lung tissue	A radiologist and your doctor
Your doctor in your doctor's office	If taken correctly and frequently elevations in blood pressure may indicate a serious medical problem	Your doctor
Your doctor in your doctor's office	Gross disease of a major organ, and indications for further tests	Your doctor
Your doctor or gynecologist in his or her office or a hospital clinic	Gross disease of a pelvic organ, and indications of further tests	Your doctor or gynecologist
Your doctor or gynecologist in his or her office or hospital cytology clinic	Early changes in the cervical cells before they become malignant, and indications for further tests	A cytologist
Your doctor in a local hospital or mammography unit	Tiny breast lumps	A radiologist
Your doctor, ophthalmologist, optometrist or optician. In your doctor's office or in a hospital	Visual defects; early signs of increasing pressure on the eyeball, and indications for further tests	Your doctor, an ophthalmologist or an optician
Your dentist or dental hygienist in your dentist's office	Early gum diseases or tooth decay	Your dentist or hygienist
Your own doctor will perform the examination and may refer you to a specialist	Enlargement of the prostate, the presence of hemorrhoids	Your doctor or a proctologist
Doctor will provide or prescribe kit for performing test at home	Presence of blood in stool; rectal cancer	Your doctor

Sleep

Our need for sleep diminishes as we get older. Whereas a newborn baby needs anything up to fifteen or sixteen hours a day, a child of eight or so probably doesn't need any more sleep than an adult. In young adulthood most of us can function on six or seven hours of sleep a day. However, by the time we reach our seventies it is quite common for us to sleep for only about two hours and to doze intermittently for the rest of the night.

Sleep researchers believe that our need to sleep is not entirely physical. There is almost certainly a chemical and hormonal component, so it is not a tired body that drives us to sleep, it is a tired brain. Think of the brain as a battery: sixteen to eighteen hours of wakefulness runs the battery down and it needs to sleep to recharge. When we have had enough sleep, our brain cells are charged with granules containing chemicals necessary for efficient intellectual function. When we are tired, however, the supply of these granules in the brain cells becomes depleted. During sleep the granules reappear.

Sleep patterns

An internal clock with a regular 24-hour rhythm governs all our body functions. For each individual, this rhythm is slightly different, but it does conform to a general pattern. It is largely determined by blood levels of cortisol, the life-giving hormone, which is secreted by the adrenal gland. By about midnight the blood level of cortisol is sinking rapidly to reach its lowest ebb between the hours of 2 and 4 a.m. Subsequently, the adrenals start to pick up and cortisol floods the body sufficiently to trigger off waking somewhere between the hours of 6 and 9 a.m. Early-morning people have an early cortisol peak. People who are slow to wake and don't really get going till midday, have a later peak.

Whether it is early or late in the morning, most of us enjoy a cortisol "kick" that makes us alert, energetic and active. Then just after lunch there is a post-prandial dip in the plasma cortisol and this accounts for the drowsiness that many of us feel in the early afternoon. Toward evening, our cortisol levels begin to increase again, enabling us to enjoy evening activities. Then as the clock moves toward midnight, the cortisol falls away, and this is one of the triggers that make us feel sleepy.

Sleep mechanism

Sleep is controlled by two centers in the brain. One is sensitive to external factors like darkness, social and domestic cues, other people saying that they are tired and going to bed, habits, and internal cues like physical or mental tiredness, and these *send* us to sleep. A second center *keeps* us asleep; this is triggered off by chemical reactions in the body and brain cells that occur toward the end of the day.

When we are asleep our body enters a state of semi-hibernation. Our body temperature drops 1°F (0.5°C) and our heart rate slows down. Our breathing becomes slow and shallow. Digestive processes and movement of the intestine virtually stop at night. By contrast, movements of the large muscles don't stop altogether. It seems that muscles have to contract now and then in order for them to recover completely and rest. During the night we move a good deal more than we think. Most of us turn approximately twenty times during our sleep. Some people, usually after fifty, can exist on cat naps. I like the Mediterranean habit of taking a siesta after lunch, a time when we are of little use to anyone, so that we are fresh for the late afternoon and evening. An hour of sleep between 2 and 4 p.m. is very energizing. Even a smaller amount of sleep, say just fifteen minutes of deep sleep, a real cat nap, can be a lot more help to the body than several hours of light, fitful sleep. While many of us may learn the trick of cat napping during the day, the majority of us cannot cat nap during the night until we are approaching sixty.

The amount of sleep we need consists of the number of hours we remain asleep if left undisturbed. On those rare occasions when we indulge ourselves in this way we sleep a couple of hours longer than our normal working days allow us. Therefore, most of us are about two hours of sleep below par each day and so it is not surprising that we feel we are not functioning properly, physically or mentally, and cannot cope with stress as well as we would like. As a general rule of thumb, our need for sleep runs parallel with our growth rate. Our sleep needs start to tail off from around seven or eight hours a night by roughly an hour every decade, until we may need as little as only four hours per night in our sixties.

If you find yourself habitually lying awake at night next to a snoring partner, don't lie there fuming, allowing resentment to build up. It's better to be constructive about insomnia and take advantage of it. Get out of bed, go downstairs and make yourself a cup of caffeine-free tea. Find a book to read or do some job that you have been waiting to do for ages. It is never a good idea to lie in bed feeling resentful if you can't go to sleep. Try and think positively about the few hours you have gained and make the best of them. After all, this is the one time in your life when you may not have to get up to get to the office by a certain time. Take advantage of your freedom and relish the fact that you can sleep till 10:30 in the morning if you wish.

TIPS TO HELP YOU FALL ASLEEP

- Avoid coffee, tea, cola drinks and tobacco after 4 p.m. Don't eat any sweet snacks before bedtime. These all act as stimulants to the body.
- Try to arrange to do something quiet and relaxing before you go to bed. Going for a walk is a good idea, so take the dog. So is half an hour of yoga. You could watch television in bed or read a newspaper or a book. Whatever it is, make sure it is not exciting.
- The temperature of your bedroom should be comfortable. It should be neither too hot nor too cold and you may have to open a window to allow the air to circulate to be comfortable.
- Dripping taps and squeaky doors can be very irritating if you wake in the middle of the night, so don't leave taps dripping and close all the doors. If you have radiators that "knock" then bleed them to get air out of the system.
- A lumpy, uncomfortable mattress, particularly if you have back trouble, is a bad idea, and don't settle for it. Invest in the best mattress you can afford. This is a health as well as a comfort measure.

- You should always wear loose fitting night clothes but choose cotton or another natural fiber.
- Try to give yourself or have your companion give you a back and neck massage.
- Many people find that a hot bath last thing at night is soporific. The blood is diverted from the brain to the skin and this makes you feel sleepy.
- A warm drink will have the same effect.
- Certain herbs like camomile in tisane or a hot pillow or herb pillow to sleep on might help.
- Here is an instant relaxation method that you might like to try when you are just dropping off to sleep. Starting at your toes, check your ankles, knees, hips, fingers, wrists, elbows, shoulders, torso, neck, face and head, and make sure all your muscles are relaxed. Now slow down your breathing to deep breaths taken at half speed. Try to make your mind a blank. My own tip is to think of black velvet.
- Remember, sex is the best hypnotic.

Smoking

While I am a very keen advocate of giving up smoking, I am not out to persuade you. I only wish to offer help to people who want to stop. Indeed, research has shown that the only people who can be helped are those who want to stop. Even such alternative therapies as hypnosis and acupuncture will fail completely if you do not want to stop.

In a way I envy smokers, because the minute you give up smoking you enter lower risk groups for death from a heart attack, bronchitis, emphysema and lung cancer. There is no other single step that is likely to improve your chances of health so significantly and so immediately as giving up smoking. Even if you feel that you are quite healthy, you are suffering without realizing it. Cigarette smoking interferes with the smooth movement of oxygen around the body.

Stopping smoking

There are all sorts of ways to give up smoking; the best way is the one that suits you. Before you start on a program to stop smoking, try to adapt it to your own framework. Here are a few tips from researchers about the best way of giving up smoking. Many experts on smoking cessation agree that you improve your chances of success if you stop smoking in steps. Others advocate stopping abruptly.

One of the best ways of preparing yourself to stop is to draw up a daily diary, noting every time you smoke a cigarette, what you were doing and how much you wanted it. At the end of each day you will find that even if you smoke more than forty cigarettes, there are only about seven or eight that are really crucial to you, and you need to concentrate on these. You can give up the others quite easily. The "tough" cigarettes have either to be avoided by breaking the situation in which you reach for a cigarette, or simply faced straight on. A good method of maintaining your will power is to sign a contract.

BENEFITS OF NOT SMOKING

- You will live longer, five minutes longer for every cigarette you don't smoke.
- You will lower your risk of getting bronchitis, emphysema, peptic ulceration, cancer of the lung and heart disease.
- From the moment you give up smoking your body will be healing itself every minute. Your lungs will no longer produce an excessive amount of phlegm to get rid of the smoke particles. Most important, the cells that have become flattened by irritation from chronic smoking will start growing normally again.
- You are likely to suffer from fewer colds and when you do they will clear up a lot more quickly. Colds are less likely to go down into your chest or cause sinusitis.
- If you have angina pectoris you can keep the pain at bay for much longer if you stop smoking.
- If you have trouble with your circulation you will start feeling the cold less.
- You are going to be fitter and more active. You can go walking, hiking, swimming and play tennis with your family once more.
- You will no longer smell of stale smoke.
- Your breathing will become easier, you won't become breathless with minor exertion. Your smoker's cough will disappear.
- You can wear contact lenses for longer.
- You are more attractive.
- Your fingers and teeth will no longer be stained with nicotine.
- You will enjoy food more, partly because it tastes better, but also because you will have a real appetite for the first time in years, and this doesn't mean that you have to gain weight if you are careful about your diet.
- Your car, house and office will be free of messy ash trays, look more pleasant and clean, and smell sweeter.
- You are setting a good example to others, particularly younger people. You have made it much less likely that your children will smoke.
- It is a source of great pride to conquer your habits because it is a real achievement, and your self-esteem will improve.
- You will save money.
- If you are a singer or an actor, or just enjoy using your voice, you will notice that it has improved.

Healthy alveoli **Nicotine-damaged alveoli**

Sign it with a friend so you feel bound to a program of stopping. If you stop, you and your friend get an enormous treat like a holiday. If you fail, you and your friend give a large sum of money to a cause you both greatly dislike.

Some people like to follow rules and a method evolved in Germany will provide you with an endless set of guidelines. If you wish to you can write your own rules, of course, as long as you are not easy on yourself. Most people when they come to write the rules do the opposite, setting themselves fairly high standards, and are strict in making sure that they are kept. In writing them you are making a contract with yourself to obey and never break them. One of the attractive things about this method is that you can start off with fairly manageable rules and then as you stick to them successfully you can make them more difficult.

Don't obey all the rules on the first day. You should choose three or four, never more than five to begin with. If you prefer, choose those that seem the easiest to achieve. Success breeds success, and once you have mastered them add one or two more rules each day. When you get to the point where you are obeying all the rules you will have stopped!

TIPS TO HELP YOU STOP SMOKING

1. Never smoke in the car.
2. Only start smoking when you are near your destination.
3. Refuse every cigarette offered.
4. Stop smoking before a meal.
5. Don't smoke before breakfast.
6. Buy one pack of cigarettes at a time.
7. Only buy ten cigarettes at a time.
8. Buy a different brand of cigarettes every time and not just your favorite.
9. Before you light a cigarette count ten.
10. Every time you take a cigarette put the pack away at a distance from where you are – in another room if possible.
11. If you run out of cigarettes, never take one from someone else.
12. After each puff put the cigarette down.
13. Never smoke out of doors.
14. Never smoke in bed or at work.
15. Don't carry your lighter or matches with you so that you need to ask for a light.
16. Stop smoking when you are using your hands for something else.
17. Stop smoking in the house.
18. Stop inhaling.
19. Stop smoking a cigarette more than half way down.
20. Stop smoking after a meal while you are sitting at the table.
21. Stop smoking while you are waiting (e.g. for a phone call or a bus).
22. When you are smoking, stop doing everything else. Don't drink coffee, watch television, or listen to music.
23. Stop smoking if someone lights up in your presence.
24. Don't smoke while you are relaxing after work with a drink.
25. Only smoke if you are sitting in an uncomfortable chair.
26. Keep a rubber band around your cigarette pack so that you are aware of opening it.
27. Time your smoking frequency. Have a cigarette on the hour, then try every alternate hour.

Alcoholism

Many of us are unaware of the fact that ten million Americans suffer from alcoholism or some form of alcohol-related problem. Although only between one and five percent of persons sixty-five and over have problems with alcohol, the percentage is significantly higher for men and women in the fifty-to-sixty-five-year old group. Most of us are aware of the physical and emotional risks taken by the falling-down-drunk-drinker – liver damage, loss of appetite, broken blood vessels in the nose, memory loss. We are less aware of the effects on our bodies and minds of moderate to heavy drinking. As we grow older, our central nervous systems undergo progressive change, and with this change comes an alteration in our tolerance of alcohol. The toxins that have been accumulating in our bodies reach a level that is damaging to our systems. Changes in our central nervous system can cause a dramatic change in our level of tolerance for alcohol. The person who could drink several beers and still feel fine when he was young and active may find, as he grows older, that even a single drink will have a definite effect on his ability to function.

Misuse of alcohol has terrible effects on the body. It can damage the liver irreparably and it weakens the nervous and digestive systems. It can cause – or exacerbate – a tremor or a condition of poor balance, causing falls and awkwardness. Eventually, the problem drinker can no longer judge distances or make coordinated hand-and-eye movements. The memory goes and there may be permanent brain damage. Sleep patterns are impaired, often to the extent of causing severe fatigue,

IS ALCOHOL A PROBLEM?

You only have to answer "Yes" to one of the questions below to realize that alcohol is affecting your life in a major way, and that you should take steps to decrease the amount of your drinking. If you answer "Yes" to more than one question, you should probably seek help.

1. When faced with a problem do you turn to alcohol for relief?
2. Are you sometimes unable to meet home or work responsibilities because of your drinking?
3. Has someone close to you sometimes expressed concern about your drinking?
4. Have you ever required medical attention as a result of drinking?
5. Have you ever had distressing physical or psychological reactions when you have stopped drinking?
6. Have you ever experienced a blackout or total loss of memory when drinking?
7. Have you often failed to keep the promises you have made to yourself about controlling or stopping drinking?
8. Do you ever sneak a drink when you find yourself in a social situation where alcohol is not provided?

irritability, and depression.

There is no doubt that alcoholism and problem drinking are on the rise. We can gain an awareness of our own use, or perhaps abuse, of alcohol through an understanding of some of the causes for this increase in drinking problems.

Economic causes

Alcohol is becoming easily available to more people because of rising income levels, particularly among the growing number of women of all ages who are joining the work force and earning incomes of their own. Advertisements on television and in magazines emphasize a connection between stylish, luxurious living and drinking; alcohol is depicted as promoting romance and as being the badge of success and sophistication. The fastest-growing market in alcohol is wine, both domestic and imported, and wine with dinner – and with lunch – is seen to be a symbol of status and cultural savvy. Research shows that the higher the income bracket, the more alcohol is consumed.

Another reason for the increased use of alcohol is that beer and wine are now sold in supermarkets in many states. It's easy to pick up a six-pack or a bottle of wine along with the groceries. This eliminates the need for a "booze budget" and masks the amount of money actually spent on alcoholic beverages. House brands and frequent sales make the purchase of supermarket alcohol seem like a bargain.

Social causes

Most drinking problems begin in a social setting. Many social groups manage to make a non-drinker feel like a spoilsport or a wet blanket. The cocktail hour is a built-in part of an evening's entertainment, and even business meetings, conventions, and conferences feature a steady flow of alcohol from the moment the sun is over the yardarm.

Stress, tension, deadlines, and the fast pace of our high-tech society contribute to a tendency to drink more in the course of a working day. Although the teacher, the doctor, and the airline pilot still have to maintain total sobriety and alcohol-free breath during the working day, many professions actually sanction drinking on the job. Long, boozy lunches are *de rigueur* for men and women in the business world, and "having a drink after work" is often part of the business day. The drink-with-lunch habit, once formed, dies hard, and the retired executive may not be able to resist the temptation – stronger when you're pouring it yourself – to tipple at lunch time when he's staying home. Lunch time, sometimes, gets earlier and earlier. If you don't cut down before all this begins to happen, you could find yourself on the slippery slope to chronic alcohol-dependency.

Psychological causes

As we grow older, our resistance to stress, frustration, loss, and disappointment is lowered. It becomes harder to pick up and start over, and a damaged self-image is tough to restore. Often we imagine that we are being passed over for a younger person, both professionally and socially; sometimes, it's true. The twentieth century seems to be bringing so many changes, so fast, that we feel super-annuated and left behind before we are past middle age. A drink gives the illusion of softening these blows.

Anyone who drinks alcohol knows that it is a mood changer and tranquilizer, and people therefore often drink to escape their problems. Many of us tend to increase our alcoholic consumption when we are faced with difficult life situations. Loss of any kind including divorce, separation, and loss of sex drive are heavily implicated in increased drinking. Threats to a woman's feminine role of mother, wife, homemaker, and lover are closely associated with alcoholism. The same applies to men if their roles as breadwinners, senior members of firms, heads of families, and dominant lovers come into question.

If you find yourself drinking more heavily when you are under stress or have suffered a disappointment, try to recognize it as a danger sign and act on it immediately.

What to do about a drinking problem

The solution is often complicated by the varying standards in the different strata of society and by regional, cultural, and religious outlooks on drinking. Some groups feel that even a celebratory glass of champagne is evil, while others consider regular consumption of alcohol a part of everyday life. But, while social drinking is widely accepted, heavy drinking – particularly when if affects work – is frowned upon almost everywhere. This taboo has the effect of encouraging troubled people to become secret drinkers. Many alcoholics perform well on the job but drink alone, during the day, and deny doing so. Not being able to handle your drinking alone or to enlist the help of your family and intimate friends is a surefire danger signal and a sign that it is time to seek treatment. There are three main lines of treatment available.

Detoxification and Medical Care

This method is suited primarily to the severely addicted alcoholic who must recover from the acute effects of drinking before being able to change in other ways. A program of detoxification is usually undertaken in a hospital or other institutions where alcoholics are "dried out" by a gradual reduction of alcohol combined with the support of sedative drugs. Medication and diet are adjusted as the drinker's physical condition improves, and after a period of hospitalization, treatment may continue on an out-patient basis. Physicians can recommend the proper facilities when a case requires such a program.

Therapy

The most important step is for drinkers to come to terms with their reasons for drinking and the problems their drinking causes. The next crucial step is to consult a doctor, or at least to admit to a friend that a problem exists. This represents a leap forward. Individual, group, and family therapy are all available through various organizations (see page 310). Anyone with a partner must involve that partner. After the initial drying-out period, one of the most successful ways of continuing treatment can be through psychotherapy. Often a "reformed" drinker who does not elect to go into long-term psychotherapy may decide to continue to attend a therapy group, sometimes as a counselor to new members. The group provides continuing support and an opportunity for communication, and can act as a buttress when the next life crisis threatens the drinker's continued sobriety.

Alcoholics Anonymous

This well-known association exists to help people who want to stop drinking. There are chapters of AA in all major cities and most towns. Meetings are held once a week or oftener. All members have been alcoholics, and are able to use and describe their experiences to help other alcoholics become sober – and stay that way – and to rebuild their lives. Alcoholics Anonymous is highly regarded by doctors, and is considered by many to offer the best, and least expensive, treatment and support, for many alcoholics. It has served as a model for other associations that treat drug addiction, smoking, and overeating.

Al-Anon, the organization that helps spouses and family members to cope with a problem drinker, also has centers all over this country. Al-Anon teaches the families of alcoholics how to deal with an alcoholic and how to give the supportive treatment he or she needs during the process of becoming sober.

Drugs

Drug dependency and addiction have been social problems since time immemorial. People take drugs to alter their states of mind, to forget their troubles, to mask pain, to achieve a "high" or to tone down excess energy and nervousness. Some people take drugs because they see others doing it, or because it is socially acceptable. Others fall into drug use by chance, due to prolonged use of drugs after an operation or a war wound. This could happen to any of us, even those of us who are actively opposed to drugs. It's important to understand how this can happen, how to prevent it, and how to overcome any dependency that may occur.

Drug dependency

We are not concerned, here, with the kind of drug addict who uses drugs for a "high" or for recreational purposes. Our concern is with the middle-aged or older person for whom dependency is an accidental result of continued use, or misuse, of prescription drugs.

This type of dependency usually develops when repeated use of certain drugs leads to a change in the way the user reacts to the drug. Awareness of the changing effects of prescribed drugs and medication, and over-the-counter medicines, is essential if the user is to avoid dependency and maintain control.

As we grow older, most of us find ourselves taking more medicines for a variety of ailments. Since the days of the all-purpose general practitioner or family doctor are behind us, we usually find ourselves going to several different specialists or sub-specialists at the same time. Each doctor may give us medication, and often they are not sure what medicines we have been given by other doctors. Also, many elderly people become confused when they have several different kinds of medication to take, each with its own timetable of dosages, and mistakes are easy to make. Once made, these mistakes can have more severe side effects on an older person than they would have on a younger one. The cumulative effects of drugs take longer to leave the body of an older person (doctors say that drugs have a longer "half-life" in the older patient) because the liver and kidneys, which do the jobs of detoxification and elimination, are less efficient as we grow older. Take, for example, a diabetic who also suffers from hypertension and angina, with a slight kidney impairment as well. This person is already taking many different kinds of medication. If another illness strikes, his doctor may prescribe yet another type of medication. The combination of drugs can cause side effects such as drowsiness, fainting, confusion, and even glaucoma. Cultivate the habit of always discussing newly prescribed medicines with your physicians in order to be fully aware of the effects and the addictive possibilities of each drug and combination of drugs you take. When purchasing over-the-counter drugs and medicines, check with your druggist, and read the instructions carefully. Monitor yourself faithfully to make sure you do not exceed the recommended or prescribed dosage.

65

How to recognize the signs of dependency

The word "addiction" derives from a Latin word that means "to be given over to a master, to be enslaved." Today the term is used to describe any kind of dependence – upon drugs, alcohol, tobacco, even chocolate. The word "addictive" is used to described any person's behavior that stems from an uncontrollable desire for those substances.

The first sign of dependency is usually a reduced ability to choose when, where, and how often to take the drug. If you experience restlessness, anxiety, or irritability for a period of time before the next dose of a drug is due, or if you find yourself watching the clock until the next pill or worrying about misplacing your medication or being caught without it, you may be on the way to addiction.

A loss of control over the use of medication leads to a feeling of helplessnesss and loss of autonomy. As control is gradually weakened, the user may become obsessed with securing a supply of the drug, sometimes hoarding and even hiding it. Even after the symptoms have been recognized, and measures taken to affect withdrawal, there is a tendency to start using the drug again.

Drug dependency is not something to be ashamed of; it can happen to anyone. The best way to avoid dependency is to keep yourself totally informed about the amount, effects, and addictive possibilities of every drug and medication you use.

Drug factors

Research has shown that biological changes occur with the use of certain drugs such as opiates and probably also with alcohol and barbiturates as well. These changes can lead to physical dependence. Many hospital patients are given opiates several times a day to relieve pain following surgery, yet very few of these patients become addicted. Why is it that some people become addicted to drugs easily, either by choice or by accident, while others find it easy to stop using them?

In almost every consistent drug taker, even those who resist the idea of taking drugs, there is a gradual escalation of drug use and dependence. Different factors – psychological, sociological, biological, and pharmacological – can affect the initial phase, when the drug is newly prescribed, the stage when the drug is a regular part of the user's daily life but not an obsessive one, and the intensive or compulsive stage – addiction. This downward spiral involves withdrawal symptoms when the drug is not taken. When a person has become dependent upon a drug and then withdraws from it, he or she will experience withdrawal symptoms to some degree. Even when withdrawal has been accomplished, however, there is still danger of relapse. Like malaria, the addictive condition may resurface at the first sign of pain, stress, illness, or relaxed vigilance. The reasons for relapse are complicated. Drug addicts who are "cured" to the point where they feel no craving in the hospital may feel the need for a "fix" as soon as they return to the home environment where they are accustomed to using drugs and where they had previously experienced the withdrawal symptoms as well as the symptoms of the disease or condition that prompted the original use of the drug.

Tranquilizers such as *Valium* and *Librium* are intended to relieve anxiety without producing the drowsiness characteristic of barbiturates. This makes them popular with professional people, both men and women, who want to reduce stress while at the same time not impairing their energy level or sharpness of mind. Many people abuse these drugs, take too many, and become addicted. Cessation of regular use produces withdrawal symptoms comparable to those of barbiturates – abdominal and muscle cramps, insomnia, anxiety, vomiting, sweating. Problems arising from the excessive use of these drugs include depression, altered sex drive, constipation, and confusion. If they are taken in conjunction with alcohol, they can be lethal. Often, a user will find the withdrawal symptoms intolerable, and will go into a relapse as a result. While giving up the drug for a few days is not terribly difficult, sustained abstention is nearly impossible for the dependent person. It is important for the dependent person to avoid stressful situations while attempting withdrawal and to enlist the support of a friend or a doctor during these times when stress is unavoidable.

Finding help and treatment

The average family doctor is usually not able to take on the whole job of detoxifying a drug user, but can certainly refer the patient to a hospital department that specializes in drug dependents, or to a self-help group. Often these groups are listed in the Classified section of local newspapers. Word-of-mouth is also a reliable index; people who have overcome addiction like to talk about it, and are good advertisers for the groups that helped them. Drug-dependent people usually prefer a group because it involves mutual support, identification, and shared experience, and because it is usually free or very inexpensive.

Self help groups concentrate on teaching self-control, social skills, and relaxation. Often they include or encourage exercise classes, shared meals, and other group activities. If a member's drug problem is too severe to be treated within the group, the group leader can usually point the way to a drug rehabilitation center or hospital situation where the addict can go for emergency treatment. Sometimes, alas, the drug-dependent person is unwilling or unable to admit that his problem is out of control and refuses the referrals. If this happens to someone you know, try to convince the user to take advantage of whatever help is available, even it if means checking into a hospital. The staffs of in-hospital drug programs have all the necessary skills for treating the physical and emotional aspects of drug dependency. Medication is given to help cope with withdrawal symptoms and depression and group therapy sessions help addicts face their problems. Individual psychotherapy is usually available from a psychiatrist or psychologist, and diet is carefully monitored and changed to allow the patient to become physically strong and to meet basic nutritional needs which might have been neglected during dependency.

Drug addiction and dependency can be cured. Often, the user must transfer his dependence to a person – a doctor, a trusted friend, a loyal spouse – or maybe even to a group or a hospital. Often, recovery comes as a pleasant and easily-won surprise, just because of a change in the person's life situation – a new job, a new friend, a move to a different location. Quite a number of formerly drug-dependent people attribute their success to a radical change in their lives. Nearly all of them point to the importance of love for someone who is special, and nearly all describe the turning point as a time when the reasons for changing their lives were greater than those for continuing the self-destructive pattern.

In other words, it's up to you – and the first step is awareness.

Maintaining Mental Agility

Happily for those of us in the fifty-plus age group, the old idea that "You're over the hill at fifty" has been discredited. Researchers who study the aging process no longer believe that the brain stops developing when we are barely adults and then goes downhill after that. In fact, it has been proven that some of the most important forms of intellectual growth can continue straight through our lifetimes, even into our eighties, provided that we are physically and intellectually healthy and active. Although our short-term memories may diminish as we grow older, our abilities to make judgments, understand both sides of issues, and deal with complicated ideas and concepts can remain as sharp as ever and may even improve with age. Experience, that greatest of teachers, continued intellectual curiosity, and active social involvement keep our minds keen and receptive. We can become wise, intellectually flexible, and able to take the long view about issues that perhaps seemed overwhelming to us in our younger years. With new ideas and new technology appearing every ten years or so, it is possible for us to have a "retread" with each decade. Bear in mind that new ideas and new technology require new learning skills from everyone, of every age group. If we take advantage of the influences from outside, we can continue to develop and grow throughout our lives without being "left back" by the younger generation.

Mental exercise

Our minds have to be exercised to remain agile. "Use-it-or-lose-it" pertains to intellectual acuity just as it does to muscle tone. Social interaction, exercise of the mind, and eagerness for new ideas, experiences, and perspectives are crucial to keep the mind healthy, supple, and alert.

Although our short-term memories tend to lose power as we grow older our ability to use accumulated knowledge and information continues to grow and develop. Our faculties can remain at peak performance and even increase if we use our minds actively and constantly.

There are three main factors that contribute to being a good learner. The first is heredity, which largely determines intellectual capacity and which we can't do anything about. The second factor is health, over which we have far more control. That's where mental and physical exercise come in. Just as we must keep our muscles in tone and follow a healthy diet in order to maintain good physical health, we must also give our brains regular exercise in order to maintain mental agility and tone. The third factor – is time. As we grow older, most of us have more time to spend organizing and processing information and ideas. An increase in the amount of free time enables us to learn more, study more, think more. If we haven't been exercising our mental faculties on a regular basis right along, or if we try to do something we haven't done for a long time, such as taking an examination, writing a report, or playing a chess game, we may feel a bit rusty. With patience and perseverence we can get our minds running smoothly again. Beginning can be tough, but the rewards will make it worthwhile.

If you have not studied or read widely for a long time, don't start by trying to educate yourself all at once, taking demanding courses, or attempting tasks that involve a lot of pressure. Preparatory courses in a new subject or refresher courses in your own field will lead you back gradually into the "think force," allowing you to flex your mental muscles and get back into shape in a protected environment. Then as your faculties tone up, you can take on tougher learning assignments and ask more and more of your mind.

Choosing a subject

If you've been out of work or mentally inactive for a long time, your first task will be to set forth your priorities: what do you want to do most? What subject really interests you to the extent that you're eager to study it in depth? Is your goal to become employed, to change jobs, to put new knowledge to practical use? Or are you learning for its own sake? How much time do you have, and how much of that time do you want to spend? Do you want to gain knowledge in a practical sense, or are you more interested in abstract ideas?

It's best to choose one field – a continuing interest – rather than to dabble in a series of short courses in widely divergent areas. We should ask ourselves, "What subject will I be interested in five years from now?" A subject that enables us to cope with the technological changes taking place is immensely useful – learning about micro-computers, for example. If possible, we should choose skills that enable us to keep up with the society, perhaps even become an authority. This makes us worthwhile not only to ourselves, but also to others, and helps us remain healthy and interesting to the people around us.

People who go back to work or take up new work in later life have the advantage of a mass of qualifications, skills, experience, and knowledge. Many employers prefer an older person to a younger one, particularly when filling a position that requires on-the-job training. Older people are less likely to marry and move away, to change jobs, or to take long maternity leaves and time off to care for small children. Older people have already passed through most of the predictable life crises and are freer from the restlessness that characterizes many young people today. We are a good risk.

Setting priorities

If we choose to rejoin the work force on a full time basis, we will probably encounter some difficulties at first. Good risk or not, older people are not fully recognized as useful contributors to the work force. Society continues to impose restrictions on older people, and these restrictions may discourage us from going back to school or trying to move back into the work force. There's still prejudice against older people, particularly in today's world where youthfulness is equated with usefulness. It will take toughness and determination to buck this prejudice, but it can be done.

Another thing that may hold us back is a network of habits we have formed and routines we have established in order to fill up our time. Family commitments and circumstances, pets, even a garden might seem to constrain us, but we should try to decide whether these are real reasons not to venture forth or merely a cover-up for the fact that we feel frightened or nervous. Some commitments are real and long-lasting, and necessary to our wellbeing; others are just a waste of our time. We must make realistic assessment of our present situation and the options that are open to us so that we can make a wise decision.

If you are already working at a job that is satisfying to you, it's usually best to keep working as long as you can rather than retiring early or trying to change fields. In most established professions such as accounting, banking, and marketing, it's often possible for a senior person to stay on as a consultant and do advisory work. Japanese research has shown that business people who continue to take an interest in their work, even going into the office once or twice a week and contributing as counselors, advisors, and senior executives, manage to keep themselves more mentally alert and to live longer than business people who retire early and cut themselves off from the stimulation of the marketplace.

Sometimes it's possible to remain in the same profession but to move sideways, say from secretarial to accounting or from buying to selling, perhaps reducing the number of hours per week so that there will be more time for outside activities and recreation or study. Many old skills can be used in a new way, if we are willing to adapt. Often, we are unaware of the skills we have, particularly if we have not been active in professional life or if we have been away from it for a long time. Running a household is a managerial skill that can easily transfer to running an office or a business. Bringing up a family is a vital qualification for working in the child-care field or becoming a teacher's assistant. Talents such as yoga, gardening, and cooking can often provide opportunities for selling, teaching, or consulting.

If you decide to adapt your hobby skills to the professional marketplace or to move into a new job field, you'll want to take some practical courses to back up your skills. Information about such courses can often be found in the Yellow Pages of your local telephone directory, or at any employment agency. Counseling is nearly always available at the Continuing Education or Community Services department of the nearest college or university. Again, word of mouth is often the best avenue to a new job or a new field of study. People love to talk about their "discoveries," and it's fun to take a course with a friend and to share the experiences, and even the frustration, of re-entry into the Real World. Don't be put off by being told there are no opportunities. Get as much information as you can from as many sources as you can locate. Go and see career advisors, prowl around the employment agencies, look for specialist advisory services, and haunt the corridors of the local community college. And keep your chin up.

Volunteer work

If you want to make a full or part-time commitment to a job but do not need to draw a salary, you may want to consider doing volunteer work. There is a wide range of possibilities in this field, and volunteer work is an area where older people are welcomed, valued, and appreciated. Hospitals, day centers, centers for the blind and deaf, and thrift shops all need volunteers and will be eager to take advantage of your skills and your energies. Sometimes, too, volunteer work opens the door to a paid job. The skills and contacts acquired while doing volunteer work often can be transferred to a "real" job.

If there are no social agencies or obvious openings for volunteer work in your neighborhood, start with your church, synagogue, or school system. Caring for the elderly is also a good way to get started; a large number of women between the ages of fifty and sixty-five find satisfaction and fulfillment in caring for older or disabled people, either at home or in a nursing facility. If you live in a city, you might apply for work as a gallery guide, an usher, or a school aide. The possibilities are limitless, the hours flexible, and the satisfaction enormous. Another side benefit is that you will meet new people, form new friendships, and be exposed to new ideas and experiences.

If you do decide to do volunteer work, here are some questions you ought to ask yourself before you agree to commit yourself to a position.
- Will this work use a skill I already have?
- Will my health allow me to spend the time, and expend the energy, that his job requires?
- Do I have the time to give the job what it need without giving up too many of my other interests?
- Will it hold my interest for a long period of time?
- Are the people involved the kind of people I feel comfortable with?
- Can I get to the place of work without transportation hassles?
- Can I really afford to work without pay?

Think about it. There are many options: formal study, refresher courses, full time jobs, part time jobs, volunteer work of all kinds. And don't forget this: Even without any of the above, you can lead a fully engaged, exciting intellectual life – on your own. Haven't you been wishing, for years, that you had more time to read?

Keeping a tranquil mind

People who are tranquil when they are young will probably continue to be tranquil as they mature; as a general rule our personalities don't change drastically as we grow older. If we are placid and easy-going, with a philosophical attitude toward life, this attitude will almost certainly extend into our middle and later years. If we are excitable, enthusiastic, and precipitous, we will probably remain that way. If we have always been anxious, timid, and inclined to worry, we will probably continue to be.

As we grow older, our mental well-being is threatened by all kinds of environmental and internal stresses. We tend to suffer deeper and longer bouts of unhappiness during and after disruptive events in our lives, and we are less resilient about recovering from them. Retirement, breakdown of marriage, professional reversals, or bereavement can throw us into a state of deep malaise, even depression. Now, as in all stages of life we will be far better equipped to deal with these crises, and the minor daily ones as well, if we are prepared for them and know where to turn for help and support when the going gets too rough. The aim of this chapter is to increase your awareness of the rough spots that may lie ahead. With this awareness and a few simple exercises, you will be better able to face the future confidently and with a fine prospect for happiness.

Growing older gracefully

One of the most important aspects of mental well-being as we grow older is adapting to the fact that we *are* older, and accepting it gracefully. Gerontologists call this "successful aging." A great deal of research has been done on the subject of successful aging, and we have much to learn from the results of studies that show what type of personalities age most successfully. From these studies we can draw up guidelines for maintaining a tranquil mind in later life.

People who perceive themselves as elderly or old are less well adjusted than those who think of themselves as middle-aged or mature. People who start thinking of themselves as old just because they no longer go to the office every day are more likely to be maladjusted than those who take retirement in stride and identify with the idea of continuing a vital and active life.

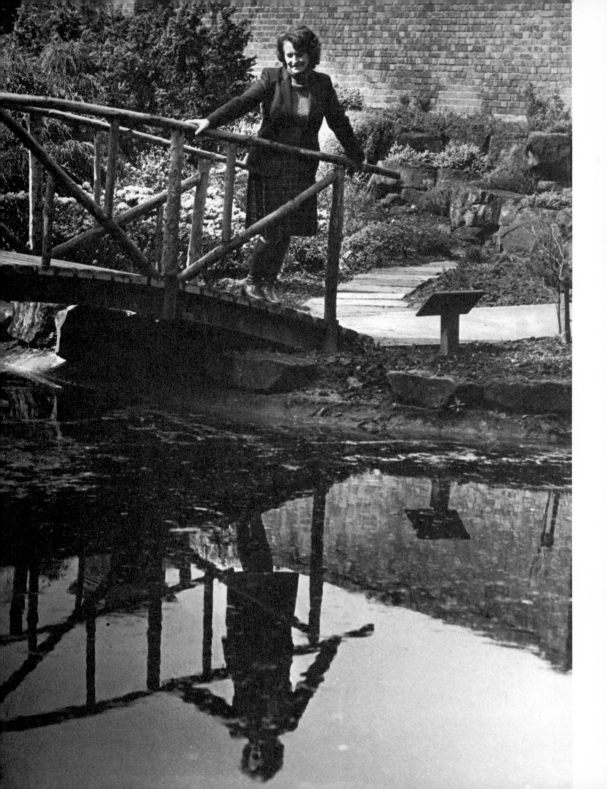

*Our
broadened
perspective*

The wisest among us don't pursue the will o' the wisp of eternal youthfulness, but accept the aging process with a calm befitting our maturity. Chasing the idea of remaining young indicates a personal inadequacy, an inability to accept the changes in body, mind, and lifestyle that are an inevitable and natural part of the life cycle. None of us can avoid the inevitable; we are going to get older whether we like it or not. It's important that we accept and enjoy the pleasures that each stage of life can bring.

I wouldn't wish to turn the clock back one single day. I finally know how to cope with life, and this knowledge makes each day seem better than the one before. I have found new ways of savoring life's pleasures, even those which, in the past I didn't find remotely interesting. Maturing gracefully means knowing and liking ourselves for what we are, with our imperfections, our foibles, and our quirks. It means being as physically active as possible, and sharing our activities, whenever possible, with a partner, a friend, or a child.

*Responses to
growing older*

Men and women, particularly those who have followed traditional male-female roles, approach the aging process in somewhat different ways. The main unheaval in life occurs at different ages for men and for women. The man, who has often pursued a career or profession for several decades and then faces retirement in his sixties or seventies, faces a different set of problems, at a different age, from the women whose duties as a mother and household manager are usually finished by the time she is forty-five. Today, with the roles of men and women changing – and overlapping – it is more difficult to predict the ways in which people will react to the aging process. But some of the old guidelines still apply.

For the woman who does not choose a career, the home and family occupy the center of attention. Though she may pursue many outside activities and interests, her heart is in her home, and when the children grow up and leave the nest there is a void that is not easy to fill. Women who elect to work instead of – or along with – raising a family, or who have their children later on, in their thirties, face a different set of problems and adjustments, and face them at a different age – often as late as fifty.

The middle years of a married woman are, traditionally, framed by her family, her job, and her community. Middle age usually signals a release from responsibility, daytime care, and constant vigilance over the children. This process is gradual rather than abrupt, and it is affected by such factors as the number and ages of her children, their schooling and employment, and how near or far away from home they live after leaving the nest. Middle age also roughly coincides with the onset of middle age for her husband, but he may not yet have reached the age where his way of life and his habits and patterns begin to change, as hers are doing. Perhaps her transition will be very smooth, if social and family activities continue to fill the time formerly occupied in looking after her children. Perhaps she will return to work or go out to work for the first time. Maybe her marriage will reach a new, serene plateau of happiness and comradeship, but there is also the danger that it will deteriorate, leaving her with a feeling of loss and sadness. In any case, her life will change, and she will have adjustments to make. She is, at this period of her life, increasingly vulnerable to emotional stress, particularly if her support system of friends and relatives is weakened. Often, this stage of a women's life requires her to cope with the advanced aging and death of her own parents and the diminution of her social group due to the fact that many friends are moving away, traveling a great deal, or changing their lives in other ways.

How men respond In middle age, most men become very concerned with their health and anxious to maintain their fitness at work and at play. They are more prone to worry about their sexual prowess than women are, and are sometimes deeply upset about such signs of aging as balding, paunchiness, and loss of muscle tone. Men watch themselves carefully for the development of symptoms and are often increasingly picky about their food, their routines, and their clothing.

Those of us who accept aging as a natural process and swing with it instead of fighting against it are more likely to find ourselves healthy, well-adjusted, and tranquil when we decide to retire from the mainstream and segue into the final decades of our lives.

Motivation and Frustration

Now that we are aware of the almost limitless possibilities open to us for work, study, and recreation, the next step is to get going and do it. How do we get started? What sort of drive and motivation do we need to take the first courageous steps toward a new and fuller life?

Our motivation and drive have a tendency to decrease as we grow older, particularly if we have allowed them to atrophy with disuse. We have less energy, less competitive drive, less need to impress and please others. We may become complacent, and show less enthusiasm, support, and encouragement before starting on a new course of action. Some of us are more motivated than others; the way we handle the changes that come with age depend upon our temperament and our previous life experience as well as upon present circumstances and opportunities.

Long-term goals and established patterns of social behavior at home and at work form the framework for our lives. When our circumstances change in mid-life or later, due to retirement, an empty nest, or other factors, some of this external framework is removed and we are forced to change our ways. If we are not prepared for these changes, adjustment can be difficult. When long-range goals and aims are thwarted, it is particularly difficult to cope with the resulting frustration. Emotional stress is often the result.

No matter what our age, emotional stress and frustration have a huge impact on our lives. Our main concern is to reduce that stress, defuse that frustration. Sometimes it is difficult, in discouraging moments, to call forth the motivation we need as fuel against disappointment and frustration. We must mobilize our inner resources, protect our interests, and find the drive to take the first step toward adjustment and avoid negative reactions such as anger, despair, resignation and apathy.

In later life, motivation has a tendency to point the way to withdrawal and avoidance of action, simply because our physical and psychological resources cannot sustain the demands made upon them. Stress becomes doubly difficult to face. Stress that is not dealt with in a positive manner leads to frustration of the worst kind.

Being aware of the typically stressful situations that are likely to occur in our later lives can help us to prepare for, and learn to deal with, these crises.

CAUSES OF FRUSTRATION

- Failure of occupational aspirations with a consequent limitation of long-maintained living standards.
- Failure to keep pace with cultural, social and scientific developments, leading to a feeling of being out-of-date and out of touch with what's happening in the world.
- Loss of youthful vigor and freedom, coupled with the uninviting prospect of growing old, usually reinforced by prevailing social attitudes.
- Restrictions on activity.
- Occupational redundancy.
- Loss of valued or stabilizing emotional relationships through bereavement.
- Loss of employment or the departure of children from the family home.
- The insoluble problem of being caught in a web of unsatisfactory circumstances from which escape seems impossible, such as family ties, physical disability or lack of sufficient funds.

A critical episode at any time of life can change our attitudes and require us to make adjustments; being older simply makes that adjustment a little toughter and makes it take a little longer. We are also more prone, in later age, to more different kinds of crises, some of which – bankruptcy, deafness, a difficult operation – can be downright traumatic. A divorce after forty years of marriage is more difficult to adjust to than a divorce after ten years. These experiences create periods of conflict in our lives, provoke frustration and sometimes despair, and demand of us that we marshal our forces and reorganize our motives and actions and the pattern of our daily lives.

The other side of the coin is the pleasant one – the happy experiences: falling in love again, coming into money, moving to a pleasanter community, achieving success or honors. We must be emotionally prepared to meet the good times, too. Any change, even a pleasant one, can cause anxiety. Being well-adjusted means that as we grow older our emotional stability allows us to be resourceful in adapting to changed circumstances, whether they be pleasant or disastrous.

To accomplish this ability to cope well, we must strengthen our basic personalities. Perhaps we must simplify our lives; perhaps we must change our ways altogether. In any case, aging is a task we must confront.

Successful and unsuccessful aging

The strategies we have used, and used successfully, for coping with stress during our youth and middle age may fail us as we get older. A first step toward learning to develop new coping strategies is to understand the pitfalls and learn how to prepare for them. There are several factors that can make adjustment difficult.

Anxiety increases steadily with age, especially among people who do not have strong support systems or who suffer from ill health, lack of sufficient money, or professional stability. As we grow older, increased anxiety can cause us to become overly cautious, less confident, and more worried about "what might happen."

'*Rigidity* is the inability to modify habits. Naturally habitual ways of thinking and behaving intensify with age, partly because the long familiarity with a stable environment has "shaped" our behavior to the point where it is no longer flexible. With rigidity comes a tendency to repeat ourselves, to ossify our opinions, and to be less and less open-minded to change and new ideas.

Intelligence, too, is an important determinant of personal adjustment. If we feel our sharpness becoming dull, our quickness of mind becoming slow, we become discouraged, fearful, and timid. It's important to realize that we are just as intelligent as we ever were; it's just that thoughts, like some actions, take us a little longer than they used to.

Personal adjustment is considered successful when a person can overcome frustrations, resolve conflicts, and achieve socially-acceptable satisfactions and achievements. As you'd expect, good adjustment expresses itself in happiness, confidence, sociability, self-esteem, and productive activity.

Personal adjustment is considered unsuccessful if the individual cannot overcome frustrations, solve problems, or find a way of life that fits in with social standards. Common signs of poor adjustment are hostility, unhappiness, fear of people, morbid anxiety, dependence, guilt, feelings of inferiority, apathy, withdrawal, and incompetence at life's simpler tasks.

There are ways to cope with stress which will help you avoid the symptoms of poor adjustment. A good way to begin is to give your mind a break; teach yourself to be mellower, calmer, and more serene.

Remind yourself frequently that your later years need not be static and unchanging. If we are prepared, personal adjustment should evolve smoothly and logically out of earlier patterns of behavior coupled with the application of new knowledge and new attitudes. If we can maintain a sense of continuity and identity in spite of those inevitable physiological, social and psychological changes, we can make our transitions easily and with grace. Normal aging is a gradual process; we don't have to cope with it all at once. If we accept the idea that old age and even death are normal and natural consequences of living, we will even begin to feel a sense of euphoria arising from our renewed sense of security and our relief from responsibilities. We will be fit; we will be tranquil; we will be ourselves.

Stress control and relaxation

Living in the twentieth century means that we feel more stress than people have ever felt before. We live in a fast-moving, success-oriented society where competitiveness and the desire to succeed dominate our working lives and even our private time. We are increasingly susceptible to stress-related illnesses, so it is important that we understand just how much pressure we are under, what effect it has upon our health and well-being, and how we can cope with it when things get out of control.

A moderate amount of stress can be good for us. Research has shown that stress can even improve our performance – up to a point. Many of us thrive on pressure, and perform more efficiently and even more joyfully when we are meeting a deadline, living up to a difficult standard, or trying to break a record. There are some people who actually need stress in order to function at maximum efficiency. For most of us, however, if stress goes beyond a certain point we start to crumble; we are on the way to mental and physical illness, or exhaustion. Before we can learn to lead an active but serene life, we must come to terms with the causes of stress, learn to recognize its symptoms, and understand the important part stress plays in our health and well-being. Then, we can either get rid of it or to cope with it. We can learn not to let it interfere with our lives.

Flight or fight Our immediate response to stress is the "flight or fight" reflex. This reflex prepares our bodies by signaling to our muscles, eyes, breath rate and heart beat either to run from our enemies or to fight them. It is primarily a hormonal response: the brain sends messages to the two adrenal glands that lie on top of the kidneys. The message is recognized immediately, and the body begins to pump out adrenalin. The physical effects of this rush of adrenalin are familiar to all of us:

• Our hearts begin to pound quickly, so that the maximum amount of blood is pumped through our bodies, readying them for any kind of action.

• The rate at which we breathe increases so that our blood carries the maximum amount of oxygen to our muscles.

• Blood pressure increases, so that our essential organs are well supplied with blood.

• Blood vessels in our skin and internal organs constrict so that a large supply of blood is available throughout our bodies. We are primed, and ready to run.

• Our pupils enlarge so that we can see whatever is frightening us and a clear path to get away from it.

• The blood sugar rises steeply, making available a large supply of energy, should we need to flee from an adversary or fight one.

Our emotional responses to stress are affected by our sex, cultural background, heredity, and the ways we have been taught to deal with stress. In most western societies it is traditionally acceptable for women to become upset and cry, or to flee, while men and even little boys are encouraged to stand and fight, and face stress with a stiff upper lip.

Knowledge tells us that most stressful situations *can't* be resolved by fleeing or fighting, even though our instincts tell us they can. All that adrenalin is being pumped through our bodies to make us ready to obey these instincts, but though our bodies are switched on, our minds tell us to repress the desire for fight or flight. The result – stress. Tension and frustration promote further stress, and a vicious cycle is set up.

Results of stress

If the blood pressure remains elevated for any length of time, there can be damage to the arteries and possibly even a heart attack. We know that certain conditions are stress-related – migraine headaches, for instance. Skin conditions such as eczema and itching of the skin, and a group of conditions such as spastic colon, dyspepsia, and duodenal ulcer may also result from stress.

There are many life-threatening diseases linked to stress – severe chronic high blood pressure, heart disease, peptic ulcers, and asthma. Research has shown that when we are under stress we are far more susceptible to viral infections and colds, and some authorities even claim that the development of certain kinds of cancer can be related to stress. Stress-related problems specific to women include menstrual disorders, pelvic pain, sexual difficulties, premenstrual tension, and disturbance of ovarian function, leading to failure to ovulate.

Dealing with stress

One of the best ways to cope with stress is to be active. Physical activity counteracts stress. Take any kind of exercise – go for a walk, jog, play a game of tennis, tackle a household chore, join an exercise class. Analyzing your problem and figuring out how to cope with it can also help. Sit down and make a list of possible solutions, narrow it down to the best three, and then choose the ideal solution. It is better to control the stress before you react to it if you possibly can, but of course it's not always possible to jump the gun on a stressful situation. A general plan for dealing with stress will help you to anticipate stressful situations and deal with them as they come up. Review your own attitudes, become aware of which important hurdles you want to get over the first, and analyze the beliefs and ideas you have to change, along with some of your habits. This may lead to a significant change in your lifestyle. You may find yourself aspiring to, and acquiring, new skills and coping mechanisms – ones that are more appropriate to our "civilized" society than the primitive instincts of flight or fight.

Two possible skills for you to learn, in the course of your stress management plan, are *deep muscle relaxation and mental relaxation*. (see page 81). Mastering these techniques will enable you to deal with stress, change some entrenched habits like smoking or drinking, and prepare you to face the problems that life presents. You might try combining the deep muscle drills and the relaxation drills. At the beginning, you should practice each drill twice a day. Once you have mastered these skills you can practice them more frequently. Don't be concerned if it takes a few weeks to become comfortable while doing them. As you go along, you will find yourself achieving the well-being that comes through relaxing and managing stress.

Two other techniques can help your body cope with stress – *instant relaxation* and *imagery training*. (see page 82). A combination of these four techniques will always help you in an emergency stress situation. Regular practice of all of them will keep you stress-resistant.

These relaxation techniques have other benefits, too. They are a sure-fire aid in giving up unhealthy habits like smoking or drinking too much – habits that at least partially result from the need to be "doing something" when stress strikes. Keeping the body and mind toned up and active will make it possible for you to resist "the most difficult cigarettes of the day" or that drink you might reach for in a tough moment. The same is true for overeating, of course – having something constructive and simple to do, such as a relaxation exercise, can help you to bypass the cookie jar.

DEEP MUSCLE RELAXATION

Deep muscle relaxation is a technique that was devised at the Stanford Heart Disease Prevention Center. It may take a little time and effort to learn but it will be well worth it. It is designed to help us to cope with stress, lower blood pressure and decrease the chance of getting headaches, thus allowing us to sleep better and feel less anxious. This is the drill to follow:

• Find a quiet place and lie on your back in a comfortable position. If this isn't possible just sit comfortably as you can and close your eyes.
• The next part of the drill involves your right hand if you are right-handed and your left hand if you are left-handed. Begin by tensing your right (left) hand for just a moment and relaxing it by letting it go loose. Actually *tell* your hand to feel heavy and warm. Moving up your right (left) side of your body to your forearm, upper arm, shoulder, foot, lower leg, and upper leg, go right round the right (left) side of your body. Then do exactly the same thing with the left (right) side of your body. Your hands, arms and legs should feel heavy, relaxed and warm. Give yourself a few seconds for those feelings to develop.
• Now try relaxing your hip muscles. Let the relaxation flow up from your abdomen into your chest. Don't try to tense your muscles, just tell them to feel heavy and warm. You will find that your breathing starts to slow down; wait for this to happen. Concentrate on your breathing.
• Let the relaxation flow up into your shoulders, jaw and the muscles in your face. Pay special attention to those muscles around your eyes and in your forehead. Actively get rid of any frowns. Finish by telling your forehead to feel cool.

If possible you should practice this drill twice a day, for fifteen to twenty minutes each time. If this isn't possible, three or four minutes are better than nothing.

MENTAL RELAXATION

This involves clearing your mind of any stressful thoughts, anxieties and worries. The drill is based on the Stanford technique.

• Just let thoughts flow through your head; let them freely associate.
• If any thought recurs; stop it by saying "no" firmly under your breath.
• Close your eyes and imagine a calm scene – such as a clear blue sky and a calm blue sea or any object that hasn't any fussy details. Blue is very relaxing.
• Concentrate hard on your breathing and become aware of its natural rhythm.

• You should be feeling calm and rested by now. You may find it helpful to repeat a soothing word such as "love," "peace," "calm" or a word with less symbolism as "breath," "earth" or "laugh." Think of the word or even a calming sound like "ah" when you are breathing outward.
• Keep the muscles of your face, eyes and forehead relaxed, and tell your forehead to feel cool.

INSTANT RELAXATION

• Arrange your body comfortably, sitting. You can also teach yourself to stand comfortably, even when you are waiting in a line, or if you are facing a stressful, worrying experience.
• Take a deep breath and hold it for five seconds. Count to five slowly then breathe out. Repeat this for several seconds.

• Tell all your muscles to relax.
• Repeat this two or three times until you're completely relaxed.
• Imagine as pleasant a thought as circumstances permit, such as learning how to relax or again imagining a pleasant scene, peaceful countryside or a beautiful view of sunset.

IMAGERY TRAINING

This helps you to use your imagination by breaking down your mental blocks. You get more in touch with your body so that you can control it. Sometimes it is quite difficult to learn, but here is a simple exercise for you to follow:

• Think of your left hand and make it feel warm. Imagine your right thigh and make it feel warm. Make it feel heavy. Now try two harder tests. Imagine that one leg is heavier than the other. It may seem odd at first but it is worth practicing to get control of the feelings in your body through your imagination. Once you can do these tests easily you will find deep muscle relaxation simple. You should be able to control your body to keep away headaches, migraine attacks and lower your blood pressure.

Depression

To some degree, depression is a universal human experience. Nobody is lucky enough to go through life without encountering situations that take him right down to rock bottom. Depression is customary in certain situations, is even an appropriate reaction when something terrible has happened.

Nevertheless, even the mildest depression is not desirable. It is often avoidable, and something *can* be done about it.

Some people are prone to depression even when things are not going wrong. For them, depression is an attitude toward life. We might describe a person as a depressed type if he or she has a pessimistic temperament, always expects the worst out of life, and usually gets it. A negative attitude like this can have a snowball effect; it can be habitual. All of us have low, depressed moods from time to time, but usually we can pull ourselves out of them. The "Monday morning blues" are usually forgotten by Tuesday. But some people get stuck in the blues groove and have a tough time getting out of it.

How do we know when we're about to go down into the dumps? The feelings are familiar – apprehension, gloom, fatigue, a sense that this is going to be a lousy day no matter what happens. Mild attacks of depression can strike any time, sometimes as a result of something that actually happens (this makes it easier to understand) and sometimes out of the blue.

Depression may be accompanied by more disturbing feelings such as a sense of not being loved or appreciated. These feelings are often turned in upon ourselves, making us feel useless, worthless, and unlovable. As the depression goes deeper, we may have a real feeling of loss. Resentfulness follows. How else can we fight back? We begin to use our depression as a defense mechanism; we switch off, retreat, until we feel better. If the protective mechanism doesn't work, and we *don't* feel better soon, our body may "blow a fuse;" a real depressive illness may be the result. This kind of depression is very different from the common blue mood or occasional day in the dumps that we all feel occasionally. Deep depression involves our physical as well as mental well-being. It is a real, dysfunction.

It's important to seek professional help if depression persists. Most forms of depression do not respond to self-help, especially if the problem that's causing the depression can't be solved.

Defense Mechanisms In order to realize that we are depressed, and to be able to assess how depressed we are, and why, we must be in touch with our feelings. To be able to explain that we are feeling depressed, we have to recognize that depression really *exists*, that we are indeed suffering from it. Many of us cannot recognize depression, and even if we could we would not be able to express what the depressive feeling is like. We have been brought up to believe that one must put on a smile and not "air one's dirty laundry," so we tend to blame our bad moods on the weather, the stars, or some minor irritation such as the car not starting. This means that many of us may be depressed without realizing it. We are masking depression.

Our bodies have protective mechanisms against physical injuries and also against psychological stresses. When our psyches "realize" that we are depressed, defense mechanisms come into play. What psychologists call *displacement* is the commonest of these mechanisms. It diverts our attention from the thing that's threatening us and onto something else – something less threatening and easier to accept or to cope with. A secondary concern, therefore, acts as a smokescreen for the first.

Many of us handle depression simply by denial. We try to persuade ourselves that something isn't so in the hope that it will go away. We tell ourselves that we are not depressed, that we are really "O.K.," and we put on a brave front. Some severely depressed people go to a great deal of trouble to look well and happy. This strategy may work for a while and the depression may even go away by itself, but usually it does not.

Causes of depression

Depression has physical, psychological, and social causes. Physical causes include head injuries and operations on certain crucial parts of the body such as the head, eyes, hands, and genital organs. Infectious diseases, particularly viral infections, influenza, and hepatitis are often followed by a period of depression. This kind of depression should be treated by a physician, as it is actually another illness added to the troubles the patient already has. Changes in the brain, such as those caused by a stroke, can lead to mood changes, alteration of behavior, and sometimes to depression.

The social causes of depression are nearly always associated with separation and loss. Being poor doesn't necessarily lead to depression, but poverty is definitely a stressor, particularly for older people: it is disheartening to have to give up an outing because of fear of slipping on the ice or hoisting oneself onto a crowded bus. As people grow older and their energies and general level of agility decrease, the ills of poverty become harder and harder to bear. One social factor – isolation – is very closely linked to depression. The older a person grows, the fewer friends he or she has. For some reason, people tend to gravitate toward their peers, not toward older people.

Depression is often associated with emotional crises. Often these emotional crises cannot be avoided; they are either emergencies or predictable stages in emotional growth. Once we have survived them, we can look back upon them as growth experiences, but while we are in the midst of them, we lack that perspective. There are two basic kinds of life crisis that all of us have to face.

Internal crises

A developmental or internal crisis occurs whenever we are about to move from one stage of our life into another, or from one role to another. There are turning-points all through our lives – going off to school, having a first love, having children, reaching middle-age, retiring, facing death. Many of these landmark experiences involve changes in the degree of independence and autonomy we have, and in our relations with others; usually we are moving toward greater and greater independence, while others – children, older parents – are becoming dependent upon us. These crises also reflect change in the roles we play; it's quite a transition to go from being a child to being an adolescent or from being a parent to being a grandparent. Sometimes these transitions go smoothly and pleasantly, and there are no physical or psychological side effects. More often, however, they cause anxiety and mild depression. Life is not easy, and it's least easy when it's in flux.

External crises

Crises that threaten us from outside ourselves are less predictable than developmental crises; it's difficult to be prepared for them, because you never know which ones are going to strike, or when. External crises are potentially threatening to our safety and our well-being. They can be failures, such as loss of financial security, being fired from a job, failing to get a promotion, standing by while the love of your life marries someone else. These crises are sometimes of our own making, but often they are the making of others, or of bad luck. Then, there are acute losses that leave painful spaces in our lives – infidelity, abortion, bereavement, divorce, loss of sexuality. When these things happen it's hard to strike back; neither fight nor flight can save us.

We also undergo a crisis when we move from one job to another, move from one location to another, or begin a new life with a new partner. Some of these transitions involve the loss of comforting guidelines or a network of supporting friends and relatives. Depression occurs when a person cannot cope with the change or the crisis, or when he or she has trouble adapting and coping but needs more support and time than are available. Such a person often views change as leaving something behind rather than as going forward to something new. The emphasis on loss rather than gain causes uncertainty, fear, and anxiety, and the depression deepens. Help becomes necessary.

Depression and aging

We are more vulnerable at certain stages of our life than we are others – more vulnerable to external changes, and also to normal, developmental crises. During these times of our life we are more prone to depression. As we grow older, our adaptability lessens, and crises become more difficult to face. A woman entering her menopause may have difficulty facing the fact that she can no longer bear children, even though her own children are grown and she has no real desire to start over again. A man cherishes his power, largely represented by his earning capacity, and letting go is difficult. For both men and women, a loss of sexuality is threatening and often depressing. As we retire and get older we start to fear that the world is passing us by.

Depression is not inevitable at any stage of life, and some lucky people avoid it altogether, but most of us will find the aging process conducive to rocky times. The more difficulties we have had in our early lives, the more vulnerable we are as we age. It is usually those people who have suffered an early loss in infancy or childhood or who have not had their needs met when they were young who are more likely, in later life, to become depressed when either external or internal change exposes them to stress.

A wide range of social and psychological stresses may contribute to the onset of depression. Bereavement is the obvious one and the most dramatic, but other causes such as our children getting married or moving away, our friends being ill or incapacitated, or the world moving in a direction we don't like can cause us acute distress. And distress may lead to depression.

No matter how well managed, the retirement process is also a time of stress. At one clip a person can lose business friends, income, a major source of satisfaction, and a position of prestige. It may seem that this is the end of useful life.

We may feel that we are valued less and less as we grow older, in industry, in recreation, and within our families. Modern society considers experience to be less important than vitality and originality, and this can fill us with a sense of inferiority that is accentuated by a lower income and a smaller house. All of this can be made worse by the pain and deprivation of a long-term illness, physical signs of the aging process, and the knowledge that the end of life is approaching.

Some people find it very difficult to shoulder the stresses and responsibilities that are peculiar to getting older. They find themselves in a new territory that has never been explained or explored, and they are bewildered. These older people, left standing on the outside of the work-force and the culture that goes with it, feel that they are unimportant, non-contributing members of society and perhaps even feel guilty that they are heavy consumers of entertainment and support services and do not "give anything back." It is hardly surprising that they are besieged by feelings of self-doubt and unworthiness. Many self-possessed people are devastated to find that they are unable to care for themselves, drive their own cars, and continue to live autonomously. It takes a stalwart emotional makeup to withstand the strains of aging.

One way to begin dealing with the stress that can lead to depression is to learn to recognize the symptoms before they take over. All of us have some of these symptoms, to a greater or lesser degree, but when one of them becomes persistent, or interferes with our well-being, it's time to take a good hard look at ourselves and to go for help if the symptom doesn't respond to our efforts to make it go away.

Symptoms of depression

Sadness and tearfulness

Sadness is probably the most common sign of depression. People who are chronically depressed always look sad; their faces are immobile and they express very few emotions. They rarely smile and they may spend long periods of time gazing into space, looking as if they were about to burst into tears. Tearfulness goes hand in hand with sadness. Crying can become a habit, and many depressed people cry a lot – most often when they are alone.

Sleep disturbance

Nearly everyone who is depressed suffers some kind of sleep disturbance. Research has shown that people who are depressed spend more time getting off to sleep, lying awake in the early hours of the morning, and waking up repeatedly during the night than people who are not depressed. The less sleep a person gets each night, the greater the likelihood that he or she will feel below par physically, which only adds to the problem of depression.

On the other hand, some people react to depression by increasing the number of hours each day that they sleep. They use sleep as an escape from their problems and take every possible opportunity for a nap, an early night, or a chance to "sleep in" in the morning. This extra sleep is not refreshing, however, and the depressed person who sleeps too much often feels more fatigue than the person whose sleep patterns are diminished.

Loss of appetite

It is very common for depressed people to lose their appetites. They can be infuriating to cook for; they pick at food, complain about it, say that they are not hungry, and push their food around on the plate. This can lead to a loss of weight which can be worrisome as well as unbecoming. Some depressed people go for days without eating anything at all.

Neglect of appearance

When depression is deep, some people let themselves go and quit caring about their appearance and personal hygiene. They may become slovenly, messy, even dirty. Formerly well-dressed women no longer bother to fix their hair or apply make up, and just throw on the same old clothes day after day. Men tend to remain unshaven and look dirty and unkempt. They may even smell.

Fearfulness

Depressed people are often fearful, timid, and unadventurous. People who have always been independent and peripatetic become housebound. Some depressed people become afraid of driving or have panic attacks in crowded shops, on trains, or while crossing bridges. A once-active husband who becomes too timid to drive the car or run an errand can cause an upset in lifestyle for his wife and family. Fear can turn a capable, well-adjusted person into a social cripple.

Anxiety

Very few depressed people are entirely free from anxiety and many of them feel anxious most of the time. Sometimes the anxiety takes the form of panic attacks, with symptoms like sweating, rapid breathing, palpitation, and dizziness. These attacks may be provoked by one of the obsessional fears that plague the person or they may occur without any perceptible cause.

Depressed people may develop a general, "floating" anxiety in anticipation of events, even those that may never happen. They become uncontrollably upset at the thought of something that may be hours or even days off. If someone is afraid to be left alone, for example, he or she may begin to worry about what will happen when everyone is out of the house two weeks hence.

Indecision

People who are severely depressed find it difficult to make even the simplest decision. It can be agony to witness a depressed person spend long minutes deciding which socks to wear or what dress to put on. Sometimes they are unable to make a choice at all and may elect to do nothing rather than decide between two alternatives.

Coupled with this lowered ability to make up their minds is a loss of good judgment; when they do make a decision, it is likely to be the worst of all the options. A depressed person cannot be relied upon to make a sound judgment, and those who care for the person must face this fact early on. It is not uncommon for depressed people to find what seem to them to be convincing or compelling ways to "get out of" their depression: they don't believe that they are suited to their wife or husband, so divorce is the answer; they don't get on with their bosses, so they quit the job; the neighbors are unfriendly, so they sell the house and move.

Agitation
Some depressed people are sad, apathetic, and slow-moving while others are agitated, nervous, and tense. They may pace the floor, wring their hands, jump from one activity to another, and run the gamut of moods from giggles to tears for no understandable reason. People whose moods shift a great deal are very difficult to live with. They usually complain a great deal and find fault with everything that's done for them. They may talk a lot and bombard people with endless anecdotes and questions, the majority of which are centered on themselves – their favorite topic of conversation. They may be so mentally agitated that their ideas follow no discernible pattern or sequence, and they may constantly suffer floods of emotion.

Tiredness and weakness
Fatigue and debility are signs of chronic depression. Some people seem to become exhausted after only the slightest effort and so they sit around a great deal, sighing and complaining that they "never get any rest." Depression can slow everything down so that thinking, feeling, and acting are all enormous, insurmountable tasks. If a person is severely depressed and reacts to it by lying around the house in a state of chronic fatigue, it is nearly impossible to get him going or to rouse his enthusiasm, even for a favorite type of activity.

Poor concentration and memory
These two symptoms are particularly annoying and frustrating. Depressed people suffer from a shortened attention span and cannot complete the simplest task without becoming distracted. They can't think straight, and their minds always wander back to their favorite subject – their problems. Their memories fail,

especially for recent and trivial things, and they forget where they put things, what they had for lunch, whether or not they remembered to take their medicine. This mental disorganization leads to a lack of confidence and self-esteem. A patient may perceive his or her depression as senility, and become even more depressed. This type of depression can often be cured by a prescription anti-depressant drug.

Loss of libido

One of the key features of depression is that sufferers stop getting pleasure out of life. One of the first pleasures to go is an interest in sex. This is exacerbated when the depressed person is getting along in years and is likely to be preoccupied about waning sexuality. Depression ranks high on the list of conditions that reduce sexual desire. A depressed man often cannot get or sustain an erection. He then becomes anxious about this, and his anxiety may further complicate the problem. Performance anxiety is a major cause of potency problems for men of all age groups. A woman who is experiencing menopause may become convinced that she has "dried up" and is no longer capable of being a sexual partner or of attracting a man. Such an attitude only serves to deepen the existing depression. As the depression lifts, she may need advice about such things as lubricants and self-stimulation.

Loss of sociability

Another main feature of depression is a feeling of flatness and loss of pleasure from those activities that normally give life a big lift. When the pleasure is lost, so is the drive to pursue these activities, and the result is inertia. Friendships suffer and eventually close family relationships cease to be important. The depressed person may stop writing letters and using the telephone. If this condition deepens, the family may even be rejected and the depressed person may retire into a world populated only by himself or herself. It is important for the family of such a person to remember that they are not at fault and that a depressive illness can control a person so totally that he or she cannot behave differently; it is the nature of the disease that the desire to behave differently is simply not there.

Once you have taken a long look at this list of symptoms, you will be more able to stop them in yourself or in someone else. Remember that depression usually doesn't "just go away," and that the wisest course of action is to get yourself, or your friend, to a doctor as soon as possible. There are several kinds of treatment for depression; the chances are, one of them will work for you.

Treatment of depression

Most depression can be successfully treated. Sometimes, a case needs to go no farther than the family doctor; perhaps he will prescribe medicine, or may be he will suggest some sort of activity or even therapy. Very few cases are severe enough to require long-term psychiatric help, but often a few sessions with a psychologist or psychiatrist are indicated in order to help the patient understand his symptoms and take the first steps back to mental health. There are drugs that work in some cases, but they are contra-indicated in others. Only your doctor can decide which are best for you.

It is of prime importance that a depressed person choose a doctor he really trusts. Since the person's outlook on life is inclined to be pessimistic and anxious during depression it's crucial that he or she select a doctor whose judgment and advice will really be valued. After an examination and consultation, the doctor will decide which kind of treatment is best.

Drugs

Anti-depressant drugs counter the changes in brain chemistry that accompany depression. The most commonly prescribed drugs are the *tricyclic antidepressants*, of which Elevil and Tofranil are examples. If the patient is apathetic and lacking in momentum, Tofranil is usually given because it is a stimulant. If, on the other hand, the patient is agitated and nervous, Elavil will probably be the drug of choice. If there is heart disease involved, Sinequan is sometimes preferred. The use of these drugs must be monitored very carefully because of the possibility of serious side-effects such as fainting, urinary retention, and severe constipation. If a patient has glaucoma, these drugs may not be used. Dosages must be smaller for elderly patients, than for younger adults.

There is a "new generation" of anti-depressant drugs which are being used increasingly for the treatment of depression in older patients. Two of these drugs are Ludiomil and Desyrel. These drugs are not more effective than the others, but they frequently work faster and may have milder side effects. Finally, lithium is a drug used for patients who have manic depressive symptoms. With the use of lithium blood levels must be monitored at regular intervals. The drug carries some risk, but its effects can be dramatic. Lithium has proven successful in many cases of severe of recurrent cyclical depression.

Electro-shock therapy

It has long been know that electrical activity in the brain can affect our moods. People with epilepsy often find that their moods improve after an attack, and in the 1930s a Viennese psychiatrist found that severely depressed patients responded positively to artificially induced seizures. Nowadays, the modern form of this treatment, electro-shock therapy, is very sophisticated. The patient's anxiety about the procedure is reduced by the use of a quick-acting anesthetic and the convulsions can be suppressed, or cushioned, by the use of specific drugs.

Although the idea of shock treatment may sound frightening, the actual procedure is usually not distressing to the patient. Following each treatment the patient may have a mild headache and a slight loss of memory, but these symptoms pass quickly. After a course of five of six treatments, usually given twice a week, the patient will feel a dramatic relief from depression. Electro-shock treatment is still the subject of continuing controversy among doctors, and, like all medical procedures, is not a universal answer to depression. It is often indicated for patients who cannot tolerate the side effects of the anti-depressant drugs, or when the suicide hazard is great and fast relief of the depression is desired.

Psychological therapy

Psychological methods are of great value in helping depression. These methods can often get to the root of the *cause* of the depression and help the patient understand the causes as well as the symptoms of the disease. Thus, the patient can take an active part in the cure.

Counseling is a form of treatment where therapist and patient sit down together, talk about the problem, and try to decide what can be done about it. A counselor finds out from the patient what is really happening and helps the patient distinguish between what is reality and what is fantasy. He or she may give advice and make suggestions, help the depressed person formulate a plan of action, and give emotional support. The patient is, to a large degree, "in charge" and will actually make the decisions, and act upon them, alone. A counselor does not need to be a doctor, but usually has had some training in psychodynamically-oriented psychotherapy. Often, a counselor is a social worker.

Psychotherapy is a specialized form of counseling that aims to promote new emotional learning. An easy way of describing psychotherapy is to say that it provides "a corrective emotional experience." For depression, therapy is used to explore the patient's inner conflicts, and learn how they gave rise to guilt, aggression, apathy, or other symptoms of depression. It is hoped that the patient, guided by the security of the relationship with the therapist, will learn to cope better and find his way back, to serenity and good adjustment. (See *Specialist help*.) Some psychologists provide this kind of therapy, but many patients are advised to see a psychiatrist, a physician who has specialized in psychotherapy and/or analysis. A family doctor can help decide which sort of therapist would help the most, depending upon the nature of the depression, the personnel available, and the patient's financial resources.

Group therapy

In this form of treatment, a psychiatrist, psychologist, social worker, or psychiatric nurse guides a small group of patients, usually eight or ten people, toward the resolution of their emotional difficulties. The group is a place for change mediated throughout the relationships that develop among individual members and the therapist, who functions as the group leader. In the group interaction, the members benefit by sharing problems and insights in a mutually supportive way. Treatment for depression is often comprehensive, involving more than one or a combination of these approaches.

Loneliness

Loneliness, unlike depression, is not an illness or a sign of emotional stress. It is a result of being alone. Some older people enjoy living alone, seeing people infrequently, and leading a very private, almost hermetic life. But these people are rare. Most of us need the close interaction we've become accustomed to, and we feel acute distress when we have to face long periods of time alone or without a confidant.

An older person who is alone and not active socially is likely to be bored and irritated at first. Then, he or she either does something about the loneliness – cultivates friends or interests – or else becomes more passive, apathetic, and inert. Stagnation leads to further decreases in alertness and interest and to a loss of mental and physical skills through disuse. Research has shown that elderly people who live with others and engage in active social interaction actually show an increase in mental abilities, while those who withdraw from life show a decline.

Prodding an older person into action and trying to overcome his or her reluctance to participate in social activities *may* be an unwarranted intrusion into that person's privacy, but it is undeniably true that a change of surroundings, the stimulation of conversation and activity, and guidance can help a person to renew and maintain an interest in life and derive a new-found enjoyment from the company of others.

Through events such as bereavement, some older people are left without any one person with whom they can enjoy close emotional contact. Such a person is prone to loneliness and is often unequipped with the coping strategies to deal with it, particularly if he or she has always been part of a couple. For a very old person, there can seem to be no hope of forming a new and satisfactory substitute. Fortunately, bereavement usually brings strong support from other people. This is vital. The ability to re-establish normal patterns of behavior varies from one person to another, but all of us need all the help we can get, not only right after the bereavement, but in months and years to come. The presence of an extensive network of sympathetic friends and family members obviously reduces the severity of loss and hastens recovery.

Loneliness is remediable. Such suffering used to be regarded as natural; people were expected to go through long periods of mourning, during which it was considered disrespectful to dance, smile, or have a good time. But those days are over, and we need not accept loneliness any more than we need fear childbirth, mental illness, or senility. Men and women no longer need to face retirement as a dramatic dislocation which will lead to a similarly dramatic loss of self-esteem. And loneliness is not an inevitable part of aging. We're tougher than we think, we live longer than people used to live, and we deserve to enjoy our later years to the fullest. Loneliness is preventable, curable, and unnecessary. There are many simple and inexpensive ways to cope with it.

TIPS FOR COPING WITH LONELINESS

One of the best ways of coping with loneliness is to face up to it. You will get great insight into just how lonely you are if you keep a diary. Get out a piece of paper and pencil and write down the times of day and night when you feel you are at your lowest ebb, when you are the most lonely. For instance, you may realize that the worst times are evenings from about six o'clock onward, Saturday nights, Sundays and holidays. Now that you have narrowed those times down, they may be much less frequent than you think.

Making new friends

You probably also miss physical closeness: holding hands, being touched, a gentle squeeze, a warm cuddle, and sexual expression. You may want company with the opposite sex but are uncertain about your feelings. You are uncertain about where and how you should meet other people, when you should begin dating, what you should do about your sexual yearnings, how to come to terms with guilt feelings about being interesed in people other than your lost companion. You may even feel anger toward well-meaning friends who seem to be betraying your dead partner by trying to arrange dates for you. Try to separate yourself from such feelings. It is absolutely right that you should remember your partner, and feel loyal to him or her. It is also quite normal to want another to hold you, comfort you and make love to you.

Planning time

You can start splitting up your evenings during the week by allocating them to different activities. You could go to night school on one and take up a new hobby, craft or subject for study. You could make one evening a time for having some friends into your house, and another for visiting someone else. You could make another evening an occasion for going to the movies, the theater or a concert with a friend. Another could be devoted to keeping fit by going to a yoga class, having a game of squash or tennis, or going to a gym for a workout. Another could be for a home hobby like painting, gardening, carpentry, or just doing odd jobs around the house. Saturday night could be something special. You could join a local club whose members are interested in the same things as you. It may be the local golf club, singles club, bridge or dancing club, with special activities on Saturday nights. Sundays should be carefully planned. Unless you invite distractions, or go out to meet others, it is a long day because it is not easy to shop or do errands. The best and most satisfying way of occupying your Sundays is to invite friends into your home for lunch or brunch. Make it a very relaxed occasion and arrange the food so that people can come and go as they like.

Finding new interests

You are never going to meet people staying alone at home. You will have to get out to meet people; otherwise you will have to rely on friends bringing new acquaintances to your own home. One of the best ways of getting yourself out of the house is to decide to take up one of your pet passions. Have you always been interested in politics? If so, go to the next local political meeting. Have you always wanted to paint, or sculpt? In that case enroll in evening classes at the local school. Is clay pigeon shooting something you have always hankered after? Join the local rifle club and buy yourself a gun. If you have oodles of self-confidence, go to the local singles club. If you are really interested in making yourself physically acceptable, accessible and striking up acquaintances with people, you could go on a cruise or take up a travel-study program where you can travel and learn while vacationing in a foreign country.

Bereavement

The grief associated with bereavement is not always a feeling that's easy to describe. There may be a good deal of ambivalence at the time; for example, sorrow and disappointment may be mixed with anger, guilt and anxiety. Bereavement is a stress that can precipitate psychiatric disorders, psychosomatic illness or suicide. Many widows, for example, experience feelings of guilt about their role in the events leading up to the death of their husband, and widowhood reduces life expectancy. The psychological and social aspects of widowhood have been the subjects of systematic studies. The reorganization called for following the death of a spouse introduces an added source of stress with regard to emotional deprivation and living arrangements, and the increased risk of death of the bereaved person. There are good reasons for supposing that preparation and psychological support help to alleviate the distress that leads to personal conflict. In older people the awareness of dying has developed slowly. There has been enough time to adapt to the prevailing circumstances and time to learn appropriate strategies of adjustment. Without such adaptation, bereavement and the awareness of dying may evoke feelings of dread associated with a sense of isolation or rejection.

A certain amount of sociological research has been carried out in connection with bereavement in general, and widowhood in particular. The situation faced by women widowed in later life is eased somewhat by their realistic anticipation of this eventuality, and by the companionship of other women of comparable age who have also been widowed. This provides opportunities for receiving support and consolation and sharing of advice, help and so on. Widowers are usually in a less favorable situation.

The importance of grief

Bereavement is the loss of someone very precious; grief is the resulting emotional experience of being bereaved. Most people think of grief as a natural response to bereavement. Indeed, they would be suspicious of someone who denied or hid his or her grief. Nearly all of us see grief as therapeutic, and we are often told "Get it off your chest and have a good cry."

Grief is a more complicated process than that. It is dynamic and we live through it. We go through several steps, each of which is hard work. It is not a passive process of letting out pent-up feelings. It is an active process of adjustment. It is a positive "letting go" of something or someone that has been very precious to you for a long time.

Grief is important in that it is a half-way stage between the experience of losing something and coming to terms with the loss. When we are grief-stricken we have strong feelings that we have to deal with so the wound can heal. I personally have found grief easier to understand and live with since I read of Ross Mitchell's stages of grief. Perhaps if these stages were talked about more freely then the subject of death would not be taboo. These feelings come in clearly defined stages, each of which has to be endured, and they are listed below.

Anticipation

It is uncommon for bereavement to strike out of the blue. Most of us live in the expectation of death, though at some distance, but there is still a shock when death confronts us and our imaginary fears become real. Even when death comes at the end of a long illness there is still the reality and shock of loss. When death and bereavement is sudden the shock is greater still.

Loss

This encompasses a feeling of emptiness. We are very aware that something has gone, that someone has been taken away. There is an empty space where that person used to be. No matter what our feelings were toward that person, there is still a feeling of loss. It is obviously greater if the person was well loved but it can still exist even if the person was hated.

Numbness

This is a protective mechanism. It is a primitive shutting down of all our emotions. All our vital functions become extremely depressed. It is a kind of mechanical cut-out that stops us from feeling any more hurt.

Anger

Here we get indignant, rebellious and resentful that something we cherished so much has been taken away. We may want to grab it back. We may feel self-pity and wonder why it has happened to us. We may wonder what we have done to deserve this grief. We may feel that we have been unfairly singled out. We want to take revenge so we look around for someone to blame because we feel we may be in some way at fault.

Searching

This is where we set out to find what we have lost. We keep looking and hoping to find the person, even though we know we will never find him or her again. This is a way of denying to ourselves that our loved one has gone for good.

Denial

Here we deny to ourselves that we are not going to find our loved one. We keep on making excuses for the fact that we can't. We may believe that he or she is just round the corner. We will find him or her tomorrow. We will just have to wait and see. He or she will come back. It is a desperate game that we are playing with ourselves and with other people.

Acceptance

This occurs when our anger eventually burns itself out. The searching ceases when we realize that we are not going to find our loved one and our denial subsides. We face up to reality.

Letting go

At last, with acceptance, we know that our loved one has gone. We start to bury him or her in our minds. We no longer enshrine our lost one. We start to feel hope that new life has to be created. We move forward into a new stage of living.

Regrowth

This stage takes a long while to complete. We don't always look forward, we sometimes look backward and even return to previous stages. Ultimately, if we have gone through all the different stages, regrowth takes place and we gradually return to normal.

In life these stages are not separated – they overlap. The length of time we stay within each stage varies for each person, and in every circumstance. Numbness may last a few hours, a few days, a few weeks. Anger, searching and denial may go on for months. Acceptance, letting go and regrowth may take another six months, so it may be a year from the death that grieving is complete. There may be anniversary reactions when temporary renewals of grief appear for a time; these may lessen in intensity as time goes on.

Indications of grief

There is no right way to grieve. Grieving varies from person to person and from culture to culture. The point about grief is not *how* it is done but that it *should be done somehow*. Things may go wrong. Grief may be denied totally, or it can begin and then be inhibited. It may be turned inward into the body instead of outward to relationships with other people. We quite often see a person who appears not to be affected by grief, but know that such good spirits are superficial, false and brittle. If grief is delayed or inhibited, superficial relief is only gained for a short time. When grieving does start it is often more severe because it has been delayed. If grief is denied altogether, the person may slip from grief, which is normal and healing, into a depressive illness that is distressing and abnormal. When grief is turned inward into the body, the person may complain of physical illness. Research has shown that during the first six months after bereavement, widowers often complain of heart trouble which may in fact develop into one or another form of heart disease and lead to death from a "broken heart". Widows tend to consult their doctors with gastric upsets and rheumatic conditions.

It is very easy to confuse grief with depression. The bereaved person feels sad and lost. Appetite goes and sleep is interrupted. There may be reproach for not having cared more for the lost one. Kind friends may tell the person not to cry, not to be upset and to try to forget it all. That is exactly what a person must not do if he or she is to go through the natural stages of grieving. People must be allowed and encouraged to grieve.

Practicalities of bereavement

While no bereaved person should have to take major decisions concerning the future immediately, there are a few things which require immediate action concerning statutory responsibilities and personal arrangements for funeral burial or cremation, and sometimes this need for immediate action can be helpful rather than burdensome.

Statutory responsibilities
If the person dies at home, your family doctor or the police must be informed of the death. They will advise you on local death certificate procedures. In some states if death occurs within 24 hours of the patient's arrival in the hospital or in unusual circumstances, it must be reported to the local medical examiner, who may order a post-mortem. A decision to hold a post-mortem examination cannot be appealed. The body does not become the responsibility of the family until the post-mortem has been carried out.

Funeral arrangements
Once you have a death certificate from the doctor, you can make arrangements for burial or cremation. A funeral director can take over the arrangements for you from this point. You have to inform the director of your various wishes for different aspects of the funeral. The director will complete the death certificate and get from you authorization for cremation if you choose. He will file these forms with the health authorities along with a request for official copies for the family. Funerals are always somewhat more expensive than expected, and it may be

101

COPING WITH BEREAVEMENT

- It is important to realize that the feelings you are experiencing are normal. It is normal to feel rage and anger. You wouldn't be human if you didn't feel guilty, so don't spend a lot of emotional energy on self-recrimination.
- Try and find an understanding person to talk to. You can work out quite a lot of your anger, guilt, shame and grief on someone who will just listen, correct you when you over-react and sympathize with what you are going through. At this moment when you are in the depths of despair, an objective viewpoint that doesn't see life as entirely white or entirely black is one of the best helps you can have.
- As I have already said it is important to grieve. Grieve in your own time. Don't take any notice of people who encourage you to snap out of it or get back to normal. You will know when your grieving work is done, because you will feel it has worked its way out of your system and you will feel like starting afresh. If you really want to have a good cry, if you even want to have a conversation with your dead partner, go ahead and do so.
- Once the grieving is over, it is important that you start to think about regaining your identity, or even possibly building a new one. Resist the temptation to live in the past and to continue living through your dead partner. You should try to become your own person and to assert your own identity. Start shaping your life as it suits you by doing things that you are really interested in rather than continuing a past way of life.
- Don't make any big decisions quickly; instead, let yourself grow into them gradually. Some decisions may be quite hard to take at first. If left for several months or a year, a problem that seemed insoluble will have a very ready solution. Trust your own judgment and go on your own gut feeling, which has always served you well throughout your life. Don't

choose this moment to start doubting yourself without reason.
- Whatever you do, try to stay mobile. Don't find yourself chained to a house unable to get out. Not only see people but do essential shopping to give yourself vital changes of routine. Keep the family car. Or if you don't have one it may be worth using up some of your precious financial resources to buy one. If you don't drive consider taking driving lessons. If you haven't driven for a little while get a friend to accompany you on the roads to give you a bit of confidence. If at all possible take the car out several times a week so that you regain your confidence on the roads. Don't deprive yourself of the satisfaction of being able to take yourself off anywhere anytime if you want to. This knowledge in itself is comforting and morale-building.
- Don't neglect your finances. This is not a time to let them get out of control and find yourself in debt. So keep an eye on them, budget your expenses and keep a good check on all your sources of income. If you have never had to budget before in your life ask a friend to explain the rudiments of budgeting to you and to have a crack at organizing yours along with you. If you have the money and your affairs are complicated, get the help of an accountant immediately. Start keeping records of all your income and of everything you spend and try to balance the budget at the end of each week or each month.
- Though it seems unlikely while you are grieving, life does go on and you will live again and you will be happy again. Meanwhile you should take good care of yourself. Reward yourself with a holiday. Take the holiday you dreamed you might always take. Perhaps a world cruise. Treat yourself. Perhaps spend some time in your favorite surroundings or take a course to study a hobby. Try and get out and see members of the family and perhaps stay for a few days.

a wise precaution to contact several firms to ask them for written quotations and to make sure that you have the arrangements as you want them.

Financial and legal considerations

It is possible that you are entitled to Social Security survivors' benefits, which include a sum that will help toward meeting the expenses of the funeral. They may also help you with long-term finances. Your children and other dependents may benefit. To find out exactly what you can claim you should get in touch with your local Social Security office immediately. If necessary, you will have to go through your partner's papers and insurance provisions to claim on policies that covered funeral expenses, life insurance and mortgage payments. If you have any difficulty, contact your partner's lawyer immediately to discuss any bequest.

Medical help

Don't hesitate to turn to your family doctor for help. Doctors are very aware of, and sympathetic to, the apathy, lethargy and depression that can obstruct your chances of recovering from bereavement. While they should never be given in the long term, short courses of sedatives, hypnotics and tranquilizers can help you over a very upsetting week or so.

The help of others

When the acuteness of your initial grief has subsided, do try to prevent yourself from becoming a recluse by seeking the company of friends and relatives. One good friend may be sufficient. It can take a lot of courage and energy to pull yourself out of your despondency but your life has to go on and it will return to normal all the more quickly for having the comforting words and presence of others.

Draw up a schedule of visits, short trips, holidays, friends to stay, that will fill up the next few months. Telephone relatives and friends and arrange visits, either you to them or vice versa. You'll find that just looking forward to this future program of being with others helps to soothe your grieving and brings you gradually back to a normal life-style.

A lifetime of loving

As we get older we don't feel very different inside about anything, but particularly about loving; we love just as strongly and as passionately and as tenderly as we did when we were youngsters. While a loving older couple may look odd to people on the outside, it doesn't seem so very different to the couple from when they were young. However, we often find new ways of expressing love.

As loving and being loved do not stop when we reach a certain age, many of us have the time to search for its expression in different ways. We may develop companionship without passion or develop the way we express ourselves sexually. Such sexual development may be personal and private or it can be in tandem with a partner. It can be a very thrilling time.

Of the many good reasons for maintaining fitness and health throughout life, one of the best is that fitness allows, and may even encourage, continuation of sexual activity. Lack of fitness certainly inhibits it, and may even preclude it. Chronic ailments affecting the lungs and the heart, muscular strength and joint mobility act as deterrents to sexual activity. So, it is worth planning well ahead of time to have a fit, healthy and agile body as we get older, in order to be able to enjoy all the benefits of fitness including sexual activity.

Partnerships

A couple who has always shared strong physical affection is more likely to share caresses as they get older than a couple who has lost the habit of touching each other in middle age. The frequency of sexual contact is much less important. As we get older the meaning of sexual contact and its frequency have little to do with each other. Between a devoted couple, sexual union is an affirmation of something that goes well beyond momentary pleasure. Years of giving and receiving love strengthen the occasion. For many couples, only one contact a month may be fulfilling enough, reflecting three, four or five decades of intimacy. It also helps each partner to have a sense of being desirable, and to create the self-image of someone who is sexually alive. Anyone who has had an enduring relationship will miss the satisfaction and meaning of this kind of experience. Maintaining sensual awareness as we progress into older age makes us more vital and attractive in all sorts of relationships, not just sexual ones, and staying sexually alive helps us to avoid the drabness and grayness that a great many people wrongly associate with old age.

It is not surprising that this should happen. Research has shown that couples who experience middle age together feel a profound increase in personal satisfaction. This is not because partners improve miraculously, but we all develop greater tolerance, which may become spontaneous once we stop blaming our partners for our own shortcomings.

At last we know our partners really well and we now have the opportunity for true companionship – something that we might not have had the time to enjoy up until now. We know now how to strike a balance between shared interests with our partners and privacy. It's a good feeling to realize that we have the chance of growing old with someone with whom we can share memories, friends, odd pleasurable moments like walking in the rain or simply recapturing earlier joys which for many years we did not have time for, by spending some time together.

Everyday occurrences such as a visit to the store can be a celebration if we are able to respect each other's privacy, but still keep the door open for companionship. It gives confidence to feel certain that we will look after each other and helps to prepare for the future with a feeling of serenity and contentment. This contentment brings security and independence. As we grow older our engagement with the world is more and more narrowed down to engagement with a partner. This is part of becoming a more private person. If a person is content with him or herself, this act of drawing back brings a new stability, especially when a loving partner thinks the same way. There again partners can take up new roles. One's mate is not only a valuable companion, he or she can take up the role of a substitute parent, if you both wish.

Sex and sexual relationships

All of us are the richer for loving and expressing love. Sexuality is one part of that love – the capacity to respond to another person physically. There are many misleading and damaging myths about what happens to our sexuality as we grow older and I should like to explode a few of them.

Sexual myths   Many people are persuaded that men approaching fifty become paunchy, consider themselves less attractive and fear impotence. Women, once the fertile period of their lives is over, feel that the sexual aspects of their lives will dwindle quite rapidly into apathy. They fear they will be bereft of sexual excitement and pleasure. Naturally enough, men and women wonder and worry about life without the special closeness that comes through a physical relationship.

These misconceptions are supported by the popular belief that as we get older, sex becomes more and more wrong, even indecent, or, at the very least, not quite the thing for older people to do. The physical side of life during our older years is generally disapproved of and is quite frequently labeled "dirty." This may be a hangover from an age when sexual activity for carnal pleasure rather than child-bearing was thought unpardonable. Today, however, we recognize that with her child-bearing life behind her, a woman can look forward to many years of a different kind of sexual activity, more beautiful, more relaxed and more leisurely than ever before.

One of the problems with the dissemination of information about sex is that the good news is kept secret. In a recent survey undertaken by the English periodical, *The Observer*, it was found that many people in their seventies and older not only need to have, but actually do have, active sex lives. Unfortunately this news is not widespread.

However, as we grow older, we can counter negative attitudes with the thought that we are beyond the reach of public moralizing and bigoted attitudes toward sex. That is all, thankfully, behind us.

WHAT THE MEDICAL TEXTBOOKS SAY

Men aged 50–89
- An erection takes longer to develop and may not be as full or as firm as it was earlier.
- Ejaculation lasts for a shorter time and is not as forceful.
- An erection subsides more rapidly after ejaculation than in earlier years.
- The volume of semen is nearly always less than it is for younger men.
- It takes longer before a man can have another erection and another orgasm.

Women aged 51–78
- A longer time is needed to respond to sexual stimulation.
- Lubrication is less effective and generally takes longer than in younger women.
- The vagina is less capable of stretching than in younger women.
- After the age of sixty the clitoris shrinks but may still remain responsive to stimulation.
- Orgasms are generally shorter and less intense than they were in earlier years.

What the textbooks say does not mean that older people cannot enjoy a good sex life. This is what should be publicized. Instead of being terrorized with the prospect of advancing years, we would look forward to them with joy and curiosity. If we did, growing older would be a great deal easier and we would do it a lot more gracefully.

What is kept secret is that more and more of us lose our inhibitions as we get older (there are surely no good reasons why we should retain them). Many of us feel a need and a freedom to enjoy sexual pleasures that we kept hidden when we were younger. There may be the feeling that time is running out so we should do as we wish as long as we don't hurt anyone. Other activities that used to consume a great deal of energy like parenting and domestic arrangements have been left behind so there is more energy left over to be invested in pleasurable activities, including sex. Furthermore, one often finds in later life that intimate situations are easier to control. There is more privacy, there are very few interruptions and many couples feel that they have the time to go more slowly and savor the most beautiful moments in sex.

The Starr-Weiner report, an excellent detailed survey of sexuality in a large group of people between the ages of sixty and ninety-one, demonstrates the inaccuracy of the old-fashioned picture of an older person being resigned to a life without much sexual pleasure (see page 110).

An important finding in this report was a clear demonstration that the frequency of sexual intercourse does not decline markedly from early adulthood. In his report, Kinsey stated that the average frequency of intercourse at thirty was 2.2 times per week and at sixty 0.5 times per week. In the Starr-Weiner reports people between sixty and ninety-one averaged 1.4 times a week, and this figure matches the one that Kinsey reported in his forty-year-olds. Desire in the Starr-Weiner group was even higher.

The facts challenge the widely held belief that older people are beyond having sex. Unquestionably, most older people still find sex a thrilling and energy-giving exercise. Contrary to the myths, neither the desire nor the capability vanishes. It may wane a little in frequency and vigor but not in sweetness and satisfaction. Just as in relationships at a younger age, attraction and love are followed by sexual desire and sexual fulfillment. These basic qualities in a relationship don't seem to falter; instead, they strengthen as we get older. This is something we can all look forward to in our maturing years and feel confident enough to carry out for many years to come.

THE TRUTH ABOUT OUR SEXUALITY

There is some good news about sexuality in our later years. In fact, the Starr-Weiner Report has confirmed that sexual drive, sexual enjoyment and sexual pleasure can be greater than they were when we were younger. This is why it is accurate to describe the years after fifty as our prime time.

- Sex is commonly considered a crucial part of life during our older years and provides a sense of well-being and a positive feeling about ourselves.
- Sex makes older people feel beautiful, desirable, exhilarated and mystical, and for some who attach importance to the youth cult, it makes them feel young. Also, sex is relaxing and relieves tension. It may be one of life's exquisite moments, driving every other problem and care out of our minds temporarily or even permanently.
- Only a minority of people (less than 30 percent) feel there is a decline in sexual response and feelings. This is especially true of men who have problems with erection and, therefore, withdraw from sexual activities.
- Nearly three-quarters of older people feel that sex is the same as it was when they were younger; more than a third of older people say that sex is better than when they were younger.

- For those of us who find sex more gratifying when we are older, the key is having the right partner, loss of inhibitions and a greater understanding of sex.
- For couples who get married for the first time or remarry in later life, love, caring and sharing and companionship are emphasized; so is sex. The majority of people consider that sex is very important in later life.
- About 80 percent of older people are sexually active; half of the people who are sexually active have sexual intercourse about once a week or more; 30 percent have sexual relations three times a week; 20 percent report sexual relations twice a week.
- Sex brings love, faith and trust, approval and warmth; these are the same needs and desires for every age.
- A staggering 99 percent desire sexual relationships at a varying frequency if they could have sex whenever they wanted to.

Mature sexuality

As long ago as Kinsey's research in the 1940s, well-worn beliefs about the decline of sexuality were being eroded. Masters and Johnson gave us excellent scientific data that proved the traditional medical picture wrong; Shere Hite made this even clearer in terms of what older people experience, feel and question. The recent Starr-Weiner Report shattered the myth once and for all with statistics and interviews showing how active older people's sex lives remain. On the basis of these reports, a clear picture of sexuality in our older years emerges. It is not a picture of decline and deprivation but one of continuing desire and fulfillment.

HOW WE VIEW SEX

- The majority of us are satisfied with our sex lives the way they are.
- We consider orgasm, which may be stronger than earlier in life, to be an essential part of our sexual experience. Most women have had orgasms in their younger years, and are still having them.
- Masturbation is a perfectly acceptable outlet for our sexual needs.
- Many of us are very happy to live together without marriage. The majority of us, including widows, widowers, divorcees and singles, remain sexually active in the last third of our lives.

- Many of us vary our sexual practices to achieve satisfaction.
- Many of us consider oral sex to be the most exciting sexual experience.
- We rarely show embarrassment or anxiety about sex if left to ourselves and not bombarded by negative messages from the media and social opinions.
- The majority of us like to be naked and enjoy nudity with our partners.
- When we think of an ideal lover, we choose someone near to our own age.
- Most of us see our sex lives remaining just the same way as we grow older.

Furthermore sexual problems are not an inevitable result of aging — the same factors that lead to sexual problems in younger people are important for older people too: factors such as fatigue, emotional problems, drug abuse, alcoholism, disease, over-eating, and these should be taken into account.

Most of us see our sex lives remaining just the same as we grow older. This is not surprising. Our older years represent a large part of our lives — one of the biggest. Many people today live well into their eighties, which means that the years from sixty to eighty-five are a quarter of the total life span. Most of us, therefore, look forward to having one-third of our lives left after we pass our fiftieth birthday. We spend relatively few years at the beginning of our lives without sexual activity. Why should we expect a curtailment of sexual activity toward the end? Despite what society and religious teaching have programmed us to believe, we never lose the need to be touched, stroked, cuddled and caressed. It has been known for years that physical contact is a basic human need, starting in the newborn infant, and, if anything becoming more powerful in sixty-, seventy- and eighty-year olds. A basic human need which we need to fulfil.

The authors of the Starr-Weiner report found the attitudes expressed in the following two statements to be fairly common among older people: "I was a widower for five years. Six months ago I remarried and everyone said to me, 'It's good that you married again because you need companionship. It gets me mad. So I want companionship, but I also got married for sex. I always had an active sex life and still do, and I am eighty-two."

A good sexual experience was described by one sixty-one-year-old woman from California as "To be really horny with a partner who is just an horny, to take plenty of time and when you can't stand it another minute, make it!"

The older woman

Older women are wrongly characterized as sexless by society, but science has recently shown that up until the age of sixty, sexual responses in women don't change at all, and even after sixty what changes take place are extremely slow and gradual. Add to this the fact that many men withdraw entirely from sexual activities for physical reasons or because they fear that they may be impotent or that they might have a heart attack or a stroke during sexual intercourse. This leaves us with too many women over the age of sixty desiring sex, but with partners who won't fulfill their needs. Many older woman find themselves without a regular sex outlet. Research has shown that for an older woman the only barrier to a more active sex life is the availability of a partner.

Another fact that has failed to filter through to the common consciousness is something first described by Kinsey. He established the sexual longevity of women by stating that a man reaches his peak early in adolescence and then shows a steady decline throughout life. This decline is consistent whatever age he is; in older years it is no faster than it was in earlier ones. On the other hand, a woman reaches her peak in her late twenties or thirties, and *remains at that plateau through her sixties*. It is only after seventy that she may show a slight decline in sexual response.

Orgasm   Nearly 40 percent of women say that orgasm is the most important part of the sexual act. This should not be surprising. Much has been written suggesting that the female is different from the male both in her capacity for, and her ability to sustain, orgasm. Dr. Jane Sherey described the human female as "… sexually insatiable in the presence of the highest degree of sexual satiation."

Masters and Johnson have reported on a woman's capacity for "…a rapid return to orgasm immediately following an orgasmic experience," and of "maintaining an orgasmic experience for a relatively long period of time." Though there are physiological changes, like vaginal lubrication taking only fifteen to thirty seconds in a younger woman, but perhaps one, two or even five minutes in an older woman, we are yet to have objective evidence that there is any real loss in sensation or feeling. The clitoris in both older and younger women remains the main organ of sexual stimulation, and the excitement generated by clitoral stimulation can be the same in older women as it is in younger ones. A woman of eighty *has the same physical potential for orgasm as she did at twenty*.

111

Another finding, which emphasizes that orgasm is a real part of the sex lives of older women, is that 86 percent of respondents in the Starr-Weiner survey said that the frequency of their orgasms was the same as or better than when they were younger.

Sexual responses

Masters and Johnson also had something to say about older women and their sexual responses. Most aspects of arousal remain identical. The arousal and erection of the nipple occurs in exactly the same way in older women as in younger ones, though engorgement of the areola (the pigmented area around the nipple) is not so intense as in younger women. What is more important, however, is the fact that the clitoris remains as responsive at least until the middle seventies, and while there is a thinning and loss of elasticity in the vaginal walls with advancing age, plus a shortening of vaginal length and width, these changes have been shown to have little effect on orgasm.

People often accept as fact that intercourse in an older woman results in pain and discomfort because of a lessening in vaginal lubrication. This appears to be wrong, as more than 80 percent of women respondents in Starr-Weiner's research report no such pain.

The conclusion is that far from being age, it is interest, opportunity and availability that control the body's response. "Use it or lose it," is an adage particularly applicable to the older age group. We must try to overcome the fact that our culture exaggerates the importance of menopausal changes, making women's fears into self-fulfilling prophecies. There is absolutely no question that powerful feelings of sexuality extend two decades or longer beyond the menopause.

Attitudes to sex

These have changed quite a lot as a result of the feminist movement. Prior to that, the majority of women accepted that sex was mainly a male domain and they were fixed in the role of passive and submissive partner. To fulfill this role, many women repressed their sexual desires and believed they were behaving in a ladylike fashion when they did this.

Today many women, particularly when older, have come to the conclusion that they have just as much passion and sexuality as men and, more importantly, that they have the right to make choices. Among older women there is a less willing acceptance of the old-fashioned male view of sex as being measured in performance only – how much, how often. Many women are now seeking equality, quality and variety. They are quite prepared to wake up their partners when they feel in the mood.

The older man

Sexual potency This is by no means a problem for every marriage but impotency can be very demoralizing if it does occur. This can be worsened when incorrect advice is given by a doctor. The news that a sixty-year-old man will no longer be able to sustain an erection can be horrifying for both partners. After all, it is tantamount to saying that their sex lives are over. The blow to a man may be so great that advice coming from a sympathetic wife to seek a second opinion may be spurned.

What is more shocking, if anything, is that doctors themselves fall into the trap of believing that it is perfectly normal for a man in his sixties to be unable to maintain an erection. Most men in this situation would be understandably depressed and needlessly feel a failure.

A doctor who takes the time and trouble to study information would be very thorough in examining such a man and he would find out as much as he could about his past medical history. It may be that the man has had his prostate removed and is looking for an excuse to end his sex life. It may be that he has had a heart attack and is afraid of having another if he attempts intercourse. This fear prevents him from having an erection. When this has happened several times, a man quite wrongly feels he is impotent.

Though the work of Masters and Johnson was widely publicized, their precise findings were not. One of their most important statements was that any kind of therapy program for impotence or premature ejaculation is as applicable to older men as it is to younger men, because most of these problems are psychological in origin and not physical. There is a lot of help available for older men and women and it should encourage us to know that the success rate in this age group is extremely high.

Masters and Johnson even made a practical suggestion to older men on how to make frequent sexual intercourse possible. They point out that it is unnecessary for a man to ejaculate every time, that men need rest periods of several days before they can have another erection and orgasm. If older men hold back instead of feeling forced by macho instincts to have frequent sex, then the frequency of sexual relations is more under their control. It becomes easier for them to adapt their sexual relationship to suit their own personal needs as well as those of their partners. To feel comfortable with this changing pattern of sexual activity it's important for men to be open and honest with their partners so that there is the understanding to maintain a loving relationship. This is the foundation upon which loving relationships are built.

113

Helping a man

You can help a great deal to make sure your man doesn't believe that his sex life is coming to an end. The most important thing that you can do is to understand the changes in the way your husband is functioning and to see them as perfectly normal. You should recognize his altering patterns of erection and orgasm as normal too. Both of you should discuss what's happening so that your expectations are realistic, and so that you can adjust your sexual behavior to whatever changes occur.

You should not become afraid because your partner takes longer to attain his erection. Should you sense that he is apprehensive you should reassure him that all is normal and if he takes longer it doesn't mean that he is unable. Your partner may become less aroused by seeing you naked or thinking about sex; skillful manual and oral caresses can overcome this. Whatever you do, don't feel rejected and panic-stricken. Don't think that because he can't attain an erection rapidly he is no longer attracted to you. Don't worry if he does not ejaculate but seems sexually satisfied. When your partner cannot attain a second erection within a short time, don't think that this is the first sign of impotence. In such a situation a woman can be a creator and an initiator. She can lead the way and introduce a changing pattern so that both partners create a new kind of sexual loving. A woman can find new ways of doing things that will fit her partner's new mood and will help to build his self-esteem rather than erode it.

Helping a woman

Few women have any difficulty in reaching an orgasm through masturbation. You can make your lovemaking techniques more successful by modeling them on the woman during masturbation. Even on a small sample, Masters and Johnson concluded that there is no time limit to female sexuality drawn by advancing years. Shere Hite argued convincingly that an orgasm achieved through intercourse is not necessarily a better orgasm than one achieved by other means. She also said that women can have an orgasm whenever they want. If intercourse doesn't work, you can help your partner reach a climax through manual or oral stimulation and this release is just as easy to accomplish for a woman as a man. Women appreciate tender stroking and kissing of the breasts and clitoris; your partner will appreciate long, leisured embraces.

POSITIONS FOR OLDER LOVERS

Experience more than compensates for any lack of energy that we might feel as we get older and there is no reason why we should not enjoy sex even more than we did when we were younger. We now understand our partner's bodily responses more fully than ever before and feel confident and considerate enough to concentrate on pleasing our partner in the years ahead.

Here the emphasis for both partners is on comfort. The woman lowers herself onto her partner's penis. She can then face him and rock to and fro gently.

Remember that lovemaking is not just about penetration; skilled and loving caresses can be just as fulfilling as intercourse itself. As the clitoris may also require a little more stimulation we will enjoy and benefit from long, loving embraces during foreplay.

Using a solid footboard as leverage during lovemaking conserves energy for both partners. Here, the woman lies astride her partner, holds onto his hands and gently pushes backward and forward using her feet. Alternatively, the man can lie astride his partner.

Sexual activity in chronic disease

Heart disease

There is absolutely no need to eliminate sexual activity altogether unless heart disease is very severe. In fact, in many cases of heart disease sexual activity can be beneficial, since sexual activity can be the equivalent of performing moderate exercises with an increased heart rate, slightly increased blood pressure and improved oxygen consumption. As each case is different, anyone with heart disease should ask his or her doctor's recommendation on the subject. Total abstinence can bring a great deal of psychological stress, which can worsen a heart condition.

All in all, the news on heart disease is extremely good. Doctors now realize that a normal sex life can actually benefit many men who suffer heart attacks, but it is important that they don't get overtired. It is possible that the pattern of sexual relationships has to change to mornings or after a good night's sleep, when both partners are feeling rested. One of the great things about being retired is that you don't have to jump out of bed at 8 a.m. The job no longer beckons and the house can wait, so you can use the mornings for sexual enjoyment.

A change in position can also help people with heart conditions. Lying next to each other on your sides, face-to-face, is more restful than the missionary position. You can find positions that avoid muscle cramps and tension, with the woman on top so that she can do most of the moving, which will prevent the man's getting overtired.

High blood pressure

Many people with high blood pressure believe that sexual activity is dangerous for them. This is not necessarily so, although quite a number of patients who take drugs for high blood pressure say that they suffer loss of potency. Most authorities attribute this impotency to the drugs. It is not known that high blood pressure itself reduces sexual desire, and when doctors are prescribing treatment for high blood pressure in older people, they should try to make sure that they are using one of the drugs that will not affect sexual potency.

Diabetes

Impotence is a fairly common occurrence among diabetics. Men find that they have difficulty in attaining erections and ejaculation and women may have difficulty with vaginal lubrication. Research has revealed lower testosterone levels in diabetic men and it has been suggested that male impotence may result from malfunction of the nerves that supply the penis. Premature ejaculation may be a symptom.

Arthritis You may find that arthritis affects your sex life by causing discomfort during sexual intercourse. Painful, stiff joints may make the ordinary face-to-face position difficult but the adoption of a new position – such as with the woman on top (if the male is arthritic) can often bring success. Taking pain-killing drugs before having sex can also help. Even if the problems involved in making love are so severe that you decide to forgo full intercourse, you should never abstain from indulging in other sexual activities if you and/or your partner desire them. Physical closeness through touching and caresses can provide a great deal of comfort and reassurance. If you are used to sleeping with someone it's better to get in an extra single bed for the occasional troublesome period than to switch to twin beds permanently. This way you need sacrifice your physical closeness only on those occasions when you feel pain.

SEXUAL POSITIONS FOR ARTHRITICS

Experimenting with some different positions for sexual intercourse is the best way to find comfort. This may lead to different feelings of intensity.

This position, where the man lies on his back and his partner assumes the more active role on top, is particularly helpful if it is difficult or uncomfortable for him to bear his weight on his knees, shoulders or arms.

A position of "spoons" may make things easier where the man lies behind his partner, who faces the same way.

Divorce

Divorce is often harder for people when they're older than it would have been if they had gone through it when they were young. In the aftermath of divorce many people feel that they are "over the hill" and unattractive. They may fear that no one will ever want them again. Many dislike going alone to dances and parties after so many years of living with a secure partner. Some people are bitter because they are left alone after thirty or more years.

The divorced woman

Women, especially after being deserted for someone younger, may feel ferociously protective about their alimony, particularly if they haven't been trained for a job and feel they are too old to begin a career. Salt is rubbed in the wound if a woman can remember it was she who put her student husband through his professional training so that he could make a good salary for the two of them. Some women feel that after bringing up the family for a man, and helping him achieve success in his career, they deserve every penny they can get.

This pessimistic approach may end up making women believe that divorce is the end of their lives. But having lived through the despair, pain, self-hatred and even self-pity, many of us find that life is better after divorce. Some get their first full-time job to keep busy and sane. Some feel self-confident enough to have dates with other men. It is possible for women to discover sex for the first time after having lived a claustrophobic life in a claustrophobic marriage. Prior to divorce and meeting men, some women wrongly believe that they have a low sex drive. They believe sex can never be really enjoyable. Sometimes they feel reborn when they have a fulfilling relationship with a sympathetic partner.

It's easy to feel cheated for having spent a long time with a rather stodgy partner, but the best view is that there is a good number of years ahead. It is the prime time of life, there is no worry about becoming pregnant, the menopause has passed. The children are married and therefore you don't have to worry about taking care of them. It is possible to have a small, efficient apartment that takes a short time to maintain. You may find that the only worry you have is how best to go about having a good time – just like your old bachelor days.

The divorced man

Now that they have discovered that they can look after themselves economically, women are leaving men more frequently than before. More and more men over fifty are being left behind by wives who always wanted to get out of the marriage. It is no longer safe to assume that an older man who is divorced is the guilty party and has left his aging wife for a younger woman. On the contrary *she* may have left him for a younger man. Men in this situation feel depressed and deserted and many seek a lasting relationship for the years ahead. Men seem to be very well suited to the marriage state. Health statistics show that they are happiest, in the best health and least depressed when they are married. So they tend to re-marry.

Remarriage and new partnerships

Widowers are much more likely to get married than either bachelors or divorced men, especially if they were happily married. Once they are over the initial shock of losing their wives, widowers begin to miss domesticity after the years of companionship and loving. Women may be deterred from marrying men over forty because they think that they are marrying a potentially disabled person, especially if their future husband has diabetes, a heart condition or high blood pressure. However, even a healthy man if he is over fifty is risky too. Women over the age of fifty are something of a health risk but these facts need not spell pessimism.

You have to decide whether the companionship of a few years of remarriage is worth the risk of living with chronic illness later. Only you can decide this for yourself. Separation is much harder when you are older and there is a lot to be said for having someone to chat to, laugh with and share life with.

Against this, you may be reluctant to share your assets, be it your salary or your alimony. Only you know how secure or insecure you feel if you have to manage on this income. Only you know how much or how little you really want to get married. Examine the kind of person you are. Be entirely honest with yourself and examine your feelings about this particular man or woman. Then make your decision. There is one golden rule that should be applied during your older years, if not at other times – there is no point in marrying *anyone* unless you would trust that person with everything of yours, and unless you are attracted to him or her. You are going to spend an awful lot of time with your new partner.

If you are over fifty your new partner may be ready to retire. He or she may already be semi-retired or fully retired. This means that you will be thrown together much more frequently than a younger couple. A woman won't have the hours off while her man is at work. Nor will he have respite from his partner's company. It will be a good deal easier if you are excited about each other and have a good time in each other's company. Being together all day and every day from breakfast until bedtime is a very long time.

In the end obstacles can be overcome just as triumphantly by older people as young. It is difficult to overestimate the importance of a long-standing loving relationship in old age. Sex on its own is not to be slighted, but love brings much more than physical pleasure. Each partner is sure of his or her identity as a person and feels able to offer something valuable and worthwhile. A body no longer young can still be a means of giving and receiving pleasure. Older lovers like and understand their bodies. People of fifty and over who enjoy an active sex life have more confidence in themselves than those who decide to go into their old age celibate.

Through a loving relationship, two people who have shared intimate years of sorrow and joy can buffer each other from the contingencies of the outside world. Through a loving partner we can find the reassurance that we are still individuals and that our emotional needs have not been forgotten. In each other's arms we can be ourselves, rather than the image of an old person that society forces us to be. This sense of togetherness against the world, the joy of small, shared intimacies and quiet conversation that insulates us from the rest of the world, is life-affirming and precious. Society's oppressive attitude toward sexual intimacy in old age is a reflection of its own insecurities and misconceptions. Most older people have come to realize this and have decided to please themselves rather than adhere to the mores of others. A few may feel the pressure to conform to society's mold, but should resist it. The fifty plus age is a rewarding time to achieve happiness because with it comes the necessary experience and maturity.

The family

Most of us became adults at a time when family, friends and neighbors automatically came to each other's rescue with whatever resources they had, no matter how little. Although bureaucracy has grown and many social services exist for older people today, the greatest strength and help for them is still the family even though family relations are not always easy. Interactions between the older and younger generations can cause stress and disturbance for both families and friends. Situations are often complex. Not enough research has been done on what happens between families and their dependents but we know that the assumption of responsibilities by younger members for their older relatives is a severe emotional, physical and economic drain and it causes a great deal of anxiety.

Most of us would confess to having questioned ourselves about failing in our responsibilities to older relatives. The children of very old parents may themselves be sixty or approaching seventy and are therefore limited in the support that they can give. By old-fashioned standards, present day families in the Western world tend to be small and have only a few relatives. The mobility of today's society means that the family is not localized in one village as it used to be, but can be scattered widely, perhaps over the whole world. Even a few minutes of traveling time can make support difficult. This can be especially so when there are commitments to other members of the family and to work, which is the case for most of us, and these are very difficult to avoid.

In recent years a growing network of support services has sprung up to help families who want to care for older relatives. Health and legal professionals specialize in bringing together families and the private or public agencies that will be most useful in each case. As there is such a maze of services available, this help can be vital, especially if the older relative lives at some distance from the rest of the family. (See page 311.)

Family problems There are several well-recognized situations in which the interaction between family members can cause great upheaval. The mother/daughter syndrome is one. A daughter lives all her life with her mother, is adoring and dependent. She seeks her mother's advice on most issues that concern her and does most of what her mother tells her to do. She bears this benign tyranny because it is stable. However, as the mother grows older, the relationship become strained due to the development of anxiety and depression or because of physical illness. For the first time the daughter sees her mother as dependent on and subordinate to herself, and she may not be ready to assume command. When tensions arise, it is usually due to the daughter's assuming more and more responsibility in the absence of any real power. Thereafter, the resentment on both sides may be rather childish.

Another pattern is the "fallen dictator." It is usually a father or husband who takes this role. He would be described as powerful, domineering, good at his job, usually well thought of by colleagues at work; but overbearing, tyrannical and rigid at home, usually maintaining his superior position by the use of fear. As such a man gets older, ill-health and loss of income and

121

status at work remove the basis of his power. To make things worse, increasing demands for help at home undermine his position further. He then tries to retain command in a radically different situation. His behavior often creates crises and even rejection by the rest of the family.

"Power reversal" affects the ideal husband, constantly helping in the house, handing over the wage packet unopened, not drinking, not smoking, not going out with the boys. He is the perfect handyman, working to improve the house, and taking great pleasure in doing what his wife and children want. He may even be viewed by the family with amused contempt. At an older age he becomes an invaluable family member, but then he may develop a heart attack, a cancer or other life-threatening disease. Then, for the first time, every minor illness and symptom demands the attention of the whole family. When he survives his illness, he will have learned a lesson. He will be aware that he has the power to be the center of attention, to frighten and to stir up feelings. Once having learned this lesson he may not be willing to return to his previous humble position in the family. War has been declared and the older person may attempt to retain power by being childish.

One of the problems is that some doctors may tend to label an emotional crisis between older people and their families as "a social problem," so older people with anxiety, hypo-chondriasis, phobias, or depression may be misguidedly offered practical help in the form of home help, meals on wheels, voluntary visiting, outings and holidays, when it is really psychotherapy they need. However, the outlook for older people with family problems is normally good. A person with a pleasant personality in the past and stable family life very often has the basis for a rapid return to normal behavior.

The family's changing nature

There is no doubt that the structure of the family is constantly changing. For many older people, the time when they really need stability and continuity may be the very time when they are confronted by a family upheaval with divorce, remarriage and new relations from various children and children-in-law. Moreover, they may have to face changing relationships with former sons and daughters-in-law of whom they are very fond. It is possible that there will be the added strain of having to decide with whom and near to whom they are going to live. The family is gradually being reconstituted and is reaching a new equilibrium. This is difficult enough for young family members to cope with, but extremely difficult for the older ones.

The new extended family will probably include children and young adults who have grown up with the idea that their

A changing family pattern often means that the members have more people of all ages to rely upon.

parents are fixed points in the universe. Suddenly they may acquire new grandparents. In the same way, grandparents may find themselves with new children. Neither may be able to understand the situation very well. As with many other aspects of changing family patterns, people often overcome these difficulties through love and generosity, and some of the newly formed family ties can be strong and good, even better than the old. However, a family upheaval can seriously affect the support system that older people receive from their relatives when they need it most.

When things go wrong in our relationships, it is not uncommon to hide them from our parents for as long as

123

possible, so as "not to worry or bother them." Usually there is another part of us that feels guilty. The younger generation, and even some adults, often underestimate the capacity older people have for forgiving and forgetting. It is possible that our childhood fears and anxieties linger on and stop us from communicating, even as middle-aged people, with our parents.

It is not only older people who experience their children's marriages breaking up; parents are still quite often middle-aged. In either case the effects of shifting membership on families need close attention and any older members must be included in this. There are those people who think we should give up the term "nuclear family" and talk instead of the "modified extended family". Some think that this label represents the family situation of many people in our society today more realistically. Even though there is greater geographical mobility than ever before, there is no evidence to suggest that kinship networks are breaking down in an emotional sense. The way we help older people when their children's marriages break down, may directly affect their confidence at a later stage when they are less self-reliant.

Stresses and strains within the changing family will be for the most part private and handled between family members themselves. Very often there is no thought or place for social workers, but in matters of divorce and child custody, they do become involved. Older family members may be called upon to take an active part. Grandparents may have an important role to play in divorce. A social worker thinking positively about what help could be offered to children might well recommend grandparental custody with benefits to children, parents and grandparents. With grandparents becoming younger all the time and with an increasingly closer identification between children and grandparents, this option of grandparental custody could become more and more common.

Being a grandparent

One of the joys that most people have in store for them as they grow older is that of becoming a grandparent. Once past the childbearing age, many women begin to look forward to their second chance for mothering, and find that few experiences exceed those of being with, teaching, and learning from their grandchildren. To my mind, grandparents are an extremely important part of the family, be it nuclear or extended. I personally see a family as a fundamentally stable structure encompassing strong and lasting relationships among an extended group in which a child can grow up feeling secure and loved, to which he or she must contribute and in which his or her voice is heard. I also consider it important that a child become able to relate to people of all ages, and, therefore, meet relatives and friends who are older.

Grandparents are vital in helping a child to do this. They also play a unique part in enabling children to develop their personalities, and are a valuable asset to a family. By virtue of their age, they are generally more philosophical, long-suffering and sympathetic than parents. Long practice means that they have learned the knack of handling children with ease.

Being a good grandparent

The best grandparents can interpret warning signs, anticipate problems, and head them off. They pacify by distraction not by insistence, and so obtain obedience more readily. Unlike those parents who rule by force, grandparents will more often than not persuade with patience. It is said that grandparents spoil their grandchildren. This must be a misuse of the word "spoil." If spoiling a child means giving explanations instead of dismissals, suggesting alternatives instead of negatives, and helping instead of ignoring, then grandparents do spoil children. The presence of grandparents in the house can often be a boon to the family and, given that they don't cause friction with the parents, they are often welcomed.

Grandparents can renew earlier joys with their grandchildren. A grandmother can teach her young granddaughter the art of sewing, bird-watching or gardening. A grandfather can once again enjoy tranquility while he is teaching his grandson to fish, and discover a new sense of purpose and usefulness if he can take the young baby for a walk and chat to his friends on the way. Grandparents should live along *with* their grandchildren but it is important that they don't live through their grandchildren rather than through their own direct experience. If they do, they may suffer an emotional setback if misfortune strikes the younger generation.

125

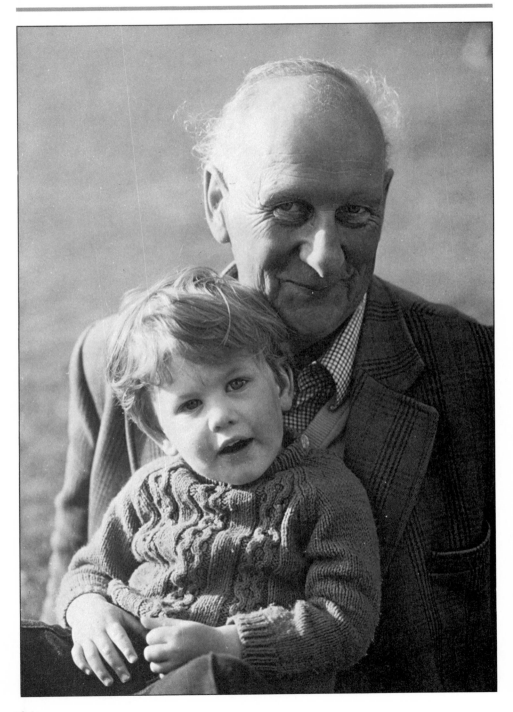

The role of grandparents

This has changed enormously since the turn of the century. Then, children, parents and grandparents frequently lived in the same house and it was assumed that the latter, as elders, were the authorities on what was right and wrong. This is no longer so. Grandparents no longer have that role. In fact, as a grandparent you may find yourself casting about as to what you can do to help. The best thing you can do is to show your children and your grandchildren how to cope with change. You have lived through the most drastic changes the world has ever known. You have lived longer than any of your family so you have had to cope with a rapidly changing society more often than anyone who is close to you. Your granddaughter may be very depressed because she can't get a job. Only you with an historical perspective on unemployment, and knowing how much it demoralizes people, can help your granddaughter to develop a healthy critical distance between the refusal she gets at job interviews and her feelings about herself. You can share with her what you remember about the depression and unemployment in your time.

You can allow your grandchildren to see you as a real person for the first time, drawing a parallel between their development and yours. In a conversation on politics, for instance, you can stop being a wrinkled, white-haired old person and describe how you were a young soldier in the army during the First World War. You can recount some of your experiences, possible moments of glory. There isn't a grandchild in the world who won't be riveted by that kind of story, and learn much from it.

You can show your family that you are not a doddering and useless grandparent. You can be independent and act so. You can be mobile and agile so that you can join younger members for a walk or a leisurely round on the golf course. You can also listen. Parents don't have a lot of time for that. But you can listen without giving advice, you can tell your family what experience you have had in your life and what it has led you to believe.

You will also find that you have a lot more in common with teenage children than you ever had thought. At opposite ends of life you may both be searching for changing identities, asking the same questions: "Who am I?" "What do I really want to do?" "How shall I do it?" Very often adolescents have more in common with grandparents than they do with their own parents. Parents often are too busy or too ambitious forging ahead in life to be self-examining and introspective. The relationship with younger grandchildren, even babies, is also very special. Grandparents can give a unique kind of loving and caring that can only come from them. Young children usually adore them, and also enjoy knowing that they have a very special place in their grandparents' lives.

You mustn't be surprised if it turns out that you and your partner are different as grandparents. After all, you might have been different as parents. One of you might have been the disciplinarian and the other more permissive. Or it might be that one was strict with a daughter, but lets a granddaughter get away with murder.

In a family this ability to change roles is a very good thing. It means you and your partner have different strengths and make different contributions to your family than you have made in the past. This results in rich relationships that are special.

Social relationships

Everyone, whether young or old, needs an active, stimulating environment and dynamic interaction with people of all ages. When youngsters are faced with lack of visual and auditory stimulation or lack of human contact, they begin to show certain signs of *old* age after only ten days of this monotonous environment. They become apathetic, mentally confused, and they may have loss of memory. One effective way of preventing, reducing or postponing social and mental deterioration in older age is to make sure that life is full and active and is set in stimulating surroundings.

Many of today's major problems connected with getting older are preventable in that they are either social or economic. Some of our present customs, such as compulsory retirement, may cause difficulties of both those kinds. A person who has been enthusiastically and gainfully employed may at the age of sixty or sixty-five suddenly be dropped into the oblivion of compulsory retirement with economic and social deprivation on the grounds that he or she lacks the ability to carry out a productive role. This stems from a value judgment common in present-day society, that personal worth can only be judged in terms of economic productivity even though it is well known that people of retirement age are able to work and learn new skills. Furthermore, they are perfectly able to adjust to such changes given the chance.

There are many opportunities for older people who are fit and mobile to enjoy an active social life beyond their own homes. Community or religiously sponsored day centers and luncheon clubs, which usually provide some care for older people, can be

Day centers and luncheon clubs often organize trips to places of interest.

a marvelous opportunity for meeting others, having chats, comparing notes, making friends, etc. They can be particularly helpful when relatives need to be at work for several hours each day and also when they need a break from everyday routine.

The day center, if the older person wishes, can provide a meeting place for local friends where everyone can socialize and be looked after. Day centers may cater to hobbies. There may be opportunities to participate in hand work, or games such as cards, billiards, bingo or checkers. There are some day centers that are organized in the form of workshops so that older people can earn enough money to give them a sense of purpose. Another type of day center provides a full daytime care where there are meals available at reasonable prices. Transport is often provided by volunteers to and from these centers.

Luncheon clubs are an extension of the meals-on-wheels service, and usually meet in a local community hall, church or home where you can buy an inexpensive hot lunch. There are clubs for people with special interests and hobbies. If you hear of a club for workmates when you retire, think seriously about joining. You may get a great deal of enjoyment from joining Old Girls' Clubs or Old Boys' Clubs run by your old work place.

I think it's important for you to make the first move; otherwise other people will be unaware of your existence let alone your needs. Once these are known it's surprising how readily people will rally round you.

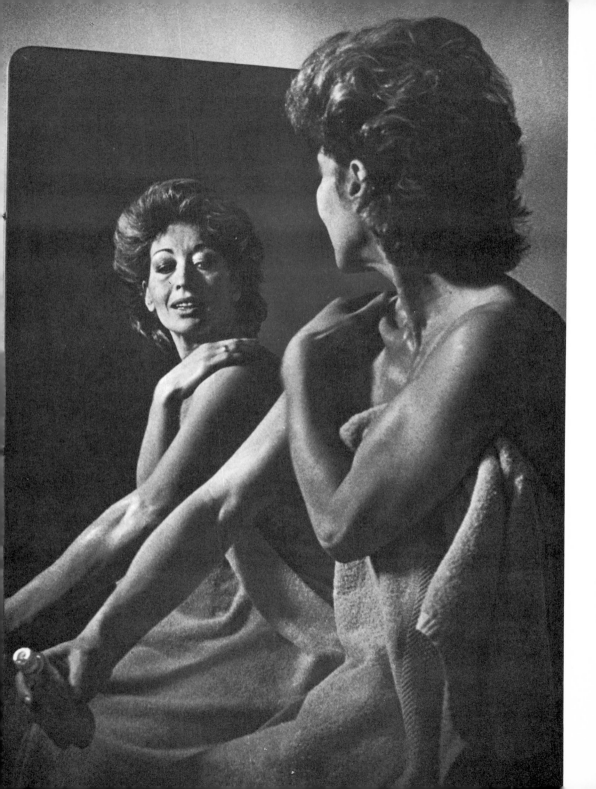

Caring for a changing body

Most experts who study aging (gerontology) agree that getting older is a continuing process that happens to us and everything else that lives – plants and animals alike. Aging can be viewed as something that goes on throughout life, beginning with conception and ending with death. It is not something affecting people reaching the age of sixty, but everyone from babies, children, teenagers, and young adults to older people. The reason for studying aging is not that it is a phenomenon that happens in any one particular phase of life; studying aging gives information about youth and middle age as well.

In addition to describing changes in individual organs and systems, this seems a good place to discuss the *menopause* – an event of great significance for both men and women. This is also the chapter to mention how we might best maintain our appearance.

General effects of aging

Our body organs show general signs of wear and tear as we continue through life. We become more aware of the physical changes in ourselves and in our partners.

Body changes   This is not to say that all functions diminish at the same rate for every individual; quite the opposite, they are different for almost every person, and of course, normal life expectancy at seventy-five may be lower if there is some pre-existing organic disease.

One of the most significant changes that occurs as we get older is an alteration in the temperature response of the body. As we age, our bodies are less able to respond to loss of heat; we produce heat less efficiently by shivering and our reflex to shiver is slower. This can result in a serious fall in body temperature if we are exposed to cold. In addition, we begin to cope less well with an excess of heat. When we were younger, as a reflex to a raised body temperature, we lost heat by opening up the blood vessels in the skin and sweating. As we get older, the response to this reflex is slower and we cannot sweat as efficiently.

There are other functions associated with aging which means that less oxygen, nutrients and antibodies are carried to the weakening parts of the body. As we grow older we are less able to move minerals like sodium, calcium and potassium around our bodies as efficiently as we did when we were younger. These solid metabolites may become deposited within and between cells. A crude analogy would be that our systems become blocked in the way that a furnace is choked with clinkers, so that it becomes difficult to maintain. This accumulation of metabolites may be a mechanical hindrance to the normal activities of the cell and the normal functioning of our bodies, causing adverse reactions.

As we get older there is a gradual decline in the function and reserves of our bodies; this increases the likelihood of our becoming ill. Most of our stabilizing mechanisms become less sensitive and less efficient as we age. The decline differs from one organ to another and from one individual to another.

Our bodies are less well able to adapt to stress, injury and disease and we take longer to recover from physical stress such as exercise, psychological stress such as anxiety and health stress such as disease. When there is increased demand during an acute, stressful incident such as surgery or an infection, this may go beyond the normal reserve capacities of our vital organs; the same stress could be easily surmounted by a younger adult. One theory on aging propounds that it is this precise "slowing down" of our bodies' ability to recover and adapt to a variety of stresses which finally kills.

Many of us don't show the signs of strain when we are resting. It is only when we are subjected to stress, or exercise, that our various functions show a decline. At one time these decreases in function were thought to be an inevitable part of getting older. Mental confusion and signs of senility were considered to be unavoidable. Now we quite rightly question this idea of automatic decline with age. Certainly, some decline can be attributed to our getting older, but much is dependent on the deconditioning of our bodies due to our increasingly sedentary lifestyles.

Skin

Our outward appearance undoubtedly alters as we get older and for most people the condition of the skin and hair is the final arbiter of age. Some of these alterations in our appearance are due to factors that are not easily controlled: the loss of the

Epidermis

Dermis

Subcutaneous layer

Hair emerges from the epidermis. The dermis nourishes the skin. The fatty subcutaneous layer holds the skin to the muscles.

layer of fat underneath the skin, the decrease in the number of cells that produce pigmentation, the gradual withering away of sebum and sweat glands, and the hardening of, or decline in, blood vessels we have to nourish the skin. Such things as heredity and hormone balance are largely beyond our control, too. However, nutrition and prolonged exposure to sun, wind or chemicals are things we can do something about.

The skin is the largest organ in the body and it serves us extremely well. With its suppleness (its collagen bundles give it almost unique elasticity), it allows us to move freely and to express our feelings. It prevents poisons from getting into our bodies, it is the major organ that keeps our bodies at a steady temperature and it contains the nerve receptors that carry messages to our brains by a series of interconnecting nerves.

Wrinkling

Wrinkling is traditionally thought to be the most obvious sign of aging skin. However, wrinkling actually begins as early as our twenties and continues at a fairly steady pace for the rest of our lives. We use our facial expressions as a way of communicating with others and recording anger, rage, disappointment, happiness, surprise, consternation, etc. These expressions are captured on our faces by lines, which begin to form in the places that move most. Very few of us get to our forties without any of these tell-tale signs.

LESSENING THE EFFECTS OF WRINKLING

For both sexes
- Splash water on your face and keep it there with a moisturizing film to prevent your skin dehydrating.
- Never go out in the sun without wearing a sunscreen - the higher the number, the greater the protection. Remember, a day on the ski slopes can do as much damage as a day on the beach.
- If you have tiny surface veins on your face, avoid eating hot, spicy food and drinking alcohol; these will aggravate face flushing.
- Stop smoking. Cigarette smoking may hasten crow's feet and causes deep lines.
- Keep your body well rested by adequate sleep to improve your complexion.

- Facial exercises can help to relax the facial muscles which cause "tension" wrinkles and lines. They can also help keep facial and neck muscles mobile and relieve tension headaches. They cannot, however, *stop* wrinkles forming.

For women
- If you don't wear make-up be sure to wear a fairly liberal covering of a heavy moisturizer that prevents water loss.
- If you can put on some make-up, it will help to reduce water loss from the skin. Avoid astringent toners; switch from cleansing soaps to creams.

Wrinking is caused primarily by a thinning out of the sub-cutaneous fat that gave our skin its original plumpness. At the same time, the disintegration of collagen bundles, caused mainly by the sun, produces a loss of elasticity. Long-term exposure to the sun unquestionably hastens aging of the skin (and more seriously is a major cause of diseases of the skin). Given a thinning, loosening skin, the force of gravity does the rest. Professions that demand an outdoor life, such as gardening, farming and construction work, would normally be thought of as healthy, but sunworshippers are simply behaving illogically. What they are really saying is "Here I am, age me" and yearly suntan can result in an irreversibly leathery skin.

FACIAL EXERCISES

These will relax your facial muscles and help to prevent "tension" wrinkles and lines. First put some moisturizing cream on your face and neck.

For your chin, upper lip and cheeks
Move the corners of your mouth upward towards your temples. Keep you mouth closed, your teeth unclenched and your lips relaxed and use very tiny, controlled movements. Carefully release your muscles in reverse.

For your chin
Jut out your chin and lower your teeth upward and forward using your chin muscles only. Relax slowly and repeat.

For the muscles in your cheeks, chin and around your mouth
Place your fists under your chin, with your face in a relaxed, normal position. Gently press down with your head and up with your fists, maintaining an even pressure.

Shortly, with practice, you will be able to wrinkle your nose upwards while smiling.

For the contours around your eyes
Focus your eyes upwards and very slowly raise the lower lids both upward and inward (as if you were trying to close them from the bottom only). Slowly lower your lids.

MINIMIZING WRINKLES WITH MAKE-UP

● Use a light-textured foundation diluted with a moisturizer and water, which won't accumulate in lines and wrinkles.

● Don't use powder on wrinkled areas—it exaggerates them. If you must, use it on oily areas only; brush it on lightly.

● Use a lipstick pencil to define mouth shape and keep the lipstick from oozing into fine lines on the upper lip.

● Lightly brush on light ivory or white foundation at the bottom of a deep furrow and blend it in very carefully to the rest of your foundation.

Major treatments for wrinkles

As the description implies, these are major procedures and should only be practiced by expert medical personnel. Never go to a clinic that advertises such treatments. In inexpert hands any of them can result in permanent scarring. Best of all, seek medical advice and consult a dermatologist who may give you the treatments. For full advice see *Specialist help*.

Dermabrasion
This is a surgical treatment that involves removing the superficial surface of the skin with a rotating, cutting instrument. Only surface wrinkles will be removed, not scars or deep pits. It is especially good for removing fine wrinkles around the mouth, eyes and brows.

A special instrument, similar to a dentist's drill, is moved over the surface of the skin. The end of the instrument has a rapidly rotating end shaped into a convex surface with a cutting edge. This planes off the skin layers. The operation takes about 30 minutes and leaves the skin baby-pink and raw. A few days of post-operative attention and bandaging may be necessary.

Skin peeling
This is a chemical treatment that involves using a highly corrosive agent on the skin to remove wrinkled layers. A more hazardous procedure than dermabrasion, it should always be done by a highly skilled expert who should take care to avoid deep burns. The scabs that form will drop off to leave red skin, and this must be kept out of the sun until it fades.

Face lifts
Pulling up loose facial skin and tightening or removing fatty tissues in the face and neck can eliminate wrinkles, jowly and wattling effects and sagging skin. Both plastic surgeons and dermatologists can perform such operations, which require general anesthetics and take about three hours. Any incisions are concealed under the hairline or around the ears.

COSMETIC SURGERY

Before considering either of these operations do read my advice on pages 197-198.

Blepharoplasty
This involves removing any excess sagging skin from around the eyes. An incision is made under the lower eyelid and the fat is removed. It's unlikely that there will be any scarring and the operation will last for up to ten years.

Face lift
This affects three facial areas: loose chin and neck; drooping eyebrows and frown line; and slack cheeks and mouth-to-nose lines. Skin is pulled back behind the ears, with any scars fading after three months.

Recuperation may involve a week in the hospital and there is much discoloration of the skin. Overtightening of the skin is not desired, as the expression becomes artificial. Face lifts are not permanent and may last eight to ten years; the skin will continue to age and sag as before. It is not uncommon for people to have repeated face lifts.

Silicone injections
Some practitioners inject small amounts of liquid silicone into wrinkles, deep lines or furrows to smooth them.

Eye lifts
Excessive skin of the upper eyelids and baggy skin of the lower eyelids can be removed to restore your youthful look. The operation known as a blepharoplasty can be performed by ophthalmologists as well as by plastic surgeons. Excess tissue is removed along the fold of the eyelid or underneath the lashes. Following the operation there will be discoloration and the sutures are not removed for about four days. The results of the operation will last for up to ten years.

Dry and sensitive skin

Normally, subcutaneous fat acts as an important insulator against loss of body heat, but when it is lost certain functions can no longer be performed efficiently. The greater the loss of subcutaneous fat, the greater the amount of body heat that escapes, leaving us more susceptible to cold. As we get older we often complain of feeling cold because our skin becomes drier as the blood circulating to it becomes more sluggish.

Our temperature regulation is affected in the other direction too, and the older we get the more likely we are to suffer from heat exhaustion. This is because we have less capacity to perspire and cool off. The loss of oil-secreting glands may cause the skin to dry and crack, perspiration is less, the moisture content is reduced and chapping often results.

● Always keep your hands and feet warm in the winter, particularly the fingertips and toes, which, being the farthest extremities of the body, are the last to get nutrients and oxygen, so the skin becomes vulnerable to cold.

● In winter a humidifier is useful for keeping the room moisture at a good level for your skin.

● Wear smooth materials next to your skin.

● Prolonged contact with water is drying to the skin – no water gets in, water is drawn out. Don't lie for a long soaking in the bath. Shower, if possible. Keep your hands out of water as often as you can possibly manage.

● Only use sufficient soap when washing, as soap is defatting and can cause itching, soreness and scaling, especially around the genitals. Don't use soda crystals or bath salts of any kind.

● It is particularly important as we get older to keep our skin supple and moist, so keep jars or tubes of handcream in convenient places around the house so that you can rub cream into your hands whenever you remember. Every time you get your hands wet, put on a liberal amount of handcream.

● Wear rubber gloves for dirty jobs, but make sure that you wear an inner lining of a cheap cotton glove soaked in hand cream or hand lotion.

Brown patches
Most of us have a few "brown spots" on our skins. These blotches are areas of irregular pigmentation affected by aging and exposure to sunlight. Typically, such spots appear on exposed parts of the body – the face, neck, backs of the hands and upper arms.

They are not dangerous but may be considered unsightly. We can cover them with cosmetic sticks or creams. Personally, I follow the golden rule that a brown spot should never be interfered with unless a doctor says so and after, only after, you've consulted a dermatologist to check that such treatments are suitable for your particular spots, they can be removed by various medical skin treatments (see page 206).

Itching and inflamed skin
After forty, itching can result merely from our skin being dry due to frequent, overzealous bathing in hot water and strong soaps and sunbathing. Sometimes, however, redness of the skin with itching and raw patches – *intertrigo* – is due to the skin

creases caused by the build-up of body fat. Where skin surfaces touch each other – as between the legs, around the armpits and, in women, under the breasts, friction and lack of ventilation can cause intertrigo and the skin gets raw and smelly and may host fungus infections.

Self-help involves keeping such areas dry and cool and not becoming overweight. Once the skin is red and sore, you should see a dermatologist who can prescribe drying and anti-yeast medications. It's even better to lose some weight. If you have a skin irritation apply a cooling lotion such as calamine, never use an itch-relieving spray, which may contain local anaesthetics.

NECK EXERCISES

Perform these once a day to relax muscles, improve carriage, prevent stooping and maintain good posture.

Neck rolls (3 times)
These relieve tension in the back of your neck while thoroughly exercising your neck muscles. Sit in a straight-backed chair or cross-legged on the floor and keep your neck and back straight and shoulders down, your face ahead. Tip your head forward and without turning your neck at all, roll your head loosely on your neck round to the other side and then back.

Chin lift (12 times)
This exercises your chin and jaw line. Sit up straight and look straight ahead without lifting your head too high, say "eee" and then "ooo".

De-sagger (6 times)
To exercise and relax your neck muscles, lie on your back on a table or firm bed with your head hanging loosely over the edge.
Now, slowly pull your head up until your chin is as close to your chest as you can get it. Hold for a few seconds and then slowly let your head fall back, but don't let it flop.

Now, put your hand lightly under your chin and feel the muscles pull and relax to the sounds.

"Crepey" necks

All of us will eventually notice that the skin of our necks is getting "crepey," This is due to two things: the neck has to be a very mobile organ, moving in all directions much of the time; its skin gets more stretching than skin elsewhere so it becomes loose. The neck is often neglected from a beauty routine, gets no special cleansing, no special moisturizing. At the same time, it's nearly always exposed, so it bears the mask of aging from the elements. The most efficient moisturizer that we can use contains sebum, which holds water in the skin.

Transparent
cortex cells

Hair

Cortex with
color pigment

The root of the hair is buried deep inside a hair follicle.

Hair is constantly being renewed from below the skin's surface; normally, 20 to 60 hairs a day fall out but are replaced. Hairs remain on the head for a period of two to six years. The rate at which hair grows, half an inch a month, slows down as we age. Also, the rate of hair loss begins to exceed that of new growth so some thinning is inevitable. However, it is felt that at least 40 percent of our hair must be lost before thinning becomes apparent.

Graying hair is a normal part of aging and most people have some noticeable graying by the middle forties. While some people may have no gray hair until their late fifties, hardly anyone at seventy has none. Gray hair is just as healthy as pigmented hair and needs no special treatment. "Old" hair does not lose its color — we don't turn gray — but rather new hair grows in without pigment.

Hair care

Use the mildest shampoo you can find and shampoo your hair only once. Make sure your head is thoroughly wet, mix a small amount of shampoo (two teaspoonfuls) in a glassful of warm water and pour this on, massaging the shampoo into your hair very gently. Make sure all the hair has been covered by the shampoo solution; it is not necessary to work up a lather. Leave it on for about a minute and then rinse thoroughly until the hair is squeaky clean. If you like, you can add a conditioner afterward. Here are a few basic tips:
- Do not scrub the scalp with your fingertips as you will loosen hairs from the soft wet hair follicles.
- Do not tug or pull at your hair as you comb it when it is wet; this will remove or tear it. Use a wide-toothed brush.
- Do not brush or comb your hair too frequently; this may irritate the scalp and the oil glands.
- Do no treat any dandruff yourself; see your doctor about it.

Hair coloring

Temporary or permanent coloring can be used to hide gray hair, though nothing can restore hair to its original shade once it grays. All the types of hair coloring below are marketed for both sexes or can be obtained from any good hairdressers.

Comb-through color "restorers," or liquid metallic salts, are sprayed onto the hair. However, they do little more than discolor hair and cover it with a dull coating that often causes the hair to become brittle and easily damaged.

Temporary colors, which can be dry or liquid, are actually rinses that can give highlights to gray hair, hide dull yellow streaks, brighten faded hair and blend streaked hair. They do not lighten or last beyond a shampoo.

Semi-permanent colors can blend gray hairs into your natural color or enhance hair that is drab. They fade over a period so re-application is necesary every few weeks.

Permanent colors penetrate the hair shaft and chemically alter the pigment so that it cannot be shampood away. This process should not be repeated more than once a month as it can damage hair or produce undesirable color shades. Permanent hair colors containing PABA have a warning on them about a possible association with developing cancer.

Hair loss

Baldness affects men most, though women may be affected to a lesser degree. If there is a familial predisposition to baldness, it cannot be prevented and there are no "cures." Some diseases, especially those which involve defects of the thyroid gland and anemia, also cause hair loss, but in these cases the hair is restored when the disease is treated.

Many people who suffer from baldness are under psychological stress. A loss of hair can cause a reciprocal loss of morale making the depression worse. The widely held beliefs that baldness is connected with virility both positively and negatively are entirely untrue.

A trio of factors including heredity, hormones and age are responsible for causing baldness; this process varies from man to man but is irreversible and progressive.

Many men suffer from male pattern baldness and some women also go thin on top – it's part of the body's genetic program. The hair gradually recedes from the forehead, temples and crown of the head, leaving a reasonably thick fringe around the sides and back.

Male baldness

Baldness usually begins in the early twenties and is pretty well established by middle age. Typically, the earliest signs of baldness are noticed in the areas on the sides of the forehead – complete lack of hair is preceded by the presence of fine downy hairs which can be seen by holding a flashlight parallel to the head's surface.

Female baldness

Although total baldness is extremely rare in women, considerable thinning does occur at the temples and over the top of the head. Again, this pattern is usually inherited although the use of hair clips, combs and bands which tug at the hair may be responsible, as may be damaging hair treatments such as permanents or dyeing. Psychological upsets, particularly around the menopause, can cause loss of hair which may take nine months to a year to recover. Certain medical conditions also may rarely be responsible for major hair loss, so be sure to check with your doctor.

You should take care to avoid using rollers and heavy bristle brushes, which may break hairs and pull at the roots, and also keep permenents, frosting and teasing to a minimum.

Many women, too, find that as they age they lose hair.

Dealing with hair loss

Hairpieces

This is the safest and least painful way (in terms of health and money) to camouflage your hair loss. A wide variety of well-cut and well-matched items are made to suit both men and women. Some hairpieces can be permanently attached to the head, either by being tied to existing hairs or by being sewn onto the scalp. These latter may result in infection and are therefore not recommended. Some wigs or hairpieces may contain adhesives to which the wearer is sensitive; other than this they cause no damage to the remaining hair.

Hair weaving

This is a non-surgical procedure that adds replacement hair to existing hair in order to cover a bald patch. The new hair is braided strand by strand on to the edges of the hair *in situ*. Hair weavings require maintenance and careful cleansing.

Hair implant

This is a quasi-surgical procedure where strips of hair are attached to the scalp in the form of surgical threads implanted in the balding area. The implants are normally synthetic so a hairdryer mustn't be used.

Hairpieces have been successfully designed to blend in with natural hair for both men and women.

141

Hair transplant

This is a surgical procedure that generally results in a permanent replacement of hair – though even when established it is not as luxurious as the hair you've lost – and has become increasingly available. Plugs of hair are cut from remaining healthy hair on the sides and back of the head and implanted in bald spots. This hair normally falls out after the transplant but it is replaced by new hair. Quite a few hair follicles must be transplanted at the same session, and the process needs to be repeated for the bald areas to be covered.

Excessive hair

Just as with hair loss, the tendency to develop excessive hair is hereditary and is usually due to hormonal influence, though it can also accompany certain diseases. It is particularly common in people with Latin or Mediterranean backgrounds. This is mainly a problem for women, as men usually worry about a lack rather than an abundance of hair. Hair may begin to appear in one or more places – chin, upper lip, around the nipples, or from the navel downward. Men often find hair growing in the ears, nostrils and on their backs. Eyebrow hair gets thicker and more noticeable.

Superfluous hair is often upsetting but there is little that can be done about stopping the growth. Remedies include lightening it with make-up or bleach, or removal. The hair's rate of growth is not affected whether it's shaved or plucked, contrary to any old wives' tales you might have heard.

Neither plucking, wax removal, depilatories nor shaving will make the hair more wiry, darker or thicker; nor will they prevent its regrowth. If your find any hair growth distressing, electrolysis is a permanent method of removal that can be used successfully on most parts of the body.

Women with very severe, unwanted hair can be investigated to see if hormone imbalance is the cause. An endocrinologist can perform a hormonal profile and, if it's advisable, hormone therapy can be tried as a remedy.

An electrical current travels down a needle placed adjacent to the hair shaft. The current destroys the follicle and prevents growth.

Eyes

The eye is one organ that does not necessarily change as we get older; this means that not all of us will suffer from deteriorating vision as we mature. Indeed 80 percent of people over sixty-five who have a visual impairment can be fitted with glasses so that they can go about their normal activities. However, it becomes more important for us to have regular checks on our eyesight as we get older so that we receive expert advice.

PRESBYOPIA

A lot of people in middle age develop a tendency to be far-sighted because the lens is less able to change its shape to bring into focus what we are looking at. This phenomenon is known as *presbyopia* or "old sight."

Normal eyesight
When the eye focuses on an object, the image is projected on to the retina upside down and back to front. The brain alters this to the way we see.

Presbyopia
This results when the lens becomes less accommodating and is less able to change its shape in order to bring objects into focus.

Eyesight with glasses
In order to remedy presbyopia your optician will prescribe convex (outwardly curved) lenses to increase the power of your own lenses.

Another difficulty aging brings is that the lens begins to yellow. This makes it difficult for us to distinguish between different color intensities. The most difficult are the cool colors such as blue, green and violet, which are filtered out by the yellowing lens. It is generally easier to see warm colors such as yellow, red and orange.

Bear in mind, too, that as we get older it takes a longer time for our eyes to adjust when we go from a well-lit area into a dark one. Don't forget that we also see less well in the dark, so don't be afraid to ask someone to go in front of you if you have to navigate steps or a bumpy path. I do.

Wearing glasses

Presbyopic eyes may require "reading glasses," which are normally focused for about 14 inches. These will reinforce the power of the natural lens of your eyes but they will have to be replaced every few years.

Half glasses may be useful for near correction but not distance. They can be worn all the time; you simply look over them to see any distance.

Bifocals contain two lenses, the long-distance lens on top and the reading lens on the bottom. They have a thin, visible dividing line, though recently blended bifocals and progressive power lenses, which have no visible dividing lines, have become available. The reading lens can be of a variable size according to taste and you should discuss this with your ophthamologist before ordering glasses. It can take some time to get adjusted to bifocals.

143

Contact lenses can also be worn to improve vision, though people over forty may find that they cannot read or see things closely with them and they may need to wear reading glasses over them. It is also possible to get bifocal contact lenses; these can be fitted after you have adapted to single ones.

Sun or tinted glasses may be useful in forestalling the development of cataracts or retinal disease, as exposure to bright light is now thought to be harmful. They should not, however, be worn while driving at night to correct the dazzle of headlamps. They will only make matters worse. Nevertheless, it is useful to wear sunglasses during the day if you expect to drive back from the beach in the evening. If headlamps do dazzle you, this may be an early sign of an impending cataract (see page 244) and the best solution is to keep your glasses scrupulously clean and windshields clear.

Loss of visual acuity

The loss of visual acuity can prove a serious problem when communicating with other people. As we go through life we become quite dependent on our eyes for receiving and processing messages about what is going on around us through books, newspapers, magazines and television. During our daily lives we have to perform tasks that largely depend on good vision. Simple things like sewing on a button, watching out for the bubbles as the gravy comes to the boil, and making sure that we have the same colored socks on each foot all become difficult, undermining our sense of security and self-confidence.

Anyone who suffers *sudden* loss of vision needs patience and sympathy if he or she is to avoid feeling afraid and isolated. Remember that anyone who is losing his or her eyesight may be hesitant in trying to do anything, especially anything new, because he or she is feeling self-conscious. Such a person feels slow and gauche in striving to do well and may draw back from getting involved in things.

Living with visual impairment

• Fit more powerful bulbs in all the lights throughout the house, especially in reading lamps and those in dark hallways; *however,* if you have glaucoma don't make your lights too bright as this can cause glare and deepen shadows. Tell those close to you what your needs are so that they can come to your assistance if necessary.

• Never leave the house completely dark at night. This can make any journey from the bedroom unnecessarily hazardous. If you can afford it, get dimmers fitted to your electric light switches in the bedroom, bathroom and upstairs hall, so that you can leave a dim light burning all night.

• Put fluorescent tape around your electric plugs and light

switches, door handles and keyholes. It will also make it easier for you to pick them out when the light is poor.

● If you suffer from glaucoma, have your eyes tested to see how much your field of vision is restricted, and then ask advice about whether or not you should drive a car. Don't forget that our reflexes slow down as we get older and in today's fast-moving traffic we can't afford not to see passing cars.

● If your peripheral vision is restricted, ask someone who is talking to you to face you directly, or if you can, make sure your face is directly in front of him or her. If someone is demonstrating something to you, make sure that all the movements are in your line of vision.

● Explain the kind of visual loss that you are experiencing to your family and friends and any social or health care workers who are helping you. They will then try to make adjustments easier for you.

Ears

At the age of about fifty most of us will have noticed some hearing loss, usually of the higher-pitched sounds. The majority of us do retain fairly normal hearing beyond the age of sixty but in our seventies and eighties we are three times more likely to have lost some of our hearing.

In the Western world men suffer much more from hearing loss than women, possibly because of a higher noise level at work. This is supported by studies of primitive villagers, who do not have the kind of age-linked hearing impairment we get in cities nor any difference in the hearing between men and women.

Hearing loss is usually due to changes in the inner ear involving the transmission of sound to the brain. The cochlea is the hearing organ in the inner ear and it transforms sound vibrations into nerve impulses through delicate hair cells. These hairs have the capability of transforming sound waves into electrical impulses, which are carried via the auditory nerve to the brain, where they are transferred back into sound. The most common cause of loss of hearing is thought to be due to loss of hair cells. This loss obviously cannot be helped by a hearing aid.

Branches of auditory nerve

Cochlea

Labyrinth

The brain receives signals from the cochlea via the auditory nerve.

Impaired hearing

Patience and kindness are automatically shown to a blind person, but someone with hearing difficulty often meets with impatience and embarrassment. People hard of hearing can see the irritation they cause, which is something spared the blind. Even long-standing relationships may be disrupted.

145

It is vitally important for our mental well-being, as well as that of those we love, that we keep in touch with the world about us. As loss of hearing jeopardizes this ability, any reduced hearing should be reported to your doctor as soon as it becomes noticeable. Loss of hearing in a young person is nearly always forgiven, but impaired hearing in an older person is frequently interpreted as stubbornness, senility and eccentricity.

When hearing begins to wane, our ability to hear higher frequency speech sounds may be affected. Consonants such as K, CH, F, SH, S and Z have higher frequencies, while vowel sounds A, E, I, O and U have lower frequencies. If there is disparity in hearing these vowels and consonants, a person can hear conversation but cannot make out the words precisely. Thus a phrase like "clean dentures" may be perceived by the person with early hearing loss as a chain of vowel sounds which he or she cannot comprehend. This presents a lot of difficulties for both the listener and the speaker. Most people try to make themselves heard by shouting, which only results in a chain of booming, unintelligible sounds. It does nothing to clarify higher frequency sounds.

A common cause of hearing impairment is failure to conduct sound waves across the middle ear through a chain of tiny bones: the hammer, the anvil and the stirrup, so named because of their shapes. *Otosclerosis,* caused by the fixation of the stirrups, can lead to a loss of hearing.

A trivial thing such as wax can harden and dry and block sound waves getting to the eardrum. Some people's ears make more wax than others, and any excess is not an indicated of lack of cleanliness. Hearing can be vastly improved simply by having the ear canal syringed and wax collected and removed by a doctor or nurse. Never attempt to remove wax by poking any object into your ear.

Hearing aids and their problems

If hearing impairment is not due to damage to the auditory nerve, then a hearing aid can help, though it is not a perfect substitute for hearing normally, nor can it give the listener a full range of sound frequencies.

It is normal for people newly fitted with hearing aids to complain that the sound seems unnatural and that the device is difficult to adjust. If you are helping someone through this adjustment period, bear in mind that hearing aids amplify all sounds and a wearer may have difficulty in distinguishing speech patterns from any other noise in the room, such as television, radio, jumble of conversation by several different people, sounds of washing up, cooking, etc. If you are given a hearing aid, seek advice as to how it works properly.

HEARING AIDS

Hearing aids are available from commercial hearing aid centers. They offer a variety of styles and prices; it is advisable to comparison shop. Medical reimbursements vary from state to state.

Internal aid
This fits snugly into the outer-ear canal and it is hardly noticeable.

Behind-the-ear aid
The earphone fits into your outer-ear canal and seals it up so that no sound is lost.

Body-worn aid
In some more powerful hearing aids, the amplifier and battery are kept in a plastic case which you can clip to your belt or place in your pocket. It's unobtrusive and connected to the earphone by a thin, plastic-covered wire.

If you don't, you might be tempted to discard it and cut yourself off from the social intercourse and companionship of others.

Another fairly common problem with hearing aids occurs when the ear-mold is fitted incorrectly. It should be an exact replica of your ear.

Making the best of your hearing

- Go and have your ears checked fairly regularly, say once a year, and have any wax removed by your doctor.
- If your hearing is going and you cannot successfully master a hearing aid, try to learn to lip read. This can be of great help in conversation. Ask the person whose lips you are reading to face you, making sure that the light falls on his or her face; it is important that you see him or her clearly, and not to exaggerate lip movements as you will find this confusing.
- Don't become defensive and withdrawn when somebody is shouting to help you hear better. Ask him or her to speak more loudly but lower his or her voice so that you can pick up he lower sound frequencies, and to speak clearly and slowly.
- If you have difficulty in hearing one particular word, ask the speaker to use another word to say the same thing.
- It does no harm at all to point out that non-verbal communication is extremely good for getting messages across. Encourage people to use facial expressions as these can tell you about their moods, feelings, excitement or disapproval when you can't get this from the tone in which the words are said.

Mouth, tongue and teeth

As we get older we begin to lose sensitivity to pain and irritation in the mouth. Many irritations, therefore, we disregard, and any that we notice are shrugged off in the false belief that they will heal quickly. This, combined with infrequent visits to the dentist, can lead to poor oral hygiene. A touch of arthritis too can prevent good care of the mouth and teeth and lead to the loss of a positive self-image and problems in the mouth.

As we get older our mouths tend to dry out because we secrete smaller quantities of saliva; the lining gets thinner and can't hold water, and we may be deficient in certain vitamins (such as vitamin A) that are responsible for the integrity of lining inside the mouth.

Loss of taste sensations   As we go through middle age we may experience blunting of our tastes due to a gradual withering of the taste buds on the tongue. A stroke, or hardening of the arteries in the brain, can also affect the way we taste.

It is possible that people of seventy have 70 percent fewer taste buds than they had at thirty. As we approach old age, in our late seventies and eighties, we feel almost an 80 percent reduction in our ability to taste. It is not until after sixty, however, that we notice any real deterioration. Salty taste does not appear to be affected by age but sweet, bitter and sour do decline. As one might expect, what goes is the ability to detect subtle differences within sweet, bitter and sour tastes. There is a loss of touch sensitivity in the mouth and any lessening of our senses of smell will also affect how we taste things. As taste becomes duller, we may find ourselves increasing the flavoring of food by adding spices and seasoning. We often eat dishes which, when we were younger, we would have considered over-seasoned and avoided at all costs.

One of the dangers of losing the ability to savor food is that our appetites may lessen and we become in danger of not eating sufficient quantities of the right foods. All of these things, plus loneliness, isolation and a loss of spirit, deter us from spending enough time shopping for nutritious foods and preparing healthy meals.

The "older" mouth   While a forty-year-old mouth may not be perfect, it should be healthy and efficient. By middle age almost all our mouths will contain fillings, inlays or crowns and we may also have a bridge or partial denture. Even a full set of dentures is no longer an indication of old age (see *Specialist help*).

Teeth have several functions. They masticate food and help to mix saliva with it so that digestion is started in the mouth. Certain sounds involve contact between the teeth and the tongue and so they are important for good speech. Even today, when there is emphasis on dental conservation, nearly 50 percent of people living in the Western world have lost most of their teeth by the age of sixty-five and about 75 percent of all people are edentulous (toothless) by the time they reach seventy-five. The main causes of this attrition are a poor diet rich in sugar, and neglect by the individual and by his or her dentist and/or hygienist to make sure that the teeth are regularly cleaned and scaled, the gum margins looked after and teeth repaired as soon as their conditions deteriorate.

As we go through middle age we begin to show a different pattern of dental problems from those we had when we were thirty-five and forty. Dental cavities, which reached their peak when we were thirty-five, are present now to a lesser extent. But after forty the most common cause for losing teeth is pyorrhoea (infective disease of the gums). During middle age the gums begin to recede and more of the teeth show so that they look longer, hence the phrase "long in the tooth."

The commonest dental changes are missing teeth, worn teeth, teeth becoming slack in the gums and badly fitting dentures. All these affect the functioning of our mouths and teeth and can lead to cosmetic changes in the appearance of our faces and to subsequent loss of self-image.

Restoring teeth

New developments in dentistry have concentrated on the restoration of adult teeth. Plastic, composite materials are available for filling and building up front teeth in an "invisible" way. New plastic-covered wire braces and those that are attached behind the teeth have led to a big increase in the number of adults wearing braces to correct their dentition. Oral surgeons can also realign jaws, making possible the correction of gaps and protruding jaws. Moreover, permanent implants have been used successfully to hold dentures in place.

Dentures

Failure to fill any gaps caused by loss of teeth can lead to complications; if dentures are not worn, any remaining teeth adjust to fill the spaces and there may be resulting changes in the underlying bony structure of the jaws. The same problems can occur if dentures are badly fitted.

Dentures are socially well accepted, and among some communities are even status symbols. The best-fitting denture is one for the upper teeth. The lower one never fits quite as well because gums recede and so the denture has to be altered.

LOOKING AFTER DENTURES

Nowadays, most bridges (see page 205) and also dentures are designed to be kept permanently in the mouth except when they need cleaning.

To clean dentures, gently brush them with a denture cleanser to remove plaque and then rinse them thoroughly before placing them in your mouth.
Removable dentures can be left to soak in water overnight.

You should go to your dentist for an assessment of your dentures about every five years or as often as he or she suggests.

Dental adhesives are almost universally unpleasant and their effects last a fairly short time. They should never be used as a substitute for periodic rechecks by a dentist.

Looking after your mouth and teeth

- Make regular visits to your dentist for the purpose of conserving your teeth and maintaining the health of your mouth. This lowers any chance of your having trouble, such as developing an ulcer due to irritation by sharp tooth edges.
- Any sore on your tongue or gums or the inside of your cheeks that lasts two weeks should be seen by your doctor.
- Drying out of the mouth can lead to problems, so if you find that this is happening to you, irrigate your mouth by sucking a sugarless sweet or having a cup of tea or coffee.
- Pyorrhoea is largely caused by calculus, the chalky white, hard deposits around the margins of your teeth where they enter your gums. You can keep this at bay by removing plaque with regular tooth brushing at least morning and night and after eating sweet food, and visiting your dentist at three-monthly or six-monthly intervals for mechanical removal of the plaque, depending on its seriousness.
- Always have the sharp edge of a tooth attended to by a dentist as soon as you feel it. Don't put off your visit.

Legs and feet

Special attention must be paid to our legs and feet in order to have an active lifestyle. Gradual hardening of the arteries and increasingly poor circulation due to aging are especially hard on feet. Feet take a great deal of wear and tear and a regular program of foot care is vital.

Looking after your feet

- Avoid blisters and sore areas on your feet or toes by **wearing** comfortable, supple, low-heeled shoes. Well-fitting shoes should grip your heel and instep but not press on your toes.
- Sit with your feet up whenever you can so that any fluid can drain out of them and their nourishment can be increased. This is particularly important if you get any kind of abrasion, cut or sore on your foot.
- Minor injuries tend to take longer to heal than anywhere else because of their dependent position. Treat even a small sore promptly with a simple antiseptic cream (no hot water soaking, please). If it doesn't clear up in a few days consult your doctor. Consult him or her *immediately* if you are a diabetic or suffer from any circulatory disease of the veins or arteries.
- Don't keep your stockings up with garters, especially **tight** ones, as they may make a poor circulation poorer.

EXERCISES TO AID CIRCULATION

Our extremities are the first to suffer as our blood circulation slows down, so it is important that we take care of our legs and feet.

Leg raising (20 times)
Keeping your legs straight, point your feet and toes upward and raise one leg 45°. Hold to the count of 3 and then slowly lower it to the floor. Repeat the exercise with your other leg.

Foot bending (10-15 times)
Point your feet and toes upwards as far as you can manage and then point them down. Repeat this action vigorously.

Foot circling (15 times)
Working from your ankles, turn your feet in a circle in one direction. Repeat in the opposite direction.

Chilblains   The older we get, the more we tend to be subject to chilblains (areas of itching, swelling and redness). You can help to avoid these by wearing thick woolen stockings or socks and, in the coldest weather, fleece-lined shoes and slippers. However, make certain that any lined shoe or boot will accommodate your foot comfortably as tightness retards circulation and may encourage chilblains. Warm trousers can also be protective. You can also help discourage chilblains by starting the day with a warm shower and massaging your feet gently with a rotary movement using foot oil before drying with a rough towel.

If you do develop chilblains, never put your feet or legs near direct heat – such as a hot water bottle. Try bathing the chilblains alternately in hot and cold water.

Nail care

Hardening of the arteries and poor circulation may make skin cool to the touch and it also leads to thickening fingernails and toenails. It is important to trim them regularly, say once a week, to keep them in the best condition.

When you are cutting your toenails, never cut them down deeply at the sides; keep the nails straight all the way across – this helps prevent ingrowing nails. If they are very thick you can file them frequently and attempt to thin them down as well as shorten them.

If you have difficulty in looking after your toenails and feet, regular visits to the podiatrist are a vital investment if you want to remain agile.

Muscles and joints

Changes in our muscles and bones are important because they can greatly affect our lifestyle by making certain everyday functions harder to perform. Even though some degenerative changes may cause pain, stiffness and difficulty with movement, there is no need for them to be disabling as long as we get the correct diagnosis, treatment and maintenance therapy. Bones and muscles give stability to the body, help it keep its shape, provide support, protect the vital organs and enable us to move and walk, jump and run freely. As we get older we find that we take these functions very much for granted; as our musculo-skeletal systems can no longer take the stresses and strains of younger life we become prey to bad posture, stooping, loss of power in our muscles, stiffness, painful and even misshapen joints, loss of mobility, and we may become prone to falls and fractures.

Bone and muscle disorders are among the commonest conditions affecting people over the age of sixty-five. It is dangerous to bracket all bone and muscle symptoms together as part of getting old; otherwise the pain of osteoporotic bones (ones that have lost protein and calcium) or the stiffness and crouched stance characteristic of Parkinson's Disease, may be dismissed as normal aging and proper treatment delayed. At no age are long-term recurrent joint and muscle pains natural. Anyone experiencing such symptoms should seek medical advice (see *Special medical problems*).

The amount of muscle in our bodies decreases as we get older. This is partly due to hardening of the arteries and a sluggish circulation, which is a result of the slowing down and/or loss of nerve cells that send messages from the brain to the muscles, and partly due to a reduction in the amount of physical activity we manage to undertake each day.

So, as we get older we may take longer to complete a job. Muscle deterioration can affect other body organs that you might not suspect. For instance, if the muscles involved in breathing become weak, this will predispose one to chest illnesses. Weakening of the bladder muscle means it never completely empties, so we feel the need to pass urine more often.

It is important that we make our limitations known to friends and colleagues so that they will recognize what we are capable of – and give us sufficient time.

Posture Often, our posture deteriorates as a result of normal aging, with gradually softening bones and loss of muscle flexibility. Our chins begin to jut forward, our backs become humped and our knees and hips bend. If this continues our breathing and lung capacities can lessen, our gaits can become shuffling and there's often a greater likelihood of fractures. The good news is that exercise can prevent, or remedy, such changes and it can help to ensure that the deterioration normally associated with old age is forestalled (see *Keeping physically fit*).

Backache can be prevented if the back muscles are kept strong by simple exercises and good posture to support the spine. Improved bearing substantially contributes to a youthful appearance (see page 37).

Posture is a matter of balance; if the body segments are properly aligned, the less strain is put on the muscles. It must be maintained when sitting and walking as well.

EXERCISE FOR CO-ORDINATION AND BALANCE

Good balance helps posture; if our body segments are properly aligned then less strain is put on muscles.

Stand against a wall with your head, buttocks and heels touching it and stretch up with your hands over your head until you are raised on your toes.

Move away from the wall, keeping your feet 6in (15cm) apart and your arms by your sides. Tighten leg and stomach muscles, extend your chest and clench your fists bringing them chest high. Take a deep breath, let it out slowly without relaxing and rotate your arms for a count of 3 (5 times).

Make sure your chair is comfortable and upright and sit back on the seat with your head and shoulders balanced over your hips. Use your hips as well as your arms when you reach for something. When walking, center your body over the balls of your feet and lead with your thigh.

Looking after joints and muscles

● Always take an injury to a muscle or joint seriously. Consult your doctor or a specialist in order to get an accurate diagnosis and specialized treatment. Make sure that once the injury is healed you learn about a maintenance program of exercising for endurance, strength and mobility from a physiotherapist.

● Most treatments for joints involve a program of combined rest and exercise. This applies just as well to healthy joints. Rest plus exercise means resting the joint at night in the position of optimum relaxation (this also prevents the joints from becoming stiff and immobile in an abnormal position) and a series of exercises repeated during the day. Anyone who feels discomfort and stiffness beginning should start on this kind of program.

● If you feel a joint becoming stiff and uncomfortable, the worst thing that you can do is rest it for any length of time without consulting your doctor. You will hasten the speed at which it stiffens and becomes immobile.

- If you find that joint or muscle pain is disabling, do consult your doctor so that any discomfort can be relieved and so that you can get appliances to help you do everyday tasks. There is special cutlery, for instance, for those who are beginning to feel stiffening joints in their fingers. There is even a gadget that can help you turn on and off the tap (see page 308).
- A program of exercise is important at all stages in our lives because it helps to increase the blood flow and promotes the health of our bodies. It may help lower the blood cholesterol and it makes the burning up of calories more efficient. It also suppresses excessive appetite. As we get older it is important to maintain a program of at least gentle exercise. People who are bedridden must be actively exercised to prevent loss of muscle strength (see *Living with long-term ailments*).
- If you fail to or cannot exercise, mobility aids such as crutches, walkers and canes become more difficult to use.
- There are conversions which you can make to your home that make life easier if you suffer from muscle or joint complaints. These are discussed in *Adapting your environment*.

Gastro-intestinal tract

In the gastro-intestinal tract some of the changes are specific to the various parts of the mouth, stomach or intestine, while others are due to general aging of the body. Digestive juices decrease in quantity and the gut doesn't move as energetically to digest and push our food along. The muscles lining the various parts of the digestive organs become weaker and when nerve function fades, messages about enzyme and hormone release don't get through to the brain efficiently. There is also less response to pain and internal sensations.

Vague symptoms from the gastro-intestinal tract such as heartburn, indigestion and discomfort at the lower end of the breastbone increase with age. Many of these symptoms are caused by normal changes but as we get older they can be linked to serious conditions which may be life-threatening. Don't be put off by a doctor who attributes rather vague stomach or intestinal symptoms to getting old. Ask for a second opinion.

Changes in the stomach From middle age onward there are changes in the structure and function of the stomach that affect digestion, but research has not yet revealed exactly what these changes are and how fast they occur. The stomach, however, gradually stops producing a normal quantity of acid, which is essential for carrying on digestion, and it may become short of acid. Mucin, which is secreted by glands in the stomach and stops the stomach from digesting itself, also has a tendency to be produced in smaller and smaller quantities.

Gall bladder and liver

Gall bladder problems may increase in frequency after we are sixty-five. When we get older, two things happen to gall bladder function that cause a predisposition to inflammation (cholecystitis). Firstly, the gall bladder no longer empties efficiently, and secondly, the bile becomes thicker, richer in cholesterol and smaller in volume. Certainly, gall stones increase with age. By the time we are seventy between 15 and 30 percent of us will have gall stones.

The liver is the largest gland in the body and it is important to our health. It has been described as a "chemical breaker's yard" because it undertakes so many functions. It builds up carbohydrates into a form which can be stored; it also acts as a reservoir for proteins, vitamins, minerals and fats; it is a chemical sieve which filters out and renders some bacteria harmless. The liver is in control of how much bile we secrete and it makes certain blood cells and antibodies. These are important in the eradication of infectious and other diseases.

As we get older our livers increase in size in proportion to the rest of the body, so that the liver's percentage of body weight remains constant until the age of seventy. Only then does it start to decline slowly up to the age of a hundred.

Changes in the intestines

There is a family of conditions affecting the large intestine that are often thought to be the natural outcome of growing older. Quite a lot can be done with plain common sense to prevent them from developing into anything serious.

Along with many other linings in the body, the lining of the intestines becomes thin and its glands get fewer in number. The resilience and elasticity of the intestines diminish as collagen disintegrates and muscles also become a good deal weaker.

The large intestine serves as a storage organ. It is the major site in the whole gastro-intestinal tract where water is absorbed from the stools and where waste collects. Both of these functions can become less efficient because the movements of the bowels weaken and slow down as we approach seventy. Constipation is an almost natural consequence unless we take care to have the right diet (see page 243). Adding bran to semi-liquid dishes, for instance, will help to overcome the discomfort. Mention the fact that you have constipation to your doctor and he will advise you which drugs to avoid, and if necessary, which laxatives are gentle enough for you to use.

Looking after internal organs

- Your stomach and liver may be less able to cope with a large, rich meal, so eat little meals, say six a day, often.
- Never medicate yourself for gastric symptoms, even mild ones, for longer than 10 days without seeing your doctor.
- When considering a diet, don't stick to a rigid plan. Accommodate your own tastes, attitudes, abilities and needs.
- Take precaution not to become dependent on alcohol, which can lead to the development of cirrhosis and death. It is never too late to stop drinking if you have a liver problem. The changes that have already occurred are not always reversible but you can often prevent further damage.
- If you are suffering from hemorrhoids consult your doctor about treatment, and in the meanwhile ask him or her for something that will soften the stool and increase its bulk. You can do this yourself by adding a spoonful of bran to your breakfast each morning. Do not use proprietary hemorrhoid products from the supermarket shelves.

Heart, blood vessels and chest

For certain heart conditions it is virtually impossible to distinguish whether they are due to age-related conditions or to heart disease. In other words, it is difficult to tell where normal changes end and disease changes begin. Finding a distinction is not merely an academic exercise – certain symptoms in an aging heart may only indicate slight weakening and not a serious threat to life.

The heart nearly always remains the same size as we advance through life, but malnourishment, confinement to bed, and the rigors of a long illness may produce some shrinkage. There is, however, a gradual lessening of elasticity in the main arterial trunk of the body, the aorta. At seventy it is only about half as elastic as it was at twenty. Also, there is a slight reduction in heart muscle cell size and a progressive weakening of the heart muscles. This leads to a reduction in the amount of blood that the heart is able to pump around the body, but these aging processes of the heart don't start in middle age, they start after the age of twenty. From then on there is nearly a one percent loss of heart muscle strength for every year lived.

Reduction in the strength of the heart muscle and cardiac output does not mean that there is an inadequate blood flow around the body. Output usually remains adequate because body requirements have fallen and there is a lower metabolic rate. An important part of cardiac function that may become defective with increasing age is the ability to respond to stress. The response may be inadequate, but it is usually sufficient if the rest of the body is not stressed. However, when the body is under stress, it may be difficult to provide for the whole body's increased fuel needs as the heart cells no longer respond as rapidly or as strongly to the chemicals produced under such conditions.

Symptoms of wear and tear

Our heart valves tend to thicken with age and there may be signs of calcium deposits. Blood pressure also rises with age. The systolic pressure usually stabilizes in the late seventies and the diastolic pressure stabilizes from the early sixties onward. Some authorities feel that a normal blood pressure for an older man is in the range of up to 160 millimeters of mercury systolic pressure and 100 millimeters diastolic pressure; for women these figures would be 170 and 90.

In the face of this list of age-related changes, you may be tempted to feel that the outlook is bleak. It is not. Usually, the changes in the heart are continuous and do not significantly interfere with heart function as long as the coronary artery system (the circulation that supplies the heart muscle itself with oxygen) is not damaged. However, diseases of the coronary arteries (ischemic heart disease) can restrict cardiac function so that symptoms such as chest pain, getting out of breath on exertion, racing of the heart, palpitation and breathlessness at night when you lie down, may show themselves. Fortunately, the power of the heart lessens in parallel with the demands that are made upon it.

Coarse artery wall

Atheroma

Blood flow

Deposits of fatty material collect at the point where the artery branches. This interferes with the flow of blood.

The following are the most important factors in heart disease: heredity, high blood pressure, diabetes, lack of exercise, cigarette smoking and being overweight. Diet is also thought to be an important factor (see page 268). Much coronary artery disease is caused by *atherosclerosis*. This consists of deposits of fatty material in the walls of arteries, thereby narrowing their cores; this can start very early in life — there are fatty streaks in the aorta of a child when only three years old. One pathologist found evidence of atherosclerosis in infants as young as three to four months. In the Korean war the average age of soldiers who were examined was just over twenty-two and more than three-quarters of them showed extensive atheroma.

Arteriosclerosis

This is synonymous with hardening of the arteries and describes loss of elasticity in the arterial wall. Arteriosclerosis occurs in every population regardless of the factors listed above. It is progressive and related to age.

Arteriosclerosis (see page 219) narrows the diameter of arteries and their ability to stretch and the amount of blood they can carry. This means that our hearts may have to work harder to push the blood through the narrowed vessels to nourish our bodies.

Hypertension or high blood pressure

This also increases with age in Western society. Diagnosis of whether blood pressure is high depends on a person's sex, age and state of health. It has been defined as a rise of pressure in the arteries that cause symptoms. It can be relieved with medication. In both men and women high blood pressure is closely correlated with the risk of coronary heart disease.

Of course, high blood pressure need not be an inevitable consequence of getting old. More primitive races than ours do not show the same trend as we in the Western world. There is no tendency among them for blood pressure to increase with age.

Diseases of the lungs

In our lungs the most important change is a reduction in breathing power and this means that the older we are, the more easily fatigued we get. These changes rarely cause symptoms when we are resting. This kind of "normal change" does not affect our lifestyles as we get older because our bodies need less oxygen; there is absolutely no reason why we should be disabled by these changes. With increasing age the airways and tissues in the lungs, including the alveoli or air-sacs, become less distensible and more inflexible. The size of the chest cavity may be reduced by a gradual softening of the bones in the spine, osteoporosis (see page 232), and the spine may become curved forward so that the chest cavity may lessen in size, making forward and downward movements of the ribs more difficult. Added to this the respiratory muscles lose some of their power as do the abdominal muscles. This means that there is extra demand on the diaphragm.

As we go into old age, diseases in the lung become more prevalent than when we were younger. The threat of a serious infection in the lung does increase with age, as does chronic bronchitis, emphysema and lung cancer. Our tendency to have lung infections is partly due to our loss of resistance to bacteria, viruses and fungi because our immune systems become weaker as we grow older. Lung cancer is influenced by smoking and by being exposed to polluted air in our everyday environment.

Breast self-examination

The point of examining your breasts once a month yourself is to find any lumps at an early stage. One of the few ways that modern surgeons have found of improving the cure rate for cancer of the breast is to treat the tumor while it is still small. When you are examining your breasts you are trying to detect lumps about ½ inch (1 cm) in diameter if possible.

Remember, most lumps are not malignant. You should also remember that most breasts become naturally lumpy during the week before a period. They usually become heavy, enlarged and tender when squeezed, and the nipples may tingle. If you are still having periods, your breasts will go through these normal monthly changes. When you feel their consistency just before a period with your fingertips you will find that there are small lumps similar to orange pips in their substance. These are only swollen milk glands, which enlarge in the second half of each cycle. They shrink again when menstruation is over. If you have stopped menstruating this cycle will not affect you.

BREAST EXAMINATION

Do examine your breasts once a month. Observe them carefully and look for any dimpling of the skin over the surface of a lump; any change in the size, shape and color of your nipples; and any discharge from your nipple.

Lie on a flat surface with your head on a pillow and your shoulder slightly raised. Hold your fingers straight and examine the four quadrants of each breast as they are illustrated above.

Starting from the outside, feel your breast with your fingertips in a circular, clockwise direction. Use your right hand to examine your left breast. Keep your left arm loosely by your side when you examine the outer parts.

Examine the inner surface of each breast with the same movement. Extend the arm you are not using behind your head to stretch the breast tissue as this will make any lump easier to find.

Feel for lumps along the top of your collarbone and in your armpit. Now repeat the examination using your left hand to feel your right breast.

Brain

The number of brain cells we have starts to drop from twenty-five onward. In parallel there is a slowing down of nerve impulses traveling to and from the brain so messages come and go more slowly. This can lead to less stimulation of all five senses: taste, smell, touch, hearing and vision, and may result in confusion and social isolation in the later years of life. Even with arteriosclerotic and atherosclerotic changes in arteries that supply the brain, nourishment can still be quite adequate as we get older. Any impairment in the circulation of the blood to the brain is called *cerebrovascular disease*; when part of the brain is deprived of blood a stroke results. The commonest underlying cause is atherosclerosis, which can lead to cerebral thrombosis in exactly the same way as a coronary thrombosis, and causes a stroke (see page 221).

If atherosclerosis of the carotid artery (the main branch to the brain via the neck) has made it so narrow that it may be denying blood to the head and neck, ask your doctor if you can be referred to a surgeon who might consider an *endarterectomy*, in which the inside of the artery is cleared of fatty plaque with something resembling a miniature version of the brushes that chimney sweeps use.

Urinary tract and genitals

The bladder capacity of people in their seventies is less than half (about a half a pint) that of a person aged around twenty-five (about one and a fifth pints). The bladder also holds about a fifth of a pint or residual urine most of the time. The desire to urinate in older people is slow to come and this can cause leaking away of urine and mild incontinence; the bladder has to be very near maximum capacity before they feel the desire to pass urine. In younger people the bladder only has to be half full before the reflex to empty the bladder is activated.

In very old women the pelvic diaphragm is weak so support around the edges of the bladder wall is deficient. The outlet may become funnel-shaped so that the bladder cannot close off completely when urine has been passed. Whenever there is an increase in pressure in the abdomen, such as during coughing, straining at stools, doing strenuous exercises and laughing, urine will leak away causing stress incontinence. Stress incontinence can occur at any age, certainly in women, where it is often due to damage caused during labor.

A prolapse, or pelvic relaxation

A prolapse, or pelvic relaxation, occurs when the pelvic musculature becomes weakened and allows part of the pelvic organs to protrude or drop out of position. It is especially noticeable when intra-abdominal pressure is increased on coughing or straining at stool, or it occurs simply due to the downpull of gravity. The affected organs include the uterus, bladder, rectum, and urethra; the uterus is the most likely one to collapse.

Urethrocele is a bulge of the lower front wall of the vagina, which contains the urethra. If it irritates the urethra lining it leads to a frequency of urination.

Cystocele occurs when the bladder bulges into the upper front wall of the vagina.

Uterus
Cervix
Bladder
Pubic bone
Vagina

Urethrocele　　　　　　　**Cystocele**

Diverticula of the bladder

These occur in about 30 percent of older men and are usually caused by an obstruction beyond the bladder, such as an enlarged prostate gland (see page 217). In women, bladder diverticula are rare.

The kidneys remain quite normal in the absence of disease, although kidney function does decline with age and the rate at which the blood is filtered slows down. The other functions of the kidney such as the reabsorption of valuable minerals and the excretion of urine decrease in line with this. There is a decrease in kidney function from our twenties onward. This rate accelerates as we approach old age. For instance, at thirty we had double the number of functioning units in our kidneys as we will have at seventy.

Infections of the urinary tract

As we age we leave a larger amount of urine in the bladder after emptying and this can act as a perfect medium in which bacteria multiply; a urinary tract infection can follow. Infections occur most commonly when people are taken into the hospital for some reason and are bedridden. The symptoms of a urinary tract infection are a burning sensation when urine is passed, having to get up out of bed at night to pass urine, an increased frequency of passing urine during the day, not being able to get to a lavatory in time (precipitancy), and possibly having a raised temperature and a feeling of nausea and a headache. Incontinence does not lead to infection; the high volume of residual urine does. This means that prostate problems have to be treated promptly and adequately (again see page 217).

The appearance of bacteria in the urine of elderly people is fairly common and it is not necessarily the cause of symptoms. Symptomatic cystitis is very often brought on by an enlarged prostate, diverticula of the bladder, bladder stones, arteriosclerosis of the blood vessels supplying the bladder and a bladder that is just more irritable than average. Cystitis at all ages is commoner in women than in men, because of their having shorter urethras and the greater possibility of trauma to the urethra during intercourse, doing gymnastics, or while riding a bike. Other characteristics of the female may contribute — features such as the close proximity of the urethral opening to the anus, dilation of the ureters and the urethra during pregnancy, the enlarging womb during pregnancy pressing on the urethra, the bladder and the ureters. In men, a predisposing factor is the gradual lessening of fluid from the prostate gland with its anti-bacterial qualities. Social and cultural factors can also increase the chances of urinary tract infection, such as the kind of sexual activities and the type of personal hygiene practiced, socio-economic status and abuse of pain killers. Some metabolic diseases such as diabetes and bladder and kidney stones will also cause a predisposition to infection.

Prostate gland There are age-related changes here. Some start to occur after the age of forty that are internal to the gland and can be felt only by an examining doctor. A gland becomes rather irregular in shape and can be nodular when felt through the rectal wall during a rectal examination. The nodular kind of growth in the prostate is fairly common from the age of fifty onward and most corrective surgical operations are carried out between fifty and seventy. Surgical removal of the enlarged prostate does not affect a man's potency.

Later on, after sixty, these changes get worse and occur throughout the whole gland. Many elderly men suffer from one kind of prostate problem or another. When the gland enlarges and obstructs the exit from the bladder a man may experience hesitancy, and then later on have to get up at night to pass urine. He may also find that the stream of urine is very thin and weak and finally he may go to the stage of not being able to pass very much urine from the bladder.

Just as cancer of the breast is the most common cancer in older women, cancer of the prostate is the most frequent tumor in older men. You should be ready to spot symptoms and go to your doctor as soon as they are causing difficulty.

163

Looking after your urinary system

The following are straightforward steps that you should take in order to keep your urinary system in a healthy condition.

• As we get older we all need to empty the bladder more frequently. Avoid embarrassment by doing so *before* you feel the urge – say every two to three hours, more often if you're drinking a lot of fluids.

• Wear a special sanitary pad if you are incontinent (see page 292) and don't drink too much coffee; it makes your kidneys produce more than usual quantities of urine and will increase your desire to empty your bladder.

• Treatment of urinary infection should always begin by getting an accurate diagnosis so that your doctor can choose the right drugs to ensure success in treating the infection. It is essential to give an adequate amount of antibiotic or urinary antiseptics. The duration of treatment will vary with severity of the infection. Anyone with a urinary tract infection must take his or her medication exactly according to instructions, and not stop when the symptoms *seem* to disappear.

• The antibiotic prescribed depends on the type and severity of the infection.

• It is essential to drink a lot of fluid if you have a urinary tract infection. This helps to flush through the urinary tract and get rid of bacteria. It also relieves your symptoms because it makes the urine less concentrated.

• Because prostate cancer is the most frequent tumor in older men, you should have your prostate checked by your doctor (this is simply done during a rectal examination) whenever you get symptoms and periodically even if you have none.

Hormone system

Abnormalities in the hormone or endocrine system are not at all frequent in old age; most endocrine disorders have their peak in early and middle adulthood. This system exhibits fewer disorders related specifically to aging than any of the other systems we have discussed. The commonest are diabetes (see page 237) and abnormalities of thyroid gland function. Despite the fact that diabetes was described in Egyptian papyri as long ago as 1500BC, it is also a disease of civilization. It becomes more prevalent with obesity brought on by lifestyles with little exercise and a Western diet. Diabetics will also benefit from modern technology and are living much longer lives. There is, therefore, an increasing number of older diabetics.

There seems to be a steady increase in the number of people with diabetes if we track them from childhood to old age. The peak occurs late in the decade between sixty-five and seventy-five and then drops again. Many cases of diabetes in old people are due to being overweight. Diabetes is not the only disease related to excess weight, a fact worth bearing in mind when you think about improving the quality of your daily diet.

Thyroid gland

This decreases in weight compared to total body weight as we get older. There are very few other functional changes. Thyroid disorders are not that common and they are most frequent in young and middle-aged people. When changes in thyroid function occur in older people, they take up quite a different pattern from that which they exhibit in young people.

Looking after your glands

● Being overweight has the strongest association with diabetes. While it is always important not to put on weight, as you get older it becomes doubly important for this reason. So you should consider your diet and take up more exercise.

● An over-active thyroid can usually be managed by treatment with drugs alone. Most doctors favor *carbimazole* as the anti-thyroid drug of choice. Treatment with radioactive iodine, which is selectively taken up by the thyroid, may be necessary. With one or other of these régimes, most patients can be successfully treated.

● With an underactive thyroid you need hormone replacements, usually for the rest of your life. The thyroid hormone, *L-Thyroxine*, is the safest and simplest drug to take. The usual starting dose of L-Thyroxine is very small but this is very gradually increased by very small amounts per day until a suitable maintenance dose is reached.

● If you are taking any kind of thyroid therapy, you should have regular check-ups: every three months for the first year or so, then less often.

● Diabetics should be regularly and fully checked every few months without fail.

The female menopause

The word "menopause" is usually used to describe the time in a woman's life, between the ages of forty and fifty, when her fertility declines and her menstruation stops. The word literally means "cessation of menstruation." This obviously cannot be applied to men, but if we consider the word "climacteric," which defines the years before, during and after the menopause, lasting anything up to 15 or 20 years, then there is a parallel to be drawn between women and men. The menopause has quite rightly been given a good deal of attention because it is a dramatic event. There are many changes: hormonal, physical, mental and emotional, which occur during the change, and there is the obvious and inescapable punctuation mark of no more menstrual periods. To feel confident it is necessary that we know what is taking place in our bodies, so that we can understand that the mechanism is normal.

For men and women, the climacteric is closely involved with gaining new insights, maturing, changing standards, choosing new lifestyles, and emergence of new opinions and priorities. It may be a confused state, or it may be plain sailing. We must draw on our reserves of serenity and maturity.

Onset of the menopause

In the US the average age for menopause is fifty to fifty-two, but it can occur anytime between thirty-five and sixty-four. At any one time there are about 39 million women over the age of forty-five in the United States. This means that about a sixth of the population is in the menopausal age group and may be suffering unpleasant symptoms because of the following.

The first half of each menstrual cycle is controlled by a follicle-stimulating hormone (FSH) which ripens an egg in an ovarian egg follicle. This ovum produces estrogen. Before ovulation a surge of luteinizing hormone liberates the ripe ovum from the follicle. From this point on the follicle produces both progesterone (in large quantities) and estrogen (in small quantities) for the rest of the month. Three or four days before menstruation begins both these hormones decline. It is this drop in hormone levels which results in shedding of the endometrium as a period.

As women approach the menopause, the ovary becomes resistant to FSH and no longer responds with a growing egg. Over the age of forty to fifty the ovary may become almost depleted of eggs and eventually it stops working altogether.

After this the levels of estrogen and progesterone swing around in an irregular way in response to the varying levels of follicle-stimulating hormones and luteinizing hormones that are attempting to coax the ovary into functioning for a little longer. It is this swinging of hormone levels that results in many of the symptoms women have during the climacteric.

Periods stop during the menopause and there are several well-recognized and acceptable patterns that cessation usually follows. *It is never normal to have frequent, heavy periods during the climacteric. The passage of clots of blood is never normal. Bleeding between periods or after intercourse or after periods have stopped for a year or so is abnormal.* You should consult your doctor immediately if any of them occur. These are the ways periods usually stop:

● Very rarely do they stop suddenly, but you may have regular periods right up to the day when you miss one and from then on you will have no more.
● It is much more common to continue to have periods for a few months and then miss a few, have a few more normal bleeds and then go longer and longer between periods until they eventually stop.
● You may find that your periods simply become scantier and scantier and shorter and shorter until they stop.
● By definition, if you are under the age of fifty and do not have a period for 12 months, or if you are over the age of fifty and don't have a period for 6 months, then it is likely that your periods have stopped for good.

Percentage of women who experience the onset of menopause at various ages.

Symptoms of the menopause

Not all women suffer symptoms at the time of the menopause. There are three classical ones – hot flushes or hot flashes, night sweats, and loss of lubrication in the vagina. Nearly all of these symptoms are thought to be caused by low levels of estrogen in the blood. It is these low levels of female hormones that are also responsible for the gradual loss of calcium and protein from the bones, osteoporosis (see page 232). Approximately 20 percent of women develop osteoporosis after the menopause if they don't take estrogen supplements in some form (see page 69).

"Classical symptoms"
A hot flash is just what it sounds like. The skin becomes hot and pink. You will feel very hot and you will start to sweat. This can be particularly bad during the night.

Night sweats can prevent you from sleeping for much of the night, making you resort to throwing off the bedclothes and getting out of bed to cool off. They can even cause sleepless nights for your partner as well. Eventually one or both of you may become exhausted through lack of sleep.

Soreness, dryness and thinning of the vagina can be very troublesome during and after the menopause and many women feel shy of discussing these complaints with their doctor. The vagina is usually kept healthy, plump and lubricated by estrogen, but when levels fall, the vagina may change dramatically. The cells of the lining become thin and dried out and they cannot protect themselves against invasion. The vagina, therefore, becomes prone to infection with the vaginal discharge. The urethra may be affected as well as the vagina, and menopausal women may suffer from cystitis or pain and burning when passing urine.

One of the most demoralizing side effects is that sex can become difficult when there is insufficient vaginal secretion and intercourse may be painful (dyspareunia). This can lead to reluctance to have sex or avoidance of it, and a consequent deterioration in your relationship with your partner. In this way dyspareunia may lead to a loss of libido.

Always try to discuss these problems with your partner and get him to understand that they should be seen as a natural part of the menopause. As a practical step you can start using a lubricating jelly. The best non-hormonal lubricant is KY jelly. It is used by surgeons and doctors to lubricate their vaginal instruments. Your own doctor may help you by giving you a hormone cream that is only available on prescription; this may help to relieve vaginal soreness and itching.

Bone changes

One of the most important changes that occurs during the climacteric is change in the bone. Estrogen contributes to a healthy calcium balance and sturdy protein architecture of the bones. As the estrogen levels fall, however, the bones become thin, weak and prone to fractures, and aches and pains may arise in the bones and joints. These bone changes can be reduced or arrested by the use of hormone replacement therapy (HRT) given as a combination of estrogen and progesterone.

The addition of progesterone may guard against most of HRT's harmful side effects, such as the association of estrogen with cancerous change in the uterus, and therefore a combined régime is nearly always employed. Hormone replacement therapy cannot repair weakened bones, but it will prevent the condition from getting any worse.

HRT should always be given along with calcium and vitamin D supplements. Calcium on its own, without HRT, is not effective. After the age of sixty-five, however, it is calcium and vitamin D that become important and they alone are probably sufficient in keeping our bones healthy.

Emotional and psychological difficulties

Emotional changes caused by hormonal fluctuations may be the predominant symptoms of the menopause. Depression, moodiness, tearfulness and irritability are common. Some intellectual functions such as memory, decision-making, speed and accuracy also deteriorate and a woman may find that she is more prone to accidents than she used to be. She is generally less stable and she may suffer a serious loss of self-confidence.

It is possible that this physiologically induced emotional upset may be worsened because of personal crises. A woman may feel that her children have grown up and left home and she is no longer needed. If she hasn't continued with her career she may feel a useless member of society. Parents may be becoming more and more dependent and this is a heavy burden, but it is not a problem that can be solved in any way by HRT.

Hormone replacement therapy

Of course, depression and anxiety during the menopause may respond to anti-depressants and tranquilizers as they would at any time, but you may need HRT as well. Some specialists in the field regard HRT as the mainstay of medication and consider the menopause to be a hormone deficiency state in which the deficiency should be corrected by hormones.

The benefits of HRT are well documented. Night sweats, hot flushes and a dry vagina, with its accompanying problems, are nearly always relieved. Very often sleep improves, there is a lessening of anxiety and depression, which helps to improve a woman's mental and physical state.

Of course there are some risks associated with HRT, including an apparent increased incidence of uterine cancer, and it is particularly unsuitable for you if you have blood clotting problems, high blood pressure or if you have a strong family history of heart disease. Before you have HRT you should discuss this whole matter with your doctor.

Doctors vary in the length of time for which they are prepared to treat women with HRT. Some doctors are so prejudiced that they won't use it at all. If this is the case you can try going to a doctor who specializes in this for an assessment of whether or not your symptoms may be relieved by the use of HRT. Sometimes it is necessary to be treated for two or three years, though most doctors agree that courses should not be given continuously. Breaks are advocated. While you are taking HRT you should have regular medical checks, your breasts should be examined both by yourself and by your doctor. You should also have internal examinations and cervical and vaginal smears.

HRT is not a way of putting off aging and preventing wrinkles and flabby breasts and it must not be used casually.

169

The male menopause

Even now, little is known about the male menopause, or better the male climacteric. We still don't know when it occurs, or if it truly develops. Do all men experience a climacteric? If there is such a thing, what are the symptoms. Drawing a parallel from the menopausal symptoms in women, should men be the beneficiaries of hormone replacement therapy? Once this question is advanced others follow. What would happen to the male climacteric if hormone replacement therapy were widely used? What would the success rate be? What are the harmful effects? What are the long-term effects? There are very few answers to any of these questions because so little research has been done in this area, though this is sure to change in the near future as more people take an interest in the symptoms.

The male menopause hasn't the same drama as a woman's. It is more gradual, gentle and in a way more insidious than a woman's; nor does it occur during exactly the same years. It is much better thought of as a male climacteric, which envelopes all the changes going on in the body and mind as the male genital system begins to wane.

Male sexuality Masters and Johnson made a very detailed study of the psychological and physiological factors that might contribute to a decline in a man's sexual prowess as he grows older. They concluded that:
• The primary factor is monotony, described as being the result of repetitious sexual relationships.
• A close second is preoccupation with career and economic pursuits.
• Mental or physical fatigue no doubt contributes to a decline in sexual response.
• The older man's penchant for over-indulgence in food and drink plays its part.
• Any physical or mental infirmities in either of the partners may lead to a further decline.
• A fear that his performance does not come up to scratch may be greater than at any other time in his life, especially during a time of stressful career decisions.

Monotony is quoted most often and most constantly as the factor that leads to a loss of interest in sex and sexual performance. The end result of this may be one of dutiful indulgence and the need for sexual release. This sometimes arises from a failure of the sexual part of a relationship to grow throughout the marriage. Both partners are responsible in this case and each must make the effort to make him/herself more interesting to the other by introducing variety and inventiveness into the relationship so that each stimulates the other. Both must be aware of the importance of making themselves physically attractive to each other. (See page 177-183).

Almost all men between the ages of forty and sixty are going through the most competitive stages of their careers. The tensions brought on by competition at work are not eased by the financial necessity to look after a growing family with multiplying needs and activities. On the one hand, men are striving for personal eminence, and on the other they are preoccupied with the security of the "family." A man in this situation often finds that he spends more time following his professional career than with his family. This leaves a smaller amount of time for loving relationships with his partner and stress may lead to a gradual lessening in sexual activity and this may eventually stop completely.

Both mental and physical fatigue are important elements in the decline of male sexuality and beyond middle age they have an ever-increasing influence on sexual activity. An active sex life in the middle years means being in good condition, for if a job requires a great deal of physical effort, a man may simply not be fit enough to have stamina left over at the end of the day to enjoy an active sex life. Sometimes, if a man is not fit, a weekend of recreation is more exhausting than the demands of his job, particularly in the age group of fifty and over. Again, this leaves very little energy for sexual activity. If a man is exposed to unaccustomed or excessive physical activity he may feel a loss of sexual responsiveness for a day or so which will add to his feeling of despondency.

As men grow older they may eat and drink more. Excessive consumption of food or drink has a tendency to repress their sex drives. Over-indulgence in alcohol has a particularly negative effect on potency.

Most men approaching middle age become concerned about performance. One of the ways of handling any concern is to withdraw from having to perform. This leads to total avoidance of sex within the marriage. If a man is also drinking excessively it only makes matters worse. A problem may arise within the marriage. A man may find that he is impotent with his wife but with another, who cannot measure present sexual performance against past, he is perfectly normal.

At any age, physical or mental infirmity can lower or even eliminate sexual drive. After the age of forty, however, physical or emotional difficulties have a very much greater effect, and above the age of sixty a tremendously negative influence. Being physically disabled in the short or long term lowers sexual responsiveness in either sex, but if the illness is acute, such as pneumonia, loss of libido is usually transient and accepted by both partners. With more long-standing disabilities, such as arthritis or emphysema, interest in sex and sexual performance may decline slowly and until it becomes non existent. Some conditions, such as long-standing diabetes, can lead to impotence in men for medical reasons. These problems do need to be discussed with a partner.

There is no doubt that "fear of failure" plays a very important part in the aging man's withdrawal from sexual activities.

Once a man has noticed that his potency is declining, or he experiences one occasion when he is unable to achieve sexual satisfaction through impotency, he may withdraw voluntarily from any kind of sexual activity. This is mainly because most men are unable to face the "ego-shattering experience of repeated episodes of sexual inadequacy." Most men are unable to accept the fact that a lessening of sexual drive and a lowering of sexual performance are parts of the normal aging process and they make all sorts of excuses and will blame many different kinds of external factors rather than face the truth that their bodies are maturing.

Masters and Johnson hypothesized in 1970 that a man who

finds his potency declining may be showing signs of lowered levels of androgens which may amount to a deficiency. They went on the say that until studies had shown that there was a general requirement by the body for androgen (testosterone) replacement therapy during the male climacteric, cases had to be treated on an empirical and individual basis.

There are endocrinologists in many parts of the world who make a special study of the male climacteric employing hormone replacement therapy for their male patients. The whole area however, still awaits clear definition and guidelines. Until then HRT for men will remain a highly specialized field not generally practiced.

Danger signs

The chart on pages 174-6 indicates certain signs and symptoms in medicine which indicate changes that become commoner as we get older. As I explain in *Special medical problems* these changes are not serious in the majority of cases and your doctor will be able to put them right. Symptoms such as a change from your normal bowel habit, change in your digestive pattern, a sudden bout where you cough up blood-specked sputum or a sudden severe headache attack are signals that the body is not working as it should and needs investigating. They are not meant to be a cause for alarm.

By noting what symptoms you have and asking yourself the questions provided you will perhaps be able to put your mind at rest. Do see your doctor if you show any of these symptoms.

DANGER SIGNS

If you have:

Blood in sputum	Blood in vomit	Blood in stools
Color and quantity	Color and quantity	Color and quantity of blood; color of stools; presence of mucus; any pain on passing; presence of black, tarry stools
What to ask yourself		
Have I had a sore throat, cough, chest pain, or recent chest infection?	Have I taken drugs? Have I eaten anything unusual, drunk a lot of alcohol or had indigestion recently? Do I have a duodenal ulcer?	Do I have piles? Do I have a duodenal ulcer? Have I had stomach or abdominal pain? Have I recently had indigestion or an intestinal infection?
What to do		
If there is a lot of blood, call an ambulance; otherwise make an appointment to see your doctor. Keep sputum to show doctor	If there is a lot of blood call an ambulance; otherwise make an appointment to see your doctor. Keep specimen of vomit to show doctor	If there is a lot of blood call an ambulance; otherwise make an appointment to see your doctor. Keep specimen of stools to show doctor
What your doctor will do		
Question you about your chest. Examine your sputum and X-ray your chest	Question you about food, your stomach and digestion. Examine your abdomen, look at your vomit and your stools. Possibly order a barium meal	Question you about your stomach and intestines. Examine your abdomen and rectum (internally). Examine your stools
What tests will be done		
X-ray, throat swab, lab tests on sputum	Lab tests on stools, possibly on vomit; barium meal	Lab tests on stools; barium enema; possibly sigmoidoscopy, colonoscopy
What it is likely to be		
If you are coughing, it's probably a small, burst blood vessel. It could be the aftermath of bronchitis or similar chest infection. It could also be the sign of a tumor or blood clot in the lung	The commonest causes are aspirin and other drugs, alcohol and duodenal ulcers	The commonest causes are piles or severe diarrhea; it may occur with diverticulitis, a tumor or polyps. Black, tarry stools occur when a duodenal or gastric ulcer bursts

Blood in urine	Sudden onset of indigestion	Sudden onset of diarrhea constipation, pipelike stools
Color and quantity of blood; any pain on passing	Relationship to food; if alkalis bring relief	Color and quantity of blood; any pain on passing
Have I had kidney or back pain; have I had a recent urinary infection?	Do I have any pain elsewhere? Have I taken any drugs, alcohol or strange foods recently? Is there any change in my bowel habit?	Have I started taking any drugs or different foods? Do I have a fever; am I in pain?
If there is a lot of blood, call an ambulance, otherwise make an appointment to see your doctor. Keep a specimen of urine to show doctor	If it persists for more than 3 days, see your doctor	Take your temperature; if it is raised, make an appointment to see your doctor. Keep specimen of stools to show your doctor
Question you about your bladder, urine and digestion. Examine your urine and arrange an intravenous pylogram (IVP)	Question you about food and digestion. Ask for a stool specimen for analysis. Try a course of treatment; order a barium meal	Question you about food and digestion. Examine your abdomen and stools. Do a rectal examination. Try a course of treatment; possibly order a barium enema
Lab tests on urine; IVP	Barium meal; lab tests on stools	Barium enema; lab tests on stools; possibly sigmoidoscopy, colonoscopy
The commonest causes are cystitis or severe kidney infection; can also be caused by a tumor	The commonest causes are starting to take medication for the first time or strange foods; gastroenteritis	The commonest causes are strange food, infection or diverticulitis; tumor

DANGER SIGNS

If you have:

Onset of persistent headaches	Sudden pain in chest	Sudden onset of breathlessness
Position and frequency. Any related signs, e.g. pins and needles in the skin, flashing lights, nausea	What makes the pain worse: breathing, coughing; or better: rest	What makes the pain worse: breathing, coughing; or better: rest

What to ask yourself

Have I had shingles of the face, or toothache, recently? Does anyone in the family suffer from migraine? Have I been working hard or am I worried?	Have my lower legs swollen recently? Do I have high blood pressure or bronchitis?	Have my lower legs swollen recently? Do I have high blood pressure or bronchitis?

What to do

Take analgesics; see your doctor	Take your temperature. If high, call your doctor or an ambulance, especially if you are breathless	Take your temperature. If high, call your doctor or an ambulance, especially if you are breathless

What your doctor will do

Question you generally. Give you a full physical examination. Take your blood pressure. Examine your eyes and your urine	Question you, examine your chest, heart, sputum, blood pressure, chest X-ray; give you a course of treatment. If you are breathless, send you to hospital	Question you, examine your chest, heart, sputum, blood pressure, chest X-ray; give you a course of treatment. If you are breathless, send you to hospital

What tests will be done

Possibly a CAT scan	Chest X-ray, sputum tests; investigations of legs and lungs to see if there are any clots; electrocardiogram	Chest X-ray, sputum tests; investigations of legs and lungs to see if there are any clots; electrocardiogram

What it is likely to be

The commonest causes are sinusitis, tension headache, postherpetic neuralgia (related to shingles), migraine, and dental problems	The commonest cause is bronchitis or tracheitis, as part of a virus or chest infection; can also accompany angina, heart attack, pneumonia or pulmonary blood clot	The commonest cause is bronchitis or tracheitis, as part of a virus or chest infection; pneumonia; pulmonary blood clot

Maintaining appearance

Both men and women, but especially women, are often upset by the effects of aging on the face and body. Sometimes, people are so affected that they no longer make any effort to help themselves. There can be few things as depressing as looking in the mirror and hating what you see, but on the other hand, if you look in the mirror and *like* what you see, your whole outlook and demeanor will improve. Such a positive sense of self-esteem becomes increasingly important as we get older, and looking after our appearance is one of the best ways of achieving this. In addition to the beneficial effects of a good diet and regular exercise, proper care of the skin and hair and attention to your body and clothing can help you both look and feel younger. It can also help you maintain an active sex life, which again can keep you feeling younger.

Hair loss in men

Whether or not it is comforting to know that human hair is probably superfluous and will disappear in future generations, it is safe to say that some men would keep theirs longer if they worried less about losing it. A positive way of looking at baldness is to realize that it can be quite flattering and may give you a forceful air – like the strong-willed personalities reflected by Telly Savalas and Yul Brynner. But there's also nothing wrong in attempting to cover up hair loss as long as your solution looks natural (see page 140). However it's often better to be bald than to look extremely artificial.

When hair loss is gradual, some camouflage can work very well. By letting the hair grow slightly longer than usual, a thinning area on the crown may be disguised; if you comb your hair forward, you may be able to cover a slight recession at the temples. A permanent can also be useful in giving body to the hair so that it looks much thicker, but if balding is severe, a permanent may only contribute to further hair loss. Probably the most successful solution is having your hair properly styled; even with relatively little hair, a good stylist can make a vast improvement to the way you look.

When there is less hair, it's usually wrong to grow the remaining hair longer as it can look stringy and unkempt. It is also a mistake to grow large sideburns as this only calls attention to what little is left on the head. Furthermore, forcing hair into an unnatural shape not only makes it look wrong, but can also put added strain on the hair remaining, gradually causing more hair loss.

On the positive side, it is a good idea to keep hair short. Short hair has more life and resilience. Trying to create a new focus in

177

a haircut, like changing a center parting to a side one, can also be successful; even avoiding a well-defined hairline can be an improvement. Or, you may try going with the baldness and foregoing style with hair cut very short and, if necessary, bleached so that it doesn't look like stubble.

Grooming for men

For all your life you have probably been conditioned not to look critically at yourself and you may have allowed your partner to choose your clothes, with you perhaps not even being present! Now is the time to take a good look at yourself full-length in the mirror to see which areas are unkempt and could be improved with a little grooming.

There is no secret formula for looking good; it is a question of thinking carefully and logically about how best to go about making the most of your good points and successfully concealing your not-so-good points. There is certainly no need to spend lots of money on expensive cosmetic products. It is much more important to look natural. Remember there are no prescribed roles for you to play. There is no set of rules for you to follow. You need not pay attention to cosmeticians' sales talk if you don't want to. As with most other things you should be starting to please yourself, so interpret the following suggestions as loosely as you'd like to. When it comes to choosing clothes, comfort need never mean shapelessness.

TIPS FOR LOOKING GOOD

- Be meticulous about hygiene; take special care of your hands and feet.
- Make sure your hair is regularly looked after – cut and styled to suit you. Gray hair can be quite attractive and you may not want to fuss with coloring.
- Keep a young figure, if you possibly can.

There is nothing that gives the impression of age more than obesity and shapelessness.
- Avoid garments or shoes in stiff inflexible materials.
- Pay attention to your posture and gait. Few things are so aging as stooped shoulders.

Clothes for women

As we grow older, comfort becomes a more and more important prerequisite of clothes. I personally am no longer prepared to go for hours in tight-fitting garments, or even to wear a belt on the tight side. This doesn't mean that a figure is not well defined. But you may like to consider going for comfortable fabrics – that is, soft, thin ones and not hard, thick ones. You might consider skirts that are gored or gathered and tops that are blouson. Never buy a size too small and avoid waistbands that are too tight. Where possible, choose natural fabrics like cotton so as not to feel sweaty.

If you are interested in clothes, try to be fashionable – it has some important pay-offs. It keeps you looking young, and more important, feeling young. It also tells the world that you are not living in the past. It has a stimulating effect on you yourself, forcing you to look at yourself in a new light.

Scan the fashion magazines and spot new fashion trends, be it in the width of the shoulder, where a belt is placed – high, low or on the waistline – the shape of the silhouette, straight, flared, A-line, or the length and shape of the sleeve. As an older woman you should never ever go for exaggerated trends, but in any outfit try to include at least one fashionable feature that will give your proportion and image a current feeling.

Avoid matronly fashions whenever you can. Any outfit that is safe, pale, with an indistinct outline, helping you to fade into your surroundings and conventional in terms of color and fabric, is unadventurous. Try to add a bit of drama to what you are wearing, possibly by color combination or with an accessory. Never be afraid to accent your femininity. Try to remember that a mature woman finds it hard to look good in a classic style, in a drab color, in a thick masculine fabric. Yes, you can wear a classic tailored style, but in a bright color. Whenever you can, avoid thick, inflexible fabrics; they make your body look stiff and unsupple, quite the opposite of young. If you have a good bustline, show it. If your waistline is attractive, display it. If your ankles and legs are good, make sure your hemlines are not too low. To stay abreast of fashion, buy cheaply, often, rather than expensive, rarely.

There are some useful tricks to flatter mature women. You should wear pretty colors next to your face and avoid too much jewelry. Go for ease and simplicity, perhaps wearing fewer pieces, parts and complications. If your body looks younger than your face, draw attention to your figure and try to keep your walk youthful; avoid a drooping posture.

The most important parts of your figure that give the impression of youth are your *bustline* – it should be midway between your shoulder and your elbow; keep it there with a well-fitting bra, and your *waistline* – if you are short-waisted and get dumpier as you get older you will look older. Stay younger-looking by choosing clothes that don't have any waistline at all or have a dropped waist, and always choose one color from top to toe. If your abdomen protrudes a bit, don't wear clingy fabrics or any that will hang heavily over your stomach. Wear A-lines or sewn-down pleats rather than straight skirts. Slash pockets are useful because they divert the eye from the stomach.

Make sure that your bra isn't so tight that there are rolls of flesh overhanging at the back, and never wear too clinging a fabric if you have a large bottom – every bulge will show. If your buttocks are too big, disguise them with long jackets and tunics and overblouses. Wear skirts and trousers that are slack over your bottom and don't pull tightly around your buttocks. Avoid garments with a flat yoke flaring out at the hips because they will give you more than ample proportion.

If you have a double chin, stay away from big earrings and avoid high chokers at the throat. Wear a long pendant low on the chest to provide distraction. Simple and flat collars that rest on your shoulders are preferable to large, stiff collars, which will crowd your neck.

MAKING THE MOST OF MAKE-UP

In my opinion a mature face cannot get away without wearing make-up. The older we are, the more we require some; not more in quantity, but more in finesse; I don't think there is a feature on our faces that we should leave unmade-up if we wish to look our best.

You might try out different cosmetics to find out what will accentuate your good features best, and what will camouflage your bad ones. If you haven't changed your make-up in the last twelve months then you should, and you should start experimenting now. This is especially true of eye make-up: nothing marks a woman's age like it. You can quite easily guess the age of another woman by the kind of make-up she wears on her eyes.

If necessary, take yourself off to a make-up expert (not a make-up salon attached to one of the cosmetic manufacturers) who will show you how to alter your bone structure with contouring; for instance, to make a fat nose less podgy, to minimize a square jawbone, to lengthen a face and to bring out your eyes.

None of these things requires layers and layers of make-up. Quite the opposite. As with good medicine, the minimum effective quantity for the maximum possible effect is all that you're after, and it need not be expensive. If you go to a make-up expert, he or she will show you how to use a particular type of cosmetic and you can either choose to buy that specific product or try to duplicate it less expensively elsewhere.

Foundation

Always apply a film of moisturizer underneath your make-up base to allow easy, smooth spreading, which is less damaging to the skin.

Use a moisturized liquid or cream make-up base in a beige tone (never pink or tan) which is one shade *lighter* than your own skin tone. This will help to reflect the light and minimize lines. Try and use a sponge if you can; all make-up experts do and it really does make a difference both to the staying power and the set of your make-up. It also stops your pulling the skin around too much.

To camouflage baggy areas under your eyes, use a light-textured shadow coverer (not the stick variety, they are much too heavy and only accentuate wrinkles) and apply this underneath your eyes, over the upper lid and the whole of your brow area. Extend it out to the upper surface of your cheekbone to cover broken veins, but then wing it out up beyond the corner of your

Use a slightly damp sponge when you apply foundation.

eyes towards your hairline. This takes the eye of the observer upward and outward over your face and counteracts any droopiness. Also apply it on top of the laughter lines which extend from your nostrils down to the lower corners of your mouth to lighten up these shadows.

MAKING THE MOST OF MAKE-UP

To make a plump nose look thinner, apply a thin line down the whole of the length of the top of your nose and put a small spot on the front of your chin to make it look more delicate.

Don't apply too much powder when highlighting your cheekbones or it will leave patches.

With a stick make-up slightly darker than your make-up base, draw in a triangle under each cheekbone with the point winging up towards your ear, and blend it smoothly into the rest of your make-up. This will accentuate the shape of your face.

Use a minimum of colorless powder to set your make-up. Powder, if applied too heavily, clogs in all the wrinkles and makes them seem more obvious than ever. Never repowder during the day, simply blot dry with a tissue or cotton wool.

Experiment with cream or liquid shaders and blushers. Never use a pink blusher, and never use too much blusher at the first application; you can always add more. Make sure it is well blended in. Go for a rather tawny apricot shade and place it just on the high point of your cheekbone and then smooth it away upward and outward toward your temples, a trick that also leads the eye of the observer upward away from your nose.

Eyes

Stop using eyebrow pencil today. There is nothing more aging than a heavily arched eyebrow drawn in a hard line with a dark pencil. Your eyebrows in general should be well plucked underneath to form a fairly high arch, again to give that upward and outward look to your face, with a fairly short downward curve. Unless your eyebrows are very sparse, all you need do is darken them with mascara. Your eyebrows should be the shade of your hair.

Try not to use an eyeshadow with an obvious color. Stick to muddy, murky, indefinite tones. There is hardly any need for anyone to vary from gray or brown as these are the most natural colors and have the most dramatic effect if used properly. Try leaving off your eye shadow from the eyelid. Eye shadow here makes the eye look smaller in the first place, but secondly, it is very old-fashioned. Eye shadow is much better applied just at the outer corner of the eye and in the eye socket and then smoothed out. A little can also be applied and smudged under the lower lashes.

If you've never worn false eyelashes, you are missing one of the greatest beauty aids that a middle-aged woman can use. They don't have to be dramatic.

When putting on your false eyelashes it is safer to use a close-up mirror.

They should be invisible when you have them in place. Start off with thin, longish eyelashes and trim them down to a natural look once they are in place. Mascara them along with your own eyelashes. Never wear black false eyelashes unless you are naturally very dark. Brown eyelashes are more flattering. Make sure that you find the best eyelash glue you can. Use an eyeliner or kohl for definition.

Lips

Place your foundation over your lips, powder them and blot thoroughly, brushing away any surplus powder. This will also help prevent lipstick bleeding.

When outlining your lips make sure that the color tones with your chosen lipstick.

If you have never used a lip pencil to outline your lips before applying make-up, start doing so now. It has two great effects. Outlining your lips and filling them in with a slightly paler shade of lipstick clearly defines them and gives your mouth a more attractive look. Also, lip pencils are generally rather dry and they stop the lipstick leaking down the small creases of the lips on to the skin of the face (known as "bleeding"). Use make-up suggestions as a basis for experimenting.

Hair

Hair, as long as it is fairly thick, looks younger if it is unpermanented, loose and fluffy, and is not lacquered. If you can't run your finger through your hair and still look good, then it needs cutting, shaping, and restyling.

Keep hair in an up-line to give it a lift and keep it away from the face. A twist or chignon is often effective as is a short feathery fringe. Pulling back the hair with barettes and other simple, straight styles is often quite successful on older women.

Get rid of all facial hair, preferably by electrolysis, but pluck it, if necessary. Shave your legs and under your arms at least once a week, and every time you wear an evening dress or something that leaves your armpits bare. Shave any hairs from around your nipples (or have them permanently removed by electrolysis, see page 150), whenever they grow.

Alternatively, you could attempt to pull any hairs out with tweezers. Make sure that you pluck in the direction that the hair is growing so as not to break it off. Waxing and depilatories have proved to be very efficient ways of removing hair from the face and body.

Keep your hair soft and if you dye it, keep the color subtle.

Retirement

For many people retirement is an important and rapid transitional period from an economically productive state to an economically non-productive and relatively dependent state. This raises all sorts of sociological, ethical, psychological and financial issues. Retirement means different things to different people, depending upon their sex, socio-economic status and psychological make-up. In general, however, we disengage from our main occupations and this brings about a number of changes in our lives in the spheres of daily activities, social contacts and standard of living.

Social disengagement

Very few of us keep up the pace and the diversity of social interaction into old age that we enjoyed in our late adulthood. Most of us begin to withdraw from the social whirl through choice. During our middle years, we live at the peak of our engagement with society because this is the time that many people depend on us and our time and energies are in great demand. We are, in essence, the establishment.

The transition we go through from adulthood to retirement age involves a natural withdrawal from the activities and obligations that had previously linked us and society closely together. To use an oft quoted metaphor – it is a kind of ritualistic dance. One partner, the person who is getting older, bows and steps back; the other partner, society, recognizes the cue, bows in return and also takes a step backwards.

The dance may continue but more slowly. The partners gradually move farther and farther apart. Soon society has found a new partner with a springy step. The old person sits down and takes a rest. He or she watches the dancers and smiles, keeping time with fingers and feet. However, interest in the dance is waning; thoughts and feelings become subjective. The older person, chooses, along with society, to become a private person who is quite willing and happy to leave the whirl of the dance to youngsters. This metaphor describes very aptly the change from active participant to interested observer that most of us experience as we grow older.

Withdrawal from the mainstream of social activity is dramatically punctuated when we decide to retire.

For many people retirement brings the time and opportunity to catch up with the advance in technology by going to adult education classes.

With the ending of paid work, or a reduction in the time devoted to it, there are a number of consequences that automatically follow. For example, we no longer meet up with colleagues or workmates and have less to do with the social side of our jobs. Ties of friendship are weakened. Relatives and children are likely to be widely scattered, especially in communities where people move around a great deal and are therefore difficult to visit. It's a sensible attempt on our part to distribute our reduced energies and resources over fewer but more personal activities. Effort is conserved and we escape from demands we don't wish to or cannot meet.

Methods of disengagement

We all disengage differently. Some of us stubbornly resist the pressures put upon us to reduce our commitments, shed responsibility and do less work. In such cases, we refuse to take advice if it means giving up activities that play a prominent part in our lives, such as running a small business, a cultural or scientific activity, or a social or civic responsibility. More of us resist the idea of giving up an independent life and our homes for residency in a nursing home. Some of us refuse to retire until we are forced to do so by ill health. Others of us die as we lived, active and involved in the world.

Although some of us fight all the way, some disengagement is bound to come. We have neither the physical nor the mental resources we had when we were younger. Disengagement, therefore, provides a solution to some of the problems of adjustment in old age and signifies a practical reappraisal of our position. Ideally, disengagement is graded to suit the declining biological and psychological capacities of the individual on the one hand and the needs of society on the other. The degree to which we can engage has as much to do with personality as it has with aging.

It would be wrong to think of disengagement as a nearly always negative process. It involves the beginning of renewal, of fresh engagements, especially those activities that involve family, friends and neighbors. The time made available by retirement from full-time employment may be easily employed through alternative activities and social relationships. Losses in social relationships following retirement, the departure of children, or the death of a spouse, may be made good by other relationships with friends, neighbors or kin. Furthermore, the activities and relationships of later life may be *more* important and absorbing because they are fewer in number and more personal in nature. There is, however, a natural inclination on the part of most of us to mix with others and participate in group and community affairs. This natural tendency is often blocked by present-day retirement practices; hence we should make arrangements to find worthwhile activities suited to our age, personal qualities and health.

However, the net effect is a shrinkage in the range of our activities and a lessening in the amount of contact we have with other people. Gradually, our lives become separated from the lives of others. We become less associated with other people, less emotionally involved and more absorbed in our own problems and circumstances.

Looking forward to retirement

Research obliges us to alter our ideas about the nature of retirement; it can no longer be thought of simply as a sudden, enforced dislocation of our working lives, almost inevitably resulting in feelings of rejection and physical or mental ill-health. A substantial proportion of us retire, or wish to retire, a few years before the usual age. After retirement age, an even larger proportion of us do not actively seek paid employment although lower levels of income are a strong inducement for us to continue to work for as long as possible.

For many of us the release from exacting, lengthy work in unsatisfactory conditions is followed not by frustration and idleness but by more enjoyable leisure time, closer family ties and better physical health. With retirement come forty or more hours in the week that we need to account for, hours previously spent in connection with work. Many retired people say they miss nothing; some miss work itself and, of course, money. To a lesser extent, others also miss the feeling of being useful. Attitudes change fairly rapidly during retirement and it is not age, but the passage of time, that explains the differences between people.

Thoughts on retirement Working men over the age of sixty-five generally seem less lonely and better adjusted than retired men, but not *because* they are working. Physical health and personality underlie both morale and working capacity in later life. Over many decades there has been a gradual but absolute improvement in the health and welfare of retired people and in their standards of living. A high level of morale is only achievable when economic status is on the level of other working adults. The reduction in living standards and income subsequent to retirement is of the greatest concern to most of us. When these are coupled with natural regrets on leaving close friends and familiar activities

187

they may bring about a temporary depression or anxiety.

However, it is often the *prospect* of retirement, rather than retirement itself, that leads to a morbid state of mind. Studies have shown that given reasonable physical health and financial resources, the average retired man or woman soon adapts to the changed circumstances and shows an improvement in physical health and outlook. It is not so much old age in retirement as the transition to old age and retirement that creates problems of adjustment. Retirement is rapidly becoming a normal and expected phase of the life path, to be looked for, prepared for, and enjoyed over a long period.

Planning retirement

Preparation for retirement is now a widely recognized need. Many firms, voluntary organizations and centers for adult education cater for this. The financial and leisure problems of retirement can be met only by long-term planning. Many people do not face up to the problems soon enough and enter retirement inadequately prepared. Preparation means putting money aside, buying and disposing of personal property and assets, attending to health needs, getting information and advice about leisure time interests, and generally changing the balance between disengagement and activity.

Intelligence, education and social attitudes play a part in this preparation. We need to acquire new skills, new attitudes and interests, and new social relationships if we are to make the most of our retirement.

The most important areas to provide for would be:
● Income and assets to provide for our material well-being when we retire;
● Some continuation of earlier working activities or social relationships to promote a sense of belonging and participation;
● Attention to physical comforts and health to make for more activity and security;
● The proper use of leisure time to provide a kind of dividend in feelings of achievement, usefulness and happiness.

Men and retirement

Disengagement works best for people who have maintained some continuity of activity throughout their lives and have vocations rather than jobs. The professional man can pursue some aspects of his life's work and maintain his professional contacts right up to the end of his life. Moreover, he has the time, money and opportunity to prepare for his retirement and to cultivate interests and activities that carry on over into later years. This continuity of activity, relationships and attitudes provides a stable pattern of adjustment, which can carry him smoothly from his busy adult working life to a more leisurely but satisfying retirement.

Most men, however, spend a large part of their adult years in fairly routine jobs that earn them a living and retirement pension but do little to provide activities and opportunities that will extend into retirement. Some men in this situation find that retirement presents problems of adjustment since it often occurs abruptly at the age of sixty-five, with neither the continuity, which is important for good adjustment, nor the time, money and opportunity to prepare for a satisfactory retirement.

Better provision for retirement and courses in preparing for retirement would enable many more men to use and enjoy their declining years. A shorter working week, longer holidays and a gradual retirement from paid work in years to come, will all give people ample opportunities to cultivate stable, long-term interests and personal activities throughout their working lives. These will carry them over into retirement. Increased opportunity for such personal outlets might do much to improve emotional stability and could lessen the social stigma attached to retirement.

Women and retirement

Problems of adjustment in later life can be met by a similar process of disengagement. Women whose careers have been as homemakers may find this task easier because they are not faced with the problem of suddenly having to adjust to an abrupt retirement. A man depends on his job and his earning capacity for status, prestige and authority in the home and the transition from work to retirement may be difficult. His disengagement from work relationship is usually followed by the renewal of kinship ties and he becomes involved in domestic chores such as shopping and cleaning. Working women are usually more closely bound than men to family life. On account of their continued activities in the home and established social patterns, they may have to cope with fewer demands for readjustment.

However, the departure of children from the home changes the environment of the middle-aged mother and a partner's retirement calls for a further readjustment. Additionally, most married women eventually become widows, which in turn creates problems of readjustment. Little research has been done into how these and other late-life problems of adjustment for women might be met more effectively through education, preparation and counseling.

Disengagement proceeds differently for most women as compared with men and some of the stages – loss of children, disability and bereavement – may occur relatively early. Apart from the differences in temperament and attitudes that are a result of sex, a man's absorption in his job and outside interests provide him with powerful supports and these can weaken his emotional involvement with his family. He may not react to family events with the same intensity as a woman. Women whose children have grown up or who have lost husbands may often find other women in similar circumstances, but retired men or widowers are less likely to have a large pool of friends and they may feel isolated unless they can turn to their families.

Planning our new found time

We must make the most of retirement by letting it make things easier for us. We can choose to be by ourselves; we won't have to adjust our schedules to meet others' needs; we don't need to answer to anyone but ourselves; we can give priorities to spending our time and money and resources in ways that we prefer; we can decide exactly where and how to live. They are solely our decisions from now on.

It has been stated that success or failure in the second forty years of life, measured in terms of happiness, is determined more by how we use or abuse our leisure time than by any other factor. It is important, therefore, to learn how to enjoy leisure activities without any guilt feelings. Some people do have to learn not to work so that they can enjoy leisure. Just like work, leisure has to be planned and we have to stick to this plan to enjoy it. Now that we have so much time, leisure is not a second-rate activity, it is very important. Thus we should adapt to it in exactly the same way as we adapt to a new job. We have to be positive and enthusiastic about it and give it all we've got, devoting all our energy to enjoying ourselves.

Just because you have more leisure time, don't fall into the trap of feeling that all your leisure time has to be spent together as a couple. It doesn't. More leisure time can mean more time for private activities as well as those you do as a couple.

Although retirement may demand a good deal of flexibility and adaptation it can lead to a time of great happiness and contentment once negotiated. The critical period for adjustment is shortly before retirement. During this time people tend to become increasingly agitated about the consequences and problems. The problem is not so much being old as *becoming* old. Some interesting findings came out of research done in the USA, which shows that we come to terms with retirement in a number of different ways, depending upon our personality (see page 195).

TIPS FOR RETIREMENT

For both sexes

• Retirement, even pre-retirement, should be carefully planned several years in advance if its actually happening, certainly in terms of housing, financial arrangements, health care, cultivating hobbies, interests and activities that can be continued into retirement.

• Take the best advice you can to make your money work for you during your retirement years; take the best counsel on investments and insurance, mortgages and wills. An accountant or a bank manager will be happy to give you advice. Try to make a budget even if you have never made one before.

• As a practice run, it is a good idea to start living on your retirement income about six months before you or your partner retires. If you start to ease into retirement this way, before you are under the strain of the other changes that go along with retirement, financial adjustments may be easier to cope with. You will also have saved up the money that you didn't use in the previous six months, which will give you a nest egg and a sense of security. You may get a pleasant surprise to find out that it isn't nearly as difficult as you thought it would be.

• If one partner retires and the other goes on working, you may find that your days get out of sync. Instead of both being up early in the morning, both getting home early in the evening and both wanting to go to bed at the same time, one may be exhausted when the other is raring to go. Sit down and talk about it. Examine the problem and find a solution that will work for both of you. Make a particular point of doing things together on weekends when your clocks become synchronized again.

• If you find yourself at home with lots of time on your hands, feel lost, lonely, unwanted and left out, then it is probably a sign that you haven't made the emotional transition to retirement. Your partner can help by sorting out with you how best to spend your leisure time together. Discuss a rota for the chores. Make a list of all your friends and relatives who are free during certain parts of the week whom you haven't seen for several years, and match up your interests with those people. What can be done with whom? A partner should be prepared to change his or her routine.

For men

• If you retire but your partner is still working, it is time for an egalitarian form of domestic arrangement. It is only fair that you should get on with some of the domestic chores while your partner is out at work.

• If you do start to take a pride in the home, you shouldn't become rigid and house proud. Men can be particularly prone to do this if they don't have interests outside of the home, and that is the best solution – to find important jobs to do that take you out of the house.

For women

• When your husband retires don't be a perfectionist. Don't keep your house spic and span with everything in its place, or always complain about newspapers or books on tables, unwashed dishes and a messy kitchen. Adjustments have to be made. If you can't relax, especially if you are working, you may have to consider premature retirement yourself.

• If you've retired while your partner is still working, start new projects and take up old interests; remember old passions and renew them. If you have lots of spare time then spend some of the time pampering yourself. Sleep late, read in the afternoon, put your feet up whenever you feel like it.

• If your partner is retired and you are still working, don't resent his freedom, though you may have to get up early while he is still sleeping.

Deciding where to live

Some older people do not want to live alone. They enjoy the companionship of others. Others should not live alone. If you are ill or unable to take care of your needs and your home, you may want to entertain another living option. One possibility is to live with or near friends and family. If that option is not available to you, you may want to consider the following:

• Retirement communities are groups of housing units planned for healthy, retired older people, usually containing at least one commonly shared nonresidential facility, such as a dining room or hall for leisure activities. Retirement communities sometimes, but not necessarily, offer medical services.

No longer look upon as "old age homes," more and more Americans of advanced age are moving into retirement communities – not to withdraw from active life in their later years, but for the positive support of others like themselves and the conveniences they provide. Today's best estimates are that there are over 1,500,000 people now living in governmental and nongovernmental retirement communities throughout this country.

● Adult homes, which fall somewhere between a rooming house and hotel. Usually, rooms are furnished, although some allow you to bring your own furnishings. Usually, there is a common dining room and leisure areas. Your room is cleaned regularly as in a hotel.

● Nursing homes are generally for the very elderly and infirm. They offer the total care of a hospital, but are specifically for older people. Nursing homes provide round-the-clock care and supervision by trained nurses as well as the companionship of other elders. Friends and family can visit during certain hours each day.

Following bereavement

This is exactly the kind of decision that you should not make quickly. Someone in a state of shock and grief after the death of a close companion is not in the best state of mind to make such an important decision about future needs. In practical terms it is better to wait several weeks or even months to see what actually happens; several unexpected things may arise which may make your decision a good deal easier.

Initially, for the sake of being taken care of, so that you won't be alone and so that you have the distraction of company, you may have decided to move in with your family or friends. Temporarily you will have escaped from your own empty home but it is unwise to give up your home irretrievably because you put yourself in a permanently dependent position. It is very important that you retain a base so that you have somewhere to go to when you feel yourself again. Nearly everyone who overcomes bereavement and grief feels strength returning and with it the desire to be independent once more and have a home of their own. Always leave this option open to yourself.

Quite a lot of people who are bereaved take the decision to live with friends or family rather than live alone. If the arrangement is anything other than on a temporary basis, then you have to take special care to make the right arrangements from the very beginning. Never forget that settling down in new surroundings means establishing a new pattern of living which has to be acceptable to everyone concerned. This means that you and the people you are living with must be honest and explain problems, difficulties, likes and dislikes as soon as they become evident. Everyone will have to make some personal adjustments, especially those who spend most of the time at home. You may have to work out timetables and job sharing. When is the most convenient time for getting up. How and when to have meals. Sharing the housework, etc.

An important aspect of this is that everyone in the household should be able to entertain friends without anyone feeling in the way. If it is going to be a room with family or friends then it should be furnished as a bed-sitting room so that you can get away from others without making it into a special issue. Have your television, radio and stereo in the room with you. Make sure that you are an equal member of the family group so that you can say how you feel about things.

Living with your children

This may seem a very tempting option immediately after your bereavement when you are grief stricken. Your children know and love you, you have been in close touch all your lives and you feel comfortable with them. Your children may even beg you to go and live with them, but there are several reasons why you should hesitate to do this.

They may start seeing you as a parent all over again, and therefore as someone who will babysit regularly, cook big meals on weekends or do the odd bit of carpentry or plumbing repair. This obviously is not the role that you want to play and you will almost certainly feel used, your feelings may hurt and you and your children will start to get on each other's nerves. As a parent you will certainly have different ideas about how children should be brought up and you may even have rows with your own children about how they are bringing up theirs. If you still feel inclined to move in do it first on a trial basis.

Move in temporarily and leave somewhere to fall back on – your own home and your own furniture. Don't get rid of either of them. If you do this, remember that it is your children's house and they are the ones who lay down the ground rules. Don't interfere, don't make suggestions and don't offer advice. Never forget that you are the guest and you have to be sensitive to your children's needs. As far as you possibly can, avoid asking favors. They soon become irksome if they are frequent. Whatever you do don't play the role of the critical parent. Look at your children as friends, not as your children. If you see them as friends they will *feel* more like friends and they will *act* more like friends. They will also be honest with you and not feel obligated to you. In other words you have to have the same sort of relationship with your children as you would with the rest of your friends. This is not always easy for parents, so weigh up the options carefully before coming to any decision because you will have to live with your decision for a long time.

HOW WE ADJUST TO RETIREMENT

Research shows that most of us come to terms with life after retirement in several different set patterns. Some patterns bring more happiness and contentment than others and while none of us is ideal, seeing these personality profiles might encourage us to take up a more rewarding pattern. These are some of the personal attributes to be found.

Constructiveness
- Had a happy childhood, little emotional stress in adult life, and a stable occupational history.
- Free of financial worries, happily married, and has made uninterrupted progress through life.
- Satisfied with achievements, self-assertive without being aggressive, and is capable of expressing feelings.
- Intelligent, well-integrated, enjoys food, drink, work and recreation and is sexually active.
- Is humorous, tolerant, flexible, aware of achievements, failings and prospects.
- Interests are well developed and has continued to enjoy some interests from earlier part of life.
- Has close, warm, affectionate personal relationships and very few feelings of hostility, self-esteem is high and he feels he can count on the support of people around him at all times.
- Constructive and optimistic attitude toward the future, accepts old age including retirement and death.
- Tolerates deprivations and frustrations.

Dependency
- Married late and had a small family, a passively tolerant partner in relationships with other people.
- Unambitious, glad to retire, happy to be free of work.
- Well integrated but tends to rely on others for material well-being and emotional support.
- Glad to be free of responsibility and effort, gets little enjoyment from the work that has to be done now.
- Eats and drinks too much, gambles, tends to live beyond means.

Defensiveness
- Stable occupational history, well-adjusted at work.
- Emotionally over-controlled, habit-bound, conventional and compulsively active.
- Works hard, but seems to work for defensive reasons rather than because the work is interesting.
- Not easy to talk to, becomes anxious and evasive when discussing social and family relationships.
- Self-sufficient, refuses help to prove independence, afraid of dependency and inactivity of old age, puts off retirement.
- Actively engaged in social organizations, good long-term planning to meet financial problems of old age.

Hostility
- Life history has a pattern of minor incompetence and neurosis, now quite often anxious, pessimistic, depressed.
- Often has a submissive relationship with parents, has grown up giving and receiving little affection, in middle age becomes neurotically dependent on wife.
- Is aggressive, complaining, competitive and suspicious in dealings with other people, tends to be depressed.
- Lacks the capacity for making realistic adjustments in retirement.

Self-hate
- Ambivalent feelings toward mother and father, not interested in other people, derives little satisfaction from heterosexual relationships, feels generally lonely and useless.
- Unhappily married or feels no warmth of affection for partner.
- Pessimistic, fatalistic, feels a victim.

195

Specialist help

Even though I was trained in the rather rigid school of orthodox medicine, I nonetheless believe in an eclectic approach to getting help from specialists like cosmetic surgeons and dentists, medical practitioners who give skin treatments, psychotherapists and certain branches of alternative medicine. Having visited many, however, I am extremely wary of health spas and beauty clinics that rely on expensive, glossy advertising and make claims that are untrue. Beware of any specialist help that promises you permanent changes in your appearance, your skin, your shape or your weight. Beware particularly of any clinic that claims to halt aging. This claim is false, because science knows of no way to halt the aging process. There is no "cure" for wrinkles and sagging skin other than surgical removal.

Most of these clinics are fairly expensive and to be fair to yourself you must have a clear understanding of what to expect from them and how well they will live up to their exaggerated claims. The truth is that no effect produced in a beauty clinic can be permanent. It lasts a few minutes, a few hours, but rarely even one day. All you can expect is to come out of a beauty clinic feeling pampered. Nothing, absolutely nothing, will have been done to change or correct any of your faults in any way at all.

Cosmetic surgery

Beware of beauty clinics' and also of beauticians' jargon. Pseudo-scientific words are created to give a false impression of medical or technical knowledge, but in nearly all cases this is artificial. In the first place the words are simply made up. They have no scientific meaning. Doctors don't understand them and are at a loss to figure out what their meanings may be. Many of the words are true nonsense, because for those people with a deep knowledge of the physiology of the skin, not only do they have no meaning, but they may even contradict themselves to such an extent that they may be dangerous.

At a consultation the surgeon assesses for himself and the patient possible changes by simulating the facelift with his fingers. This he does by pulling loose skin upward and backward.

I have included the various types of specialist help in the order in which I give them credence and so start with cosmetic surgery and cosmetic dentistry, medical skin treatment, psychotherapy and biofeedback. I have not found any scientific information to show that health spas, beauty treatment and beauty clinics are any better than a placebo. Oh yes, you may *feel* better but it will not necessarily be because you *are* better. You may feel better

197

because your attitude to yourself has changed, but you don't have to go to a clinic to experience that kind of change. It can happen without a beauty clinic. It can happen because of your own will power.

Choosing a cosmetic surgeon

Before you even approach a cosmetic surgeon, examine yourself closely. It is important that your motives for having the operation are the right ones. For instance it is no good thinking that cosmetic surgery will be the cure-all for a disaster that has overtaken you. It is going to make you no better able to cope with divorce proceedings. Having your nose straightened will not be able to make you give up alcohol, so don't look at cosmetic surgery as an emotional crutch. It is important to give a lot of consideration to cosmetic surgery, so do weigh up the possible risks (page 204) before you make a final decision.

When trying to decide who should be your cosmetic surgeon, first see your own doctor for a professional, objective opinion; he or she is the one whom you should listen to. Next best is recommendation from a friend who can show you the results of cosmetic surgery and describe his or her own experiences. You will be able to make a "before and after" judgment if you have known your friend for some time. It is very inadvisable to take any notice of advertisements in newspapers or magazines. A good surgeon or a good treatment needs no advertising because he or she will have acquired a good reputation.

When you are in the process of choosing a surgeon look for the following points. If you spot any of them move to another surgeon.

● A surgeon who is unrealistic about the possible results of the operation. No good surgeon will guarantee his or her operation to be 100 percent successful.

● A surgeon who will not explain in detail what the operation involves and what he is trying to achieve, with a realistic estimate of the chances of success.

● A surgeon who offers no professional opinion as to what you really need and is willing to perform exactly the operation you want. Any surgeon worth his salt will want to do the operation that has the best results for you and should offer his own suggestions about what he thinks should be done.

● A surgeon who will not answer your questions in detail with illustrations and photographs of other clients' surgery.

● A surgeon who is not prepared to take many and detailed photographs of the feature you require altering with surgery. Many cosmetic surgeons will say they need photographs to study in order to decide exactly how and what they have to do to make the correction.

COSMETIC SURGERY

Eyes
Blepharoplasty will improve puffy or drooping eyelids, remove the bags beneath eyes and reshape eyelids

Nose
Rhinoplasty will alter the size or shape of the nose, strengthen or straighten it

Cheeks
Cheekbone augmentation will make them more prominent

Ears
Otoplasty will pin back sticking-out ears

Chin
Remodelling will correct a receding or prominent chin and reduction will remove sagging skin beneath the jaw

Neck
A face lift pulls back loose skin, making the neck look healthier

The face Cosmetic operations performed on the face are usually to remove signs of age or to improve features. Cosmetic surgeons will tell you that the classical patients are no longer the vain, rich women with nothing better to do with their money; they are more likely to be energetic, active women who are less interested in hiding their age than in looking as youthful as they feel. People in their fifties and onward no longer resign themselves to being thought of as aging. Many feel that growing older would be more comfortable if they could avoid looking old in the process. Many others justifiably feel it is unjust that they should begin to show signs of deterioration when they are just reaching intellectual and emotional maturity. So when fine lines, wrinkles and sags appear on their faces they decide to fight back with cosmetic surgery.

The illustration on page 199 shows the facial features which you can have altered by a cosmetic surgeon. In the USA a new approach to face lifts has been developed for older patients, *total facial rejuvenation* (see chart, pages 202-203). The latest techniques can eliminate frown lines by a modification of the muscle structure under the skin.

The body Expense is not the only factor that should make you pause before contemplating body surgery. It should always be considered a last resort in the search for beauty – it's far better to exercise or diet your bulges away. From a medical standpoint, cosmetic surgery on your body will be more serious than on your face. The operations are lengthy; some involve a considerable spell of post-operative pain and immobility. All of them leave scars, though they vary in their degree of conspicuousness. Furthermore, the technology for these operations is confined to the main centers for cosmetic surgery in the USA and it is difficult to find good surgeons with all the best facilities elsewhere in the world.

Breast uplift or mastoplexy
This will correct drooping breasts. With age, the suspensory ligaments, the skin and the breast tissue itself will thin and become inelastic. Once this has happened nothing can make the breast regain its former shape. Not even exercises, no matter how much you are encouraged to do them. There is no muscle tissue in the breasts, and by strengthening the pectoralis major and minor you are doing nothing to improve the shape of your breasts. Occasionally breast uplift is combined with breast augmentation or breast reduction or the correction of a minor idiosyncracy like lopsidedness. A general anaesthetic is always needed. The length of stay in hospital is about three days, but in the USA clinics are offering breast uplift operations to outpatients. The technique used is virtually the same as for breast reduction, but only skin rather than skin fat and breast tissue is removed.

Breast augmentation is the most popular body operation in cosmetic surgery anywhere in the world. A request for surgery is usually made by someone who has tried every other conceivable method to improve her bust, including exercises, massage, bathing the breasts alternately in hot and cold water and hormone creams. None of these work. The only way to enlarge breasts successfully is through surgery. Before the operation, patient and surgeon should establish the shape and size of the breasts without being over-ambitious. Too large breasts make you look unnatural and top heavy. Study pictures of the various operations that the surgeon can perform and ask his advice about which will best suit you. Then ask to see a specimen of the implant material that the surgeon will use.

The operation is usually performed under an anesthetic on an in-patient basis, and your hospital stay will probably last a few days. An incision is made around the areola where it will heal without leaving any obvious scar. The implant is then placed *behind* the normal breast tissue so that it lies against the pectoral muscles. The deep layers of the wound are stitched together with soluble nylon that does not have to be removed and the stitches closing the incision around the areola come out a week after the operation. There is usually very little discomfort and any bruising disappears within a few weeks. There may be a slight tingling or numbness around the nipple, but this will gradually wear off.

Start wearing a bra in your new size as soon as it is comfortable to do so. Make sure you buy one in advance to take into the hospital when you go for the operation.

For about a month after a breast augmentation operation it is better to avoid very active sports like swimming, tennis and volley ball. Any movements that extend the arms high above the head and those that pull the elbows out at right angles should be avoided, but the operation should not interfere in any other way with your mobility. Your breasts should look and feel natural and they should not become hard after insertion. If they do, you may need further surgery, but this change is exceedingly rare with the new type of inflatable implant currently available.

Breast reduction
This operation is for women who are embarrassingly well endowed. Occasionally, some breasts are so pendulous that they hang down to the thighs and so heavy that the bra straps ulcerate the skin of the shoulder. Most cosmetic surgeons would agree that these breasts should be reduced for psychological if not medical reasons. You should first have photographs taken of your breasts from every angle, then agree with the surgeon on a new outline for them. An incision is made around the areola just as for breast augmentation and all the way down the front underside of the breast to where it meets the skin covering the chest wall. Skin fat and breast tissue are removed, leaving enough to fashion a breast of normal shape and size. The nipples have to be moved upwards to an appropriate position on the reshaped breasts, but this should not affect their sensitivity. Any scars can easily be hidden under cover-up make-up.

POPULAR COSMETIC OPERATIONS

Operation	In/Out-patient. Length of stay	Preconditions	Anesthetic. Time taken	Post-operative effects
Face lift Lifting skin of whole face	In-patient 3 days	None	General 2 hours +	Face red and swollen
Total facial rejuvenation Face lift, neck lift, eyelid repair, dermabrasion	In-patient 5 days minimum	None	General Up to 4 hours	Face red and swollen
Breast reconstruction Building new breast(s) after mastectomy	In-patient 3 days + for each stage	Psychological preparation. No indication that cancer has spread	General May be in 2 stages	Soreness, bruising
Breast augmentation Enlarging the breasts	In-patient; rarely out-patient. 3 days minimum	None	General; rarely local 2 hours	Occasionally soreness, bruising, tingling round nipple
Breast reduction Making breasts smaller	In-patient; rarely out-patient. 3 days	None	General Up to 3 hours	Bruising, tingling, soreness and numbness of nipple
Abdominoplasty Removal of folds of fat from lower abdomen	In-patient 7 days	First discuss operation with surgeon	General 2 hours	Drainage tubes in wound for 3-5 days
Buttocks, hips and thighs Recontouring of shape by removing fat and skin	In-patient 5 days if possible	Diet to lose fat first	General 2-3 hours depending on operation	Can move and sit same day but some discomfort likely for 2 weeks
Total body lift Removal of sagging skin from abdomen, buttocks, thighs, arms, neck and face	In-patient 5-7 days on each occasion	Diet to lose fat first	General 1-2 hours each session	Depends on operations
Hair transplants Transplanting skin from back of scalp to bald area	In-patient 7 days	None	General or local 1-2 hours each session	Swelling and crusting
Upper arms Removal of loose fat and skin	In-patient 48 hours	None	General 1 hour	Hardly any discomfort

Stitches removed	Care and dressing	Time of full recovery	Possible complications	Results
Some at 5-7 days rest at 2 weeks	Can eat immediately, fully active in 3 days. Large dressing for 2 days	Superficial swelling subsides in a month	Feeling of tightness usually gone in a few months	Generally very good. Only fully apparent in 3 months.
Some at 5-7 days rest at 2 weeks	Can be fully active in 3 days. Bulky dressings for 48 hours	Swelling subsides in 3 weeks	Tightness around neck and numbness ; around ears, subsiding in few months	Good. May take up to 6 months to see best effect
5-7 days	As breast reduction	3 months	Visible scars. Rarely reduction in sensitivity of nipple	Good
1 week	No active sports or stretching for 1 month. Light dressing and antibiotic ointment	2 months	Hardening of implants. Any bruising and discomfort usually goes in a few weeks	Very good if up-to-date methods are used
1 week	No active sports or stretching for 1 month. Dressing for 3-5 days	2 months	Visible scars. Swelling, discoloration, infection possible	Very good
14 days	Keep body bent for 3-5 days. Mobility restricted for 4-6 weeks. Daily dressing	3 months	Scarcely visible scars	Good
7-10 days if non-soluble	Ordinary activities in 14 days. Sport in 1 month. Light gauze and antibiotic ointment	2 months	Significant scars	Very good if up-to-date methods are used
Depends on operations	Depends on operations	3-4 months after last operation	Significant scars	Good
7 days if used	Careful shampooing and combing. Bulky bandage for 7 days	1 year	None	Repeat may be needed. Better for men than women
5-7 days	No stretching for 2 weeks. Light gauze and antibiotic ointment	2 months	Visible scars	Very good

203

RISKS OF COSMETIC SURGERY

- Be aware that all surgery carries a risk. With any surgery there is risk of dying under general anaesthetic and a risk that the operation will give you a shock from which you will never recover. Both of these risks are very small.
- A proportion of patients over fifty undergoing cosmetic surgery can no longer be classified as young and are certainly less robust than people in their twenties and thirties, so it could be argued that the risks involved are higher.
- Remember that the period immediately after any operation can be unpleasant and cosmetic surgery is no different – the area involved may be uncomfortable and painful for days or weeks. You may have a period of complete immobility or at least severely restricted activity. With older people it is essential that you combine a régime of rest with activity, otherwise joints will stiffen and there is a possibility of pneumonia just from sitting in bed.

- Keep at the back of your mind that the operation may not turn out exactly as you had thought. Though it's very rare, they may be disastrous. You should be prepared for the results being not quite as you had expected. Occasionally, there are complications that delay recovery, and while these risks are slight in the hands of a good surgeon they must be taken into account when you consider the pros and cons of cosmetic surgery.
- Cosmetic surgery is not exempt from scars. They may be well hidden under the hairline or inside the mouth, but very occasionally a scar will be visible. If this is an aspect of cosmetic surgery that troubles you, try and talk to someone who has already had the operation so that you can get an idea of the probability of scarring. In my experience, the more expert the cosmetic surgeon, the more likely he is to take pride in leaving no scars, or only the faintest.

Cosmetic dentistry

Bridge | Missing tooth

Bridge in position

Fitting a bridge
This involves shaping the teeth on either side of the gap so that a bridge can be cemented to them.

As we get older our teeth tend to yellow with age and because of gum recession we might be described as being "long in the tooth." Both of these things can be mitigated by good dental hygiene and regular visits to the dentist. Avoid using toothpastes that claim to whiten your teeth, unless your dentist recommends otherwise, because this "whitening" is an optical illusion. The toothpaste contains a red pigment that turns our gums pink, making our teeth look whiter by comparison. Toothpaste that claims to give a white, polished smile makes the teeth shine by use of abrasives, including a very strong one known as "jewelers' rouge."

Avoid these toothpastes at all costs – they are much too harsh on teeth and work by scratching the surface enamel. Prolonged use of such toothpastes damages or wears away teeth. The safest and by far the most efficient way to give your teeth a new look is to visit a dental hygienist. When we were younger we should have gone every six months; now our dentist may recommend that we go every three months to remove calcium deposits.

Eventually these cause inflammation in the margin of the gum and pocketing, which leads to a loosening of the teeth in their gums. The hygienist will also polish your teeth and make them several shades whiter, particularly if you smoke.

A good cosmetic dentist can alter the look of your teeth, your smile, the set of your mouth and therefore your facial expression. As we get older our teeth tend to be ground away simply by use or by having an especially strong masticating muscle or perhaps by night grinding. Whatever the cause, our jawbones tend to become closer together and this accentuates the folds on either side of our mouths – and most of us would agree that this makes us look older. A cosmetic dentist can correct this by widening the distance between the jawbones by re-positioning the teeth and stretching out the skin in your laughter line. Even an increase as little as half a millimeter will make a substantial difference to our appearance.

Repositioning teeth

We think of cosmetic dentistry as involving complicated techniques with bridges, wires and crowns, but many dentists use common sense and simple methods and materials to achieve their effect. For instance, it is quite possible to move the roots of the teeth within the jaw bone by anything up to a millimeter if they are pulled or pushed in one direction for any length of time. Even such tiny adjustments can make quite a difference to the overall effect.

Caps, crowns and bridges

Any badly positioned, ugly or broken tooth can be given a new cosmetic appearance by *capping* or *crowning*, terms that dentists use synonymously. Your dentist fits a cap by first filing away the tooth to form a peg, onto which the cap is cemented. This can still be done if your tooth is snapped off or has had to be removed right at the gum margin. Then, three or four posts are drilled into what is left of the tooth and the cap or crown can be fitted to them.

A bridge (page 204) is clear plastic molded to fit over the hard palate. The teeth required are fitted onto various parts of the bridge and this slips easily into place, held snugly in the mouth by wires that fit around your existing teeth. You should remove it and clean it in a sterilizing solution.

Shortening or lengthening teeth

If your teeth are too long they can soon be filed away and given caps that will make them look a little shorter than they were originally. The reverse problem is common too. The gums grow too high so that they make teeth appear to be too short. In this instance your gum margins can be cut away and your teeth lengthened with caps that are slightly longer.

MEDICAL SKIN TREATMENTS

These chemical and surgical techniques can be used to alter or repair the surface of the skin. I am very firmly of the opinion that they should be administered by medical specialists only, such as plastic surgeons or dermatologists; a non-medically qualified person cannot possibly judge how radical they can be with their treatment nor deal with side-effects.

Dermabrasion

Dermabrasion is used to remove or improve pitted acne scars on the face and to treat large, flat birth marks. It may even produce good results for stretch marks and fine lines around the mouth.

Great advances in dermabrasion have been made in the past twenty-five years largely due to high-speed rotary drills and better cooling techniques.

During the operation a strict procedure must be followed to avoid any accidents. The patient is sedated or tranquilized and then the area involved is chilled with cold packs. It is cleansed first with soap and water and then with spirit. Plugs of gauze, impregnated with ointment, are inserted into ears and nostrils while hair is carefully protected with towels. Eyes are covered with ointment and a lead shield. The area to be treated is frozen with a stream of cold gas and then the drill is used to abrade the skin to the required depth.

Crusts usually separate in seven to ten days and the wound heals more quickly if it is left open and dry. It is possible to treat the same areas again after a period of four weeks.

Chemical treatment

Skin peeling can be done for cosmetic or medical reasons by various chemicals. The area to be treated may be fairly extensive and so you may have to spend time in the hospital. In the hands of an expert, skin peeling can make blemishes, fine lines, wrinkles and acne pit marks much less obvious and it can occasionally be used to treat discolored areas of skin and freckles. It may soften the facial line temporarily; it will wear off within a year.

Curettage

In the right hands this procedure is straightforward. A curette, or a tiny spoon with a sharp cutting edge, is used to destroy or remove some skin conditions that are well circumscribed and embedded. The curette can enucleate small cysts and successfully remove warts and verrucae. The sharp edge is applied to the buried lesion at an angle and gradually separates it from the normal surrounding skin. It should shell out without any bleeding.

Electro-desiccation/coagulation

These involve destroying tissue in two ways. By producing a spark that solidifies the skin or by heating it up to a temperature at which it coagulates. In the former, cells are shriveled, while in the latter they simply solidify in the same way that the white of an egg does when it is boiled. By varying the current, the same apparatus can be used for both processes.

This treatment can be used to remove broken veins in the skin of the face and leg and it can also be used to treat warts that stand proudly above the surface of the skin. It is particularly useful for treating those little skin tags that appear as we get older and large numbers can be treated in one session.

Excision

Treating surface skin conditions involves complete surgical removal of a piece of full-thickness skin. Only a dermatologist or plastic surgeon can decide when this technique is necessary. A general rule is not to interfere in any way with pigmented skin such as a mole.

PSYCHOTHERAPY

Psychotherapy aims to help us acquire insight into ourselves and our behavior so that we can learn to deal with our own difficulties. The following forms of psychotherapy may bring useful insights. The first three forms often overlap in practice.

Psychoanalysis
This is the best-known form of psychotherapy but it has certain disadvantages. It is expensive and it takes a very long time; sometimes the duration is five years at a rate of five days a week. Undoubtedly it has helped a lot of people, but friends and relatives are not always as enthusiastic about the results, finding that the person has not necessarily changed for the better.

Interpretive psychotherapy
This helps people to understand the causes of their difficulties and the symptoms they are suffering. Psychotherapists cannot do this without understanding every aspect of a person's life, including childhood, adolescence, family and personal relationships. They may interpret the significance of a person's symptoms as they relate to his or her present life, but quite often a special technique is employed involving the *transference* of relationships between a person and his or her therapist.

Suggestive psychotherapy
This relies on resolving a person's difficulties by making direct suggestions. Hypnosis is one of the most intense and dramatic suggestive therapies in which a person's state of consciousness is altered and active directions are given. Although hypnotherapy is often used to change patterns of behavior, it can also be used to encourage a person to release repressed memory. This use is based on the theory that it is possible to make closer contact with the subconscious mind when someone is hypnotized.

Group therapy
This started after the second world war and quickly gained popularity. Small group therapy involves seven or eight people, usually strangers, who meet together with the therapist under strictly defined conditions. They all have in common the fact that they are unable to cope with the stress in their lives.

Group therapy aims to help a person to discover, rationalize, adjust and finally to cope with his or her problems. Talking gives a valuable insight into problems.

Thus it follows a logical, purposeful development with the end product a person who no longer depends on a group for inner confidence and social stability.

Behavioral therapy
This will greatly benefit phobias. A phobia is an overwhelming, unreasonable fear about certain situations – most people who suffer from a phobia are aware that they are behaving irrationally but are quite unable to control their fear. Very often a phobia can be the result of an earlier distressing event that has been forgotten. Phobic patients can be helped particularly by the different forms of behavioral therapy such as *aversion therapy, desensitization* or *modeling*.

Encounter group therapy
This gained prominence in the early 1960s. It involves complete openness to any impulse, whether it is touching, caressing, undressing or cursing, and such is the variety of groups available that anything promoting this openness such as nudity or screaming will be used.

Hormone treatments

At any age, but usually around fifty when their levels of estrogen decrease, women frequently experience emotional and physical discomfort. Hormonic replacement therapy can be useful in relieving such symptoms. As there are risks associated with it, be sure it is administered by a doctor whose speciality it is and only after contra-indications in your medical history have been screened out.

Men produce less testosterone as they get older – a hormone they need to function in all areas, particularly sexual, and testosterone replacement therapy (TRT) can correct this deficiency. It is never prescribed routinely and very little research has been done in this area. Many doctors disagree with it because they believe it might cause prostatic pain during ejaculation and difficulty with orgasm. So far the risks of TRT are generally felt to be greater than its benefits.

If you feel that TRT might be of use you should go to your doctor to talk it over. If he or she doesn't know a lot about TRT, ask to be referred to someone who does or get a second opinion. Don't be afraid. The more you find out about your body and the way your body changes and also the kind of treatment that is available to reverse these changes, the more you will benefit.

Regenerative cell therapy This also made extravagant claims about rejuvenating or revitalizing the skin. Such are people's insecurities that these treatments often become widely used in the absence of any proof that they are effective. A currently popular treatment is one that was developed in the 1930s by Doctor Paul Niehans. It involves injecting patients with a mixture of cells from ten glands of freshly-slaughtered animals. Basic physiological factors do need to be considered. Our bodies have mechanisms to protect us from invasion by live foreign cells and also it is highly unlikely that an injected substance will reach a specific organ in any undiluted quantity.

Biofeedback

Biofeedback is a technique that teaches us to be aware of our bodies' inner workings through the use of machinery and it is currently the subject of research among scientists of all disciplines. It was initially the subject of much hostility but now that it has shown that we can achieve "mind over matter," it has revolutionized many previous beliefs about the nature of nerve function. Some biofeedback enthusiasts would now go as far as to claim that this discipline is a way of eradicating all need for conventional medicine, by teaching people to gain complete control over their bodily functions, but this is absolute nonsense. By fewer people it is considered to be a means of reaching in a matter of hours a state of inner awareness and peace, spiritual and mental, which the practitioners of yoga, Zen, and other forms of meditation are only able to reach after many disciplined years.

Biofeedback suggests that information about our inner state is being relayed to us in the same way that information about our surroundings is fed back to us by our senses. This means that we can learn more about our environment and how to control behavior in reaction to it. The sort of information gained by biofeedback concerns the structural activity of the heart, for instance rate of heart and blood pressure, and the brain and indicates to us the way they function.

Various instruments such as an electro-encephalograph, which records brain waves, an electro-micrograph, which charts muscle tension and an electro-cardiograph, which records heart beats, can all make us aware of what is happening in our bodies and help us develop personal techniques to maintain physical and mental control. This way it may be possible to gradually feel the way our internal organs work.

Uses for biofeedback

We can't all cart around an electro-encephalograph with us during our normal daily lives but there are much smaller and more convenient instruments that can monitor inner body functions. A small machine can be attached to one finger only and it will monitor and give a visual display of heart rate and blood pressure. What we can try to do is to relax, breathe regularly, clear our minds of anxiety (try the relaxation drills given on pages 80-81) and when heart rate and blood pressure are back down to normal we must take note of the kind of feelings that we have. Then when blood pressure and heart rate rise again we can attempt to recapture the feeling that accompanied our heart rate being slow and our blood pressure being normal.

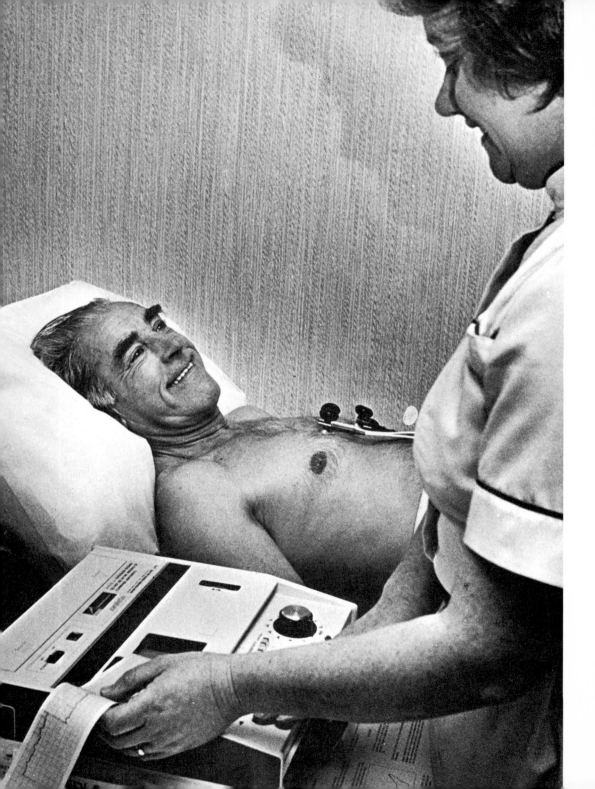

Special medical problems

Just as there are special diseases in infancy and childhood, so there are certain conditions that begin to show as we get older and become commoner as we age. Naturally enough, fear of these diseases also increases and the fear of getting heart disease or having cancer may grow to the point of irrationality, even to being a phobia. Medical conditions of age are largely those that occur because our bodies' machinery is shifting down a gear and this alters the way it works.

Because the aging process continues on through life, it is not as easy to identify a single malfunction in an older person as it is in a younger person. Many of the medical conditions of this age are those of wear and tear; and the ones that affect our vital organs are often dramatic, for instance heart disease, strokes and cancer. Most of the common medical problems of fifty-year-olds and upward will be mentioned in this chapter. The accent will be on how to manage a medical problem yourself if you have it, what you can do to minimize its encroachment on your activity and enjoyment of life, how to slow its progress, how to deal with possible serious outcomes, and some tips on how others can help you. For the management of chronic illnesses in yourself and others see *Living with long-term ailments*.

There are certain signs and symptoms in medicine that indicate change: change from a normal bowel habit, change in the digestive pattern, a sudden bout of coughing up blood-specked sputum, severe headaches that strike out of the blue. In the majority of cases they are not serious, and whatever has gone wrong can easily be put right, but in some cases the underlying cause can be degenerative as in atheromatous arterial disease, or inflammatory as in rheumatoid arthritis, or cancerous as in a malignant tumor.

For this reason all the following warning signs represent something serious until proven otherwise when you take them to your doctor. Please don't let them alarm you. They are described as warning signs and they are only a warning. In the majority of cases they will turn out to be easily explained and eminently treatable but any symptom or sign of change needs investigation, proper diagnosis and appropriate medical help. This list will help you to be alert to changes so that they need not be an unnecessary source of worry. To a doctor, change always represents a signal that the body is not functioning as it should. This doesn't necessarily mean danger.

Cancer

Cancer is not the worst problem facing us as we get older, but it causes a great deal of concern. It is common enough for almost every person to fear it as he or she gets older and to imagine that it is the cause of any symptoms he or she may have. Anyone who is aware of this should be sympathetic.

Cancer accounts for about 20 percent of all deaths and the proportion increases as we grow older. In many organs such as the skin, the lungs and the digestive tract, the chance of cancer developing rises steadily with age, as do certain leukemias. Cancer of the prostate gland is even more strikingly connected with the age of a man, but many tumors, such as those of the cervix and womb, are more usually found in younger women.

There are some hereditary factors involved, so that your chances of developing cancer are greater if it runs in your family. Some cancers are caused by harmful agents like tobacco and industrial chemicals, most of which take a long time to show their effects. It is not surprising, therefore, that some cancers tend to appear latterly, as older people will have had more time for this to happen. Even though an aging population will probably have more cancer than a youthful one, cancers in older people are often less malignant and grow much more slowly, and some even seem to get smaller.

While I will not discuss individual cancers in detail, there are certain facts about cancer in later life that are well worth mentioning. Cancer of the breast is fairly common and very often it is missed by the woman herself. Many of these cancers go undetected and we cannot avoid the conclusion that women know of lumps, more than suspect what they are, but decide to say nothing either because of embarrassment or because they are afraid to hear the truth and undergo treatment. Many tragedies result from this, from ignorance or fear. As most cancers in old age grow slowly, it is quite common for an older woman to have had one developing for many years.

Breast cancer　Breast cancer can be curable. As the breast is almost a separate organ supported on the chest wall, it is easy to get at. This means that a small tumor of the breast that hasn't spread can be cured by surgical removal of the lump alone if it's small, or of the breast or part of it.

Factors related to breast cancer
Many factors are known to affect the development of breast cancer. If you are white you run a higher risk than women of other races. If other members of your family have breast cancer

then your chances are higher. Women who have no children are at a fairly high risk, but breast feeding may have a protective effect. There is an undoubted connection between a western diet and the development of breast cancer. It is generally agreed that the risk of developing breast cancer increases with age. Under the age of twenty-five it is very rare and up to the age of about thirty-five it is not so common, but then between the ages of thirty-five and fifty its incidence increases and after the age of fifty the risk is greatest.

You should examine your breasts monthly (see *Caring for a changing body*). You should go to your doctor and have your breasts examined regularly, especially if you fall into a high risk group. Many authorities recommend yearly mammography examinations after age forty.

Discovering a lump
If you discover a lump in your breast it may feel clearly defined. It may feel hard and stony or it may feel round and cystic. It may or may not be associated with pain and the most malignant tumors are painless. It may involve the skin and send up constricting bands so that it is tethered to it, pulling on a small area of skin making it dimpled. It may also tug at the nipple and alter its shape. All of these changes have important significance for your doctor, whose first concern is to exclude the possibility of your having a malignant tumor as rapidly as possible.

Your family physician will certainly refer you to a surgeon who specializes in treating breast cancer, and he or she will probably approach the lump in your breast as being malignant until able to prove otherwise. Your doctor will need to act with speed and efficiency, and will also try to find out if the tumor has spread and, if it has, to what extent. Ask your surgeon to keep you informed of the plan of action he or she has in mind for treating the lump in your breast and to give you reasons for why such a decision is made. You should be part of these decisions, and you need quite a lot of information to participate intelligently.

The surgeon may decide to perform some tests to confirm what the initial examination has already suggested. One of the most important that can be performed is a fine needle biopsy. It is a painless procedure where a fine needle is inserted into the lump and a little fluid is withdrawn. If the tumor is malignant, cancer cells will be found in the breast fluid in about 85 percent of cases. Some surgeons consider lumpectomy (removal of the lump alone) as an acceptable preoperative investigative procedure. Once the lump has been removed it will be examined in the pathology laboratory and a diagnosis can be confirmed. It is also possible to do a breast biopsy where a little part of the lump is taken out to be examined for malignant cells.

You should not agree to surgical removal, partial removal or treatment of your breast until a diagnosis has been confirmed. Try to avoid going to the operating theater having agreed to removal of your breast should the surgeon find it necessary when you are on the table. Have a clear understanding of the possible courses of action and their consequences.

Any of the preoperative investigative techniques I have mentioned can be and are performed in the most modern units so that women have time to adjust themselves to having a malignant tumor of the breast and also to the form of treatment that the surgeon wishes to follow.

Treatment for breast cancer
There are almost as many ways of treating cancer of the breast as there are surgeons, but they usually involve one or any combination of three types of approach.

Surgery involves removing all or part of the breast and some of the underlying muscle, the lymph glands from the arm pit and lymph glands from the neck. All of these operations are given the general name "mastectomy" and then prefixes of "partial," "simple," "total," "modified," "radical," etc., which describe the extent of breast tissue removal. Naturally, the greater the extent of the operation, the greater the amount of scarring.

MASTECTOMY OPERATIONS

There are seven different operations performed today for breast cancer. All require the removal of some, if not all, of the breast tissue, but they differ in the amount of tissue, muscle and lymph nodes removed.

Lumpectomy
The whole lump is removed plus a little of the breast tissue. Your breast will not look very different.

Partial mastectomy
Here, an amount of breast tissue, plus the overlying skin and underlying tissue are removed.

Total or simple mastectomy
In this operation the whole of the breast is removed, but the axillary nodes and the pectoral muscle are left untouched. The last lymph node in the breast is routinely taken out to see if the cancer has spread to the axilla.

Radiotherapy (deep X-ray therapy) is sometimes given before the operation; quite often it is given after the operation both to the breast itself and to the glands in the armpit or the neck. Further courses of radiotherapy may be necessary over a period of weekly visits to kill off any cancer cells that may remain in the area.

Hormone therapy has been found to diminish the size of breast tumors in a proportion of women if they are given courses of estrogens or anti-estrogens (which have the reverse effect of estrogens). This is because the normal growth of the breast is influenced by estrogen levels, its sensitivity to estrogen varying with age. Estrogen-sensitive tumors will require treatment with anti-estrogens.

In older women the approach to treatment of breast cancer is rather different from that in younger women. In younger women there are more mastectomies, and mastectomies plus X-ray therapy, whereas in older women, where tumors seem to have a closer dependency in estrogens and anti-estrogens, the tendency is to treat more often with hormone therapy with or without radiotherapy.

Hormone therapy takes various forms and in the best centers hormone therapy is tailor-made to suit each individual person's hormone profile. Endocrinologists, working closely with surgeons and radiotherapists, perform studies on an individual hormone balance and may even do tests on the tumor itself to see whether estrogens or anti-estrogens are more likely to be successful as a therapy.

Estrogen is usually considered the treatment of choice for women who are more than five years beyond the menopause. Anti-estrogens, often given in the form of androgens, are usually reserved for post-menopausal patients between two and five years beyond the menopause. Patients and doctors can usually see a response within six weeks from the beginning of treatment to hormone therapy of this kind.

The most popular form of treatment is di-ethyl-stilbestrol at a dose of five milligrams, three times a day. Tolerance to this régime is most easily achieved if the patient has a low dosage for a few weeks or takes a coated tablet. The commonest side effects are nausea and vomiting.

Anti-estrogen therapy can be given by mouth, but if androgens themselves are used, injections may be necessary once or twice weekly. There are other hormones that can be used to promote appetite, increase in weight and remission of the tumor. Anabolic steroids are sometimes used along with corticosteroids and synthetic progesterone.

Women who are more than ten years beyond the menopause have an excellent chance of a cure. The older you are when the tumor is discovered and the more slowly it is growing, then the better your chances of a complete cure.

Cancer of the prostate

This is the most common cancer in men; it is not uncommon in forty-to-fifty-year-olds, and becomes marked in seventy-year-olds and over. As many as 20 percent of men over sixty have prostatic cancer. In its easily stages it may be tentatively diagnosed on routine rectal examinations. Biopsies of suspected tissues are then needed to confirm the diagnosis. Treatment by surgery and irradiation is very successful when the cancer is detected in its early stages, but the prognosis is poor once it has spread outside the prostate. Therefore, routine rectal examinations every year for men fifty and over are strongly advised.

This cancer usually develops in a normal gland, but it may also grow from a gland that is enlarged through benign prostatic hypertrophy (see page 217). No one yet understands the cause of carcinoma of the prostate fully. At the moment it seems likely that an imbalance in the ratio of androgen versus estrogens circulating in the blood plays an important part in its development. It is probably the amount of androgen that is critical. The tumor may lessen in size if estrogens are given to a patient to restore the estrogen-androgen balance. It appears that androgens are responsible for inducing cancerous changes, while enlargements of the prostate may be under the influence of estrogens.

When the prostate gland grows because of a cancerous tumor it obstructs the urethra so men suffer difficulty with passing urine, retention of urine and possibly urinary infection. Eventually any of these conditions may go on to chronic kidney failure if they are not treated to relieve the obstruction.

On the other hand, some men may have fewer urinary symptoms and mainly complain of pain in the lower back and sciatica going down the back of the leg. This happens when deposits of the cancer have spread from the prostate gland into the bone at the lower parts of the spine so they are pressing on the sciatic nerve.

When a doctor examines a cancerous gland through the rectum, the surface will feel hard, irregular and fixed. It may even be possible to feel an extension of the cancer out to the side walls of the pelvis, around the rectum and sometimes down to the bladder. When the blood is examined an enzyme, acid phosphatase, may be raised to confirm the diagnosis.

Unlike the procedure for some other cancers, biopsy is rarely

Thickened
bladder
wall

Enlarged
prostate

Urethra

An enlarged prostate reduces the flow of urine by blocking the urethra. The bladder gradually thickens and strengthens as it works harder to force urine through the urethra.

CANCER OF THE PROSTATE

It is generally agreed by doctors that it is not necessary to attempt special treatment if the cancer remains confined to the prostate gland because it rarely spreads and removal is a radical operation with serious risks.

The prostate gland is a small organ, the size of a chestnut, which straddles the urethra. If enlarged it restricts the flow of urine.

Stomach

Prostate

Urethra

Cancer of the prostate does not spread in the same way as other cancers. Symptoms are indistinguishable from those of a benign enlarged prostate and this is a harmless result of aging. If the cancer is not discovered it may spread to surrounding areas (left). Your doctor will advise you.

There are four kinds of prostate operation: a, surpubic, where the bladder is opened; b, supra pubic, where the bladder is bypassed; c, transurethral, where a slender tube is passed through the urethra into the bladder; and d, perineal, where an incision is made between the legs.

performed to confirm a diagnosis in a difficult case. A biopsy is usually done by passing a surgical knife through a fine tube by the urethra but it's risky. Sometimes, if the diagnosis is very doubtful, it may be attempted through other operative routes.

It is rare for a cancer of the prostate to cause symptoms until it has spread through its capsule into the surrounding areas. This means that there are few patients who are suitable for radical surgery. This kind of tumor is fairly resistant to deep X-ray therapy, and treatment is usually based on hormonal therapy. As the normal prostate gland depends on androgens for its proper growth and functions, hormonal therapy can be very successful against carcinoma of the prostate.

It is possible to reduce the secretion of the body's own androgens significantly by giving large doses of estrogen, up to 30 milligrams of stilbestrol a day. The action of the estrogen dampens testosterone production. Shrinkage of the cancer usually follows.

About 70 percent of patients will do well with this treatment, but it may be necessary to give more than one course. A patient who continues to have difficulty with passing urine may have part of the prostate gland cut away by a small operation through the transurethral route.

Cancer of the lower bowel

This is quite common but very slow to develop. It sometimes produces unusual symptoms to which you and your doctor should be alerted. It is not a very invasive kind of tumor and can be treated in its very early stages with a good chance of a cure.

Cancer of the rectum is also slow to develop but it may become inoperable because the patient is just too shy to mention rectal symptoms, or believes that rectal bleeding is just trouble with piles. The fault may be with some doctor or nurse who doesn't bother to make a rectal examination for symptoms of diarrhea or constipation. Warning signs include constipation and/or diarrhea; blood or pus in the stool; pain in the bowel; anemia; loss of weight and general ill-health.

Cancer of the skin

This is very slow to develop in older people and it's not likely to spread very far or very fast, with the exception of *melanoma*, a rare form of skin cancer that can spread quickly. Usually, skin cancer occurs in those parts of the skin that have been exposed most to sunlight, and it's especially noticeable in old farmers. One kind of skin cancer that appears on the face, usually near the eyes, is called *rodent ulcer* and it is most commonly a small, raised area with a dark scab in the middle, which forms after bleeding. This cancer responds very well to treatment and will heal with scarcely a mark, so you should seek attention if you ever spot anything like this on your face. If it is not treated, it may cause considerable disfigurement.

Cancer treatment

In the older person, there is probably the greatest chance of a cure from cancer of all age groups. Because cancers grow very slowly, they can be detected at an early stage and therefore the chances of successful treatment are greatly improved. As we get older we shrink from troubling nurses and doctors with little things, but little things may be the first sign of something that may develop into a serious illness.

The obvious treatment for cancer is surgery, but not all cancers in older people need surgical intervention. There are many groups of drugs that are effective against cancer. The full course of drugs may be long and they may make the patient feel unwell. Some cancers, for instance cancers of the prostate or breast, can be held in check for many months or years by using hormones that do not have a serious effect on the patient's general well-being. The extent of the efforts depends on the cancer; some are far more treatable than others. Never think that cancer is the end of the world – do be alert for early symptoms and see your doctor. There's no need to feel intimidated by doctors and ultra-modern clinics with their high technology – they are there for the sole purpose of helping us.

Heart disease

In the United States deaths from cardiovascular disease have been declining since 1968. Nevertheless, one-half of all deaths in most Western countries are cause by *atherosclerosis*, which in turn is responsible for coronary heart disease, strokes and other blood vessel disorders. This condition, whereby fatty deposits cause vessel walls to thicken and narrow, is definitely related to age. It is rare before thirty, but by fifty most of use have some degree of atherosclerosis. It is more extensive in men up to fifty, after which women begin to draw even. The deposits in the blood vessels, or *atheroma*, restrict the blood supply flowing to the heart so that it is put under strain. Additional burdens are added by physical and emotional stresses, which may precipitate a heart attack because the heart is not being supplied with sufficient oxygen. Risk factors have been identified: heredity, diabetes, high levels of fatty substances (cholesterol and triglycerides) in the blood and high blood pressure and cigarette smoking. Except for heredity, which cannot be altered, a change of lifestyle can protect everyone against heart disease.

Areas affected by heart disease
Hypertension can lead to a stroke, heart failure or kidney failure.
The tell-tale sign of angina is pain in the center of your chest or, less commonly, in your arms.
The main symptom of a heart attack is a dull, heavy pain in the center of your chest.

Hypertension   **Angina**   **Heart attack**

A heart attack When some of the blood supply to the heart muscle is cut off, a portion of the heart muscle dies from this lack. This incident may be small and never suspected by the person, or it may do significant damage which can be fatal. Most often a person will experience excruciating and crushing chest pain. In other instances the only symptoms may be shortness of breath and dizziness. A heart attack is often caused by a thrombus in a coronary vessel, or a blood clot from elsewhere in the body (an embolus), which cuts off the blood supply causing the heart to be thrown out of gear.

Most deaths caused by heart attacks occur within minutes or hours of the attack. If you show no sign of heart failure or heart rhythm disturbances six hours after the pain disappears, you have a 90 percent chance of recovery. Even after a severe attack, if you are alive one month afterwards, you have a 70 percent chance of surviving five years.

Heart failure A heart that is "tired out" and weakened so that it cannot pump blood around or provide sufficient circulation to the body tissues is said to be "failing." Untreated high blood pressure, coronary artery disease, chronic lung disease, anemia, infection and alcoholism can be contributory factors.

Treatment is based on drugs that eliminate excess fluids in the body, thus relieving strain on the heart and increasing its pumping ability, and on those which strengthen the heart muscle. Heart failure does not necessarily mean you will be restricted for the rest of your life. You should reduce your physical activities, however, and get sufficient rest to conserve energy, but you should never let yourself become bedridden.

Angina pectoris This condition, with classic brief pains over the mid-chest region that may radiate to one or both arms, the back, neck or jaw, is caused by a temporary inadequacy in the blood supply of the heart muscle. An attack is usually brought on by exertion, emotion, heavy meals or smoking. It goes away with rest and can be difficult to distinguish from indigestion.

Angina can be relieved by medical treatment with drugs and certain operations. Bypass operations in which the blocked vessel can be replaced by a portion of a vein removed from another part of the body (see below) can be successful, but only if the person attempts to alter his or her lifestyle to avoid worsening the condition.

CORONARY ARTERY BYPASS

This operation relieves pain but it does not cure the underlying cause of the disease. You will be under a general anaesthetic, your breathing and circulation being taken over by a heart-lung machine. The surgeon then transfers a length of vein from your leg to bypass the blocked artery.

Afterward, a few days in an intensive-care unit will be necessary to check your heart beat.

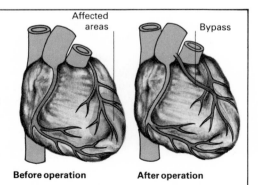

Affected areas

Bypass

Before operation　　**After operation**

High blood pressure (hypertension)

As we age our blood pressure increases and, if it is very high, it can complicate many other conditions, notably coronary artery disease, and kidney and brain disorders. About 75 percent of hypertensives are over the age of forty, but their condition is not often diagnosed until they are fifty or sixty. It is associated with excess weight, affects blacks more than whites, and men more than women, though after fifty women do complain of it.

The first signs of high blood pressure may be dizziness or headaches, though usually there are no symptoms at all, making regular check-ups vital, especially after age forty. Salt and stress have been found to be contributory factors, as is being overweight. The treatment normally consists of weight reduction, a low-salt diet, and possibly drugs.

Strokes

Diseases of the blood vessels of the brain (the commonest causes of strokes) rank high among our disabilities as we get older. Though not often fatal, they can deprive us of the pleasures of independence and the dignity of self-sufficiency. Responsible for about 9 percent of deaths in the United States, cerebrovascular disease is exceeded only by heart disease and cancer. Most reports show clearly that there is an increase in the incidence of cerebrovascular disease with increasing age. Although this represents both hemorrhages and blood clots, the major cause is undoubtedly blood clots. The chance of dying as a result of a stroke is related to our age; even when other factors affecting survival are taken into account, the final outcome is worse the older we are and the poorer our physical condition.

In 1981 there were 1,870,000 strokes in the U.S. Of these, 164,300 resulted in deaths.

Types of stroke

Even in the acute stroke, the underlying abnormality is a narrowing of the cerebral blood vessels, either by atheroma or arteriosclerosis, which is insidious and progressive, long in advance of the stroke. Most of us think of a stroke as a debilitating illness that may paralyze half the body, disrupt speech, sight and hearing, and virtually leave its victim helpless. This is true of a very few cases, indeed. The term "stroke illness" covers a number of patterns. Below is a list of some of the more common ones.

• A transient and minor attack, say a drooping eyelid or paralyzed side of the mouth, which gets better within 24 hours.

221

- A transient attack of blindness in one eye that gets better very quickly.
- A stroke that is gradually evolving over a period of several days and getting worse.
- A very severe, sudden stroke affecting parts of the brain on both sides of the body so that there is loss of speech, difficulty in swallowing, an unsmiling and staring appearance because the eyelids cannot blink.
- An inability to make coordinated movements and a hesitant gait, a condition that does not improve without help.

Strokes are associated with certain illnesses such as anemia, high blood pressure and a coronary thrombosis. It is always important to ask "Why has this stroke occurred?" If there is an underlying cause, treatment should be directed towards it and not to the stroke, which is only a symptom.

When a stroke develops it may be in an early part of its evolution, making diagnosis difficult. This may prevent urgent treatment and proper investigation and it may not be for several days that the full extent of the damage from a stroke can be clearly seen. Here are some of the grades of disability that can result from a stroke:

- Complete paralysis;
- A flicker of movement;
- Movement possible when the force of gravity is removed;
- Unaided movement possible against the force of gravity;
- Movement possible but weak when it is resisted;
- Movement normal when compared to the unaffected side.

The amount of damage done by a stroke will depend on two things. Firstly, which part of the brain is denied a healthy blood supply – only those functions controlled by that particular part will be affected. Secondly, the type of incident that caused the stroke – either a hemorrhage or a blood clot.

Hemiplegia is the commonest disorder. It is a paralysis down one side of the body, usually the arm and the leg together. The lower half of the face muscles may be affected, too.

Monoplegia is the paralysis of an arm or a leg on its own, meaning that only a small branch of an artery may be blocked.

Hemianesthesia is a loss of sensation of various kinds down one side of the body. It is much less serious than loss of muscle power, and usually passes off quite quickly. In a straightforward stroke, hemianesthesia usually occurs on the same side as the paralysis, but less than one in ten strokes has this kind of loss of sensation.

Hemianopia is loss of half the visual field formed when both eyes see correctly. In strokes, it is the same side of the field of both eyes that becomes blind, and the same side as any loss of power or sensation. This is particularly important to know if you are looking after a stroke patient who is unable to see you approaching from the blind side and cannot be interested in anything if it's done on his or her blind side. Such a person is startled by someone unexpectedly appearing in front of him or her from this side, so as a general rule you should try to appear from the sighted side. Usually the central field of vision, which is the part used in reading, writing and handwork, is preserved and can be used as before.

Cerebral hemorrhage

A hemorrhage is usually more serious than a clot because if the blood pressure is high blood will pour into the substance of the brain doing a great deal of harm. In its most severe form this kind of stroke is usually dramatic, starting off with a violent headache and vomiting, and then the person quickly falls unconscious with uneven "blowing" breathing. Usually his or her head and eyes are turned to one side and one cheek is "puffing." Often the neck is stiff and there may be limpness and paralysis down one side of the body.

An *embolus* causes a similarly sudden attack, but probably not as extensive in terms of body involvement. A thrombosis is usually a slower and gentler event.

Cerebral thrombosis

A cerebral thrombosis can come on at any time of day, but it is not unusual for someone to wake up, start to get out of bed, and fall down because his or her leg has lost its strength. Or he or she may be sitting at a table having a meal and suddenly drop a cup or a knife because his or her hand has lost its strength. So loss of conciousness is quite rare. It is fairly common for a stroke due to cerebral thrombosis to develop over several hours.

People suffering a cerebral thrombosis have a good outlook for recovery even though they may have lost significant movement. They can usually regain some function with several weeks of physical therapy and rehabilitation.

It is important that the diagnosis be clear because as there is no hemorrhage taking place with a thrombosis, there is no need to keep the person quiet and in bed. Most physicians advocate a régime in which the person starts getting out of bed the very next day. There is no sense in wasting precious time.

As soon as possible, a physiotherapist should move the limbs through a full range of movement on both sides, affected and normal, to maintain joint mobility and preserve normal muscle health. These passive movements are so important that they can

The physiotherapist will patiently teach a person how to move his or her limbs through a full range of movement.

be taught to husbands, wives, children, friends, neighbors, and anyone else who is interested so that they can be performed repeatedly during the day. They should be taught to the person so that they can be practiced while he or she sits in a chair using the sound hand to manipulate the weak hand and arm.

Whenever somebody notices as much as a flicker of returning movement it should be reportd to the physiotherapist, who will devise exercises to encourage it.

Effects of a stroke The side of the body that is damaged in a stroke lies opposite to the side of the brain that has been damaged. This is because all nerves controlling movement and sensation cross from one side of the brain to the other before they go into the spinal cord to travel to other parts of the body. It follows that damage in the left half of the brain produces most of its effects on the right side of the body and vice versa.

Dysarthia is a fairly common disturbance of speech that is not confined to stroke cases. It may consist of slurring of words, but the meaning is usually clear enough to us. In severe strokes, involving both sides of the brain, it may be so severe as to make communication extremely difficult.

Aphasia is a more complicated group of speech disorders and it is rarer than dysarthria, but basically there is a failure in the use of words we employ to name things. These difficulties are characteristic of certain strokes or other destruction of the brain. This can be exceedingly frustrating to a stroke victim; he or she may get very angry at any apparent stupidity, and that of anyone else in not understanding what is being said. Such a person may not understand that his or her speech may be nonsense to us, and relatives who do not understand the situation may think that this is a sign of mental derangement in the person. They have to be reassured that it is only part of the person's stroke problem. Many aphasic people are quite capable of understanding what is said to them, and it is a common and humiliating mistake to speak about them in their presence assuming that they do not understand. Aphasia is a great handicap. Sufferers have to be cured of it by being taught how to read and use words from scratch, as if they were children. This really is an area that should be tackled by an experienced speech therapist.

Dysphagia is a disturbance of swallowing, so that victims are in great danger of choking and inhaling food or drink. This is as terrifying for them as it may be for someone looking on, and when there is doubt about safety in swallowing, doctors may pass a tube into the stomach. The tube may have to be left in place for quite a long time. Usually, safe swallowing returns.

Emotionalism is a very common difficulty for patients who have suffered strokes. They tend to be emotional and to weep when people talk to them or try to help. A few do the reverse and burst out laughing. This is all part of the stroke illness and has occurred because the normal "brakes" that we apply to all our emotions to keep them hidden are released when the brain is damaged. Relatives may quite wrongly suppose that these floods of tears are because they are doing something wrong.

Muscular difficulties The state of the muscles, whether they are tense or floppy, is dependent on whether the nerves to opposing muscles, which bend and straighten joints, are paralyzed. However, when the nerves and muscles recover, they may not be in perfect balance, so the muscles that bend the joint may be stronger than those that straighten the joint. In this case the arm feels tense and may resist movement. When the opposite happens it stays floppy.

Brain failure

Brain failure, or dementia, has been described as "impairment of memory and personality but without impairment of consciousness." This kind of illness can be the result of a number of causes, with variable rates of progression. In the case of the two commonest forms of brain failure, one cause is thought to be the cumulative effect of small strokes over a long period of time. The other is the Alzheimer type, for which there is no known cause. It may run in families and be inherited through genes. A belief still commonly held, though quite wrongly, is that once a patient has been labeled as having dementia, then deterioration is inevitable and early death unavoidable. This is untrue.

Brain failure is one of the greatly underdiagnosed conditions in older people. A survey in the UK has estimated that about 13 percent of the population over the age of seventy-five have a significant degree of brain failure. In a group over the age of eighty, the proportion rises to 22 percent. Cases of pre-senile dementia are not uncommon in the early fifties and there are some cases recorded prior to the age of fifty. Aside from the Alzheimer type, there are many causes of chronic brain failure that are eminently treatable, such as dehydration, drugs, renal failure, an underactive thryoid, diabetes, vitamin B12 deficiency, thiamine deficiency, lack of a good oxygen supply to the brain, sudden isolation, anesthetics, epilepsy, stroke, chronic infections due to conditions like syphilis and poisons in the form of alcohol.

The symptoms of failure

A fairly typical picture of a person suffering from chronic brain failure would be a man between the ages of seventy and eighty. Everyone who is close to him has noted that he has a failure of memory, particularly an inability to deal with recently given information. Sometimes worse than this decline in memory is a decline in initiative, and the quantity and quality of constructive activity. Speech may be difficult, there may be frequent repetitions, and favorite stories and anecdotes out of the long, distant past may recur. To personalize this picture even more, he might have been a proud gardener who has become totally apathetic about his favorite hobby. The garden is overgrown and disordered as the seasons go by unheeded, and the diasarray escalates. A lady who has been a proud housekeeper may have a very untidy kitchen where every surface seems cluttered. For her, life is limited to waking, drinking tea, eating bread and butter, and laying utensils aside unwashed until they have to be used again. Making plans for balanced and varied eating by organizing major shopping expeditions that take account of tomorrow and the rest of the week have become a thing of the past. Conversation hardly exists because an exchange with a neighbor about weather, chatting over recent happenings in the neighborhood, even discussing intimate details with a relative, will gradually deteriorate to nothing but monosyllables and nods.

One of the things frequently noticeable in a person with brain failure is that the mood that has predominated throughout his or her life tends to persist, but such a person has very little flexibility and cannot withstand changes that may be demanded in or outside the home. Sensitive people may therefore feel victimized; a timid person becomes patently fearful, and the life and soul of the party may lose all inhibitions and be bad-tempered and miserable to boot. Any kind of pressure in life that demands a rapid change cannot be dealt with and results in an explosion of hysterical behavior.

Some unrelated conditions may be confused with brain failure. A patient who is very depressed, having been through a traumatic experience such as the loss of a partner, may give the appearance of being demented. Similarly, someone who is suffering from paranoia or any person who lives alone with no visitors, dim lighting and no other means of communication, may behave abnormally and even be diagnosed as demented, though there is immediate improvement when a social program is organized and the person is given more psychological stimulation.

One of the best ways of assessing the amount of brain failure in a person is to ask him or her some very simple questions such as those in the questionnaire below. Any number of different questions could be included.

MENTAL QUESTIONNAIRE

This is useful for relatives who notice any strange behavior in an older person in their family. Many doctors find that it is one of the best methods of assessing the amount of brain failure in somebody.

Name	Mr. John Brown	Name of town	Date of World War I
Age	42 West Street	Recognition of two	(year sufficient)
Time (to nearest hour)	Salem, Oregon	persons	Date of World War II
Time of day	Day of week	(doctor, nurse, etc)	(year sufficient)
Name and address for 5	Date (correct day of	Date of birth (day	Name of present
minutes recall:	month)	and month	president
this should be	Month	sufficient)	Months of year
repeated by the	Year	Place of birth (town)	backward
patient to ensure	Place:	School attended	Count 1-20
that it has been	Type of place (i.e.	Former occupation	Count 20-1
heard correctly:	hospital)	Name of next of kin	

Arthritis

This is one of the oldest diseases known. Paintings done by the Neanderthals more than 40,000 years ago illustrate an arthritic relative who is stooped and walks with bent knees. Arthritis occurs in all races at all ages. Just as most functions in the body begin to show measurable decline around the age of thirty so does joint functions. All of us over thirty-five and possibly over twenty-five have some degree of osteoarthritis. It also occurs in animals.

Osteoarthritis is a thinning, wearing down or roughening of the cartilage that covers the ends of the bones at the joints. This damage may also be complicated by chemical changes in the cartilage that can cause a joint to become inflamed.

Nobody knows exactly why osteoarthritis occurs, but it does become more frequent as we get older and has been described as part of the aging process that affects us all. It is unusual for it to show before middle age, except if there is previous injury or prolonged stress to a joint. Other factors, such as being over-weight and having bad posture, are implicated as causes of the condition. It occurs most frequently in those joints that are subjected to the most stress: knees, hips, ankles, feet and hands.

The cause of arthritis is not clear. The synovial membrane of a joint gradually becomes inflamed and swollen, eventually leading to inflammation of other parts of the joint. The result can be severe disfigurement as shown here.

The main symptoms of arthritis are painful, creaky joints. The small joints of the fingers and toes are affected as well as the bigger, weight-bearing joints that take the most wear and tear during life. One of the most familiar places to see osteoarthritis is the final joints of the fingers and thumb. As a sort of defense against the arthritis, the body quite often builds up little pieces of bone around the joints. These pea-sized swellings at the side of the joints are characteristic of osteoarthritis. They are called Heberden's nodes after the man who first described them.

Far and away the commonest weight-bearing joints to be involved are the knees and hips. In the knee you often can hear a grating sound as the rough cartilages grind together. Later on there may be so much pain that the range of movement of the knee is limited. Then there may be loss of stability in the knee joint. I have often heard people say that "their knee lets them down", and this causes them to fall. Just as the joints build bone to form Heberden's nodes in the fingers, they do in the knee, and it may become swollen and deformed and fluid may collect.

Osteoarthritis

Osteoarthritis of the hip is probably the most disabling type of arthritis because the pain and stiffness interfere so crucially with everyday life. It makes getting out of a chair very difficult, climbing on and off a bus very slow, walking up and down the stairs an act of endurance and getting in and out of the bath quite hazardous.

Sometimes it is difficult to pinpoint osteoarthritis in the hip because pain doesn't always occur there – it is often referred down to the knee. The arthritis progresses in exactly the same way as in the knee. There is, however, one ray of hope for anyone suffering from osteoarthritis of the hip. When the joint becomes very stiff and painful, unable to bear weight and causes disability when walking, an orthopedic surgeon will consider replacing the joint with an artificial one and this can be done whatever your age.

There is no known cure for osteoarthritis. Relief is achieved through the judicious use of analgesics and anti-inflammatory agents. Quite often the initial changes in osteoarthritis cause no symptoms whatsoever, so it is essential that you embark on a life-long program, certainly from your twenties onward of looking after your joints.

If your osteoarthritis is going to be a long-term condition, then your treatment and management should also be viewed in the long term. The mainstay of treatment is pain-killing drugs. Some of the newer ones need not be taken more than once or twice a day, are very effective in relieving pain and help to increase mobility and strength. Physiotherapy is also extremely important in encouraging full movement of the joints thereby

HIP REPLACEMENT

Replacing a damaged hip is very common nowadays – the majority of operations are successful. This is a constantly improving form of treatment, the joints being made of metal or a combination of metal and plastic.

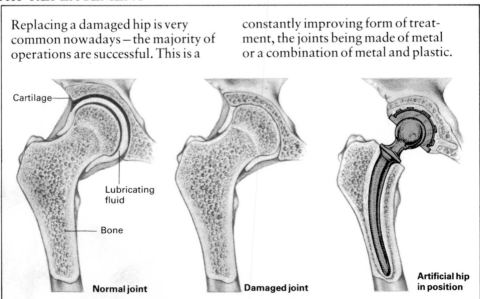

Cartilage

Lubricating fluid

Bone

Normal joint

Damaged joint

Artificial hip in position

increasing the muscle strength in the limbs, leading to greater stability and mobility. A wider range of movements, particularly for the hip and knee joints, helps to distribute forces such as weight-bearing over a larger area of the joint's surface and this helps prevent the gradual deterioration.

Occasionally, shoulders are affected by osteoarthritis so that they become less maneuverable and people suffering from this kind of arthritis are unable to raise their hands up to their head and neck. This means that they lose the ability to dress, to do their hair and to feed themselves.

Rheumatoid arthritis

This is quite different from osteoarthritis. It affects small joints like the fingers, hands, toes, ankles, wrists, shoulders and elbows, whereas osteoarthritis mainly affects large joints. The pain is worse in the morning – the oppposite of osteoarthritis. It's common in women and may appear early in life. Not so with osteoarthritis. There is active inflammation of the lining of the joints (causing them to become inflamed and swollen) and other tissues such as the tendons. It also affects organs other than joints such as the lungs, kidney and heart. It often starts at around forty to fifty years of age, and it is not uncommon for older people to be attacked. Unlike osteoarthritis, we know it is caused by an inflammatory reaction in the joints. Why some of us develop such an inflammation is only partly understood.

Rheumatoid arthritis can start slowly, or it may be very abrupt, even explosive. Very often the first joints to be affected are the finger joints, but not the same as those in osteoarthritis. In the case of rheumatoid arthritis, it is the middle joint of the finger that is affected and it may become very tender, swollen and "spindle-shaped." Later, the arthritis may affect the wrists, the ankles, the knees, the elbows and the shoulders. The main symptoms are pain, stiffness, swelling, and a loss of the full range of movement. During the early stages pain is usually aggravated by movement and lessened by rest. Stiffness is a problem of the disease as it progresses. It is usually worst in the morning (morning stiffness) and following periods of rest. It usually gets better with exercise. In the long term, people with rheumatoid arthritis may suffer loss of appetite, depression, weight loss and a slowly developing anemia. Round, yellowish nodules may develop on the elbow joints and the surfaces of the limbs that are rubbed most.

The aim of treatment is to dispel pain and try to halt inflammation. There are many anti-inflammatory agents now available for the treatment of rheumatoid arthritis. There is a menu for your doctor to choose from and he or she is therefore able to select the medication that is particularly suitable for you.

It is generally agreed among physicians that steroids are hardly ever used for the treatment of rheumatoid arthritis, though they were used to a great extent in the USA in the past.

An important element of physical therapy for rheumatoid arthritis is the maintenance of a very careful balance between rest and activity to keep joints mobile and in shape. If a joint is immobilized for any length of time, especially if it is in a faulty position, severe disability and crippling can occur. In the active phase, however, rest is essential and the joint should always be placed in the optimum position of rest and function. It sometimes can be helpful to wear light PVC splints molded to the limb, especially for the wrists and knees, partly for comfort and partly also to prevent deformities. Sometimes joints are so sore that the patient may feel that the weight of bedclothes is too much and you can relieve this by using a bed cradle.

As the active phase wanes – this may be anything from a few weeks to several months – the physiotherapist will teach you how to carry out a wide variety of exercises to keep you mobile and agile. Generally, your physiotherapist will make sure that the exercises are related to the various activities that you perform during your daily living. They won't only help you when you get home, they will improve joint function and keep your muscles up to strength for a very long time if you keep doing them at your own steady pace.

Gout

Gout is caused by a higher-than-normal level of uric acid in the blood. The first attack of gout usually occurs in middle age, but the kind of gout or arthritis which leads to deformities in the joint is usually seen in older people. The joints that are affected are the big toes, the ankles, fingers, knees, elbows and wrists, the big toe being by far the commonest. An acute attack of gout or arthritis is extremely painful, sometimes described as "exquisitely" painful. It usually lasts about four or five days and then eventually subsides completely, leaving the joint apparently normal. Sometimes, several joints are involved at the same time or in sequence.

If you have a number of episodes of this kind of arthritis, it becomes chronic and may deform the joints and limit their movement. It may also damage your kidneys. The treatment of an acute attack is with a strong anti-inflammatory agent or with special gout medication such as *colchicine*. There are

Avoid rich foods high in protein and eat carbohydrates.

other drugs which can reduce the amount of uric acid in the blood, and they are well tolerated in older people. Long-term management of gout will require a special diet from your doctor which is low in proteins and fortified wines, and possibly a maintenance dose of an anti-gout agent, or a uricosuric agent, to keep the level of uric acid in the blood and joints down to a low level.

Osteoporosis

Dowager's hump
Collapsing vertebrae leaves a rounded back.

As a person grows older, this condition – the thinning of the bone substance – becomes increasingly common. It is found more often and earlier in women than men: 1 out of 5 post-menopausal women will experience this gradual softening of the bones caused by loss of calcium and protein. This condition is sometimes also linked to the thinning and flattening of the spine's vertebral discs, its gradual curvature and loss of height. Colloquially, this condition is known as "dowager's hump" in women.

Prevention lies in getting sufficient exercise and taking calcium and vitamin D supplements; women should do this both before and after menopause.

The management of osteoperosis is well worthwhile in that it may prevent some kinds of arthritis and alleviate others. The most effective treatment for menopausal osteoporosis is hormone replacement therapy (see *Specialist Help*), which restores calcium balance and can stop any weakening of the skeleton, though it will not restore it to its previous condition. In women a régime of female sex hormones will reduce the number of fractures that they suffer on falling and will prevent any further loss in height due to softening and flattening of the vertebral bones. It is also necessary to back this up with a high calcium intake and moderate doses of vitamin D.

Osteomalacia

This is a change in the bone which occurs with increasing age due to insufficient calcium being deposited around the architecture of the bone. While it is not confined to any age group, during old age there are many predisposing conditions which can give rise to it and therefore it is not uncommon. Osteomalacia is more common in women than in men and in one study the ages of patients ranged from thirty-nine to eighty-nine, so you can have it while you are still young.

Anemia

As we get older there are remarkably few changes in the blood. For instance, the normal range of hemoglobin is unaltered by age. As it should be 12.0g/100ml in a younger person, it should be exactly the same in someone older and a low reading should never be though of as simply due to aging. There are two types of anemia that are commonly seen as people get older.

Iron deficiency anemia

This accounts for nearly half of all older anemic patients. The blood becomes deficient in iron mainly due to blood loss from the stomach or intestine due to a hiatus hernia, peptic ulceration, diverticulosis and hemorrhoids. Sometimes it is due to minute ulceration of the stomach wall caused by drugs such as aspirin, and other medications used for the treatment of arthritis. As ulceration may be symptomless you should always take a specimen of your stool to your doctor. If you are anemic, he or she can test it for hidden blood which, if found, suggests that you are losing small quantities from the stomach or intestines. If you have had a partial gastrectomy for the treatment of a peptic ulcer this may contribute to your becoming anemic because of inefficient absorption of iron.

Pernicious anemia

This is due to the poor absorption of vitamin B12 from your food. It is found in 1 in 10 patients who go to their doctors with anemia. Many people in their older years suffer from pernicious anemia without having any symptoms at all.

Treatment

Living with your anemia may mean living with fairly long-term treatment or a treatment that has to be repeated on several occasions. Many patients with iron deficiency anemia relapse after treatment and this is mainly because people forget to or won't take iron tablets by mouth. Make sure that you are not one of these people. A course of six to eight weeks on iron tablets should bring your blood back to normal. However, it may be necessary to continue therapy with iron for another three months so that your body can replenish its iron stores. Iron medication is sometimes complicated by constipation, nausea, and mild discomfort at the top of the abdomen, though these side-effects may be reduced by always taking the iron tablet after a meal. There is no harm in halving the dose for a little while until discomfort subsides. Occasionally it may be necessary for you to get iron by injection as this gives a faster rise in your hemoglobin level.

Pernicious anemia may be quite severe and you may have to go into the hospital to have a special blood transfusion. You are committed to having injections of vitamin B12 for the rest of your life. When you start the treatment you have an injection every other day for two weeks, which will correct the anemia and replenish your body's stores of the vitamin. After that you will only need one smaller injection every three months. Supportive therapy for both of these kinds of anemia is obviously to take plenty of food rich in iron.

Parkinson's disease

About 1 percent of the population over the age of sixty has Parkinson's disease to one degree or another. It is due to biochemical and structural changes in certain parts of the brain that control our movements so that they flow smoothly and are well coordinated.

A person with Parkinsonism has a combination of tremor, muscle stiffness and a noticeable slowness of movement. The tremor is always worst when he or she is relaxed, and improves when he or she is engaged in some kind of activity. The tremor of Parkinsonism can be controlled by carrying a newspaper or glass in the hand that trembles most. Such a person's face is often expressionless, arms motionless, and the walk is a shuffling gait without swinging of the arms. The body is bent forward with the arms held rigidly at the sides. The person rushes along with small, shuffling steps – a kind of battle to keep up with him- or herself. There may be excessive production of saliva, and the skin may be oily due to overactivity of the sebaceous glands.

The treatment of Parkinsonism was revolutionized by the introduction of *L-dopa*, which relieves some of the biochemical abnormalities in the brain. It is very effective in controlling tremor, rigidity and difficulties with movement. L-dopa does not cure Parkinsonism, it only alleviates it. Nor should it blind you to the importance of good physiotherapy and occupational therapy. Walking has to be practiced and lost skills re-learned.

Hypothermia

This is a mysterious condition in which the body loses heat and is unable to maintain the temperature balance necessary for normal working. It has been known for many years that even young men exposed to intense cold for long periods experience a severe fall in body-core temperature (the temperature of the vital organs such as the heart, the lungs, the kidneys, the liver and the brain), but it is only in the last fifteen years that it has become clear how widespread this condition is among the elderly. Instead of the usual 37°C (98.6°F), temperatures have been recorded as low as 21°C (78.5°F) and there have been many cases in the range between 24° and 32°C (75°-90°F).

At one time it was thought that hypothermia was the result of falls and lying in the cold, and of course these cases do occur, especially if an older person breaks a limb when falling and has to lie there because he or she cannot move. The same thing can happen after falling at night in a cold bedroom, if the victim doesn't think to pull the bedclothes on top of him or herself.

However, recent research has revealed that there are other circumstances in which hypothermia appears. At first there may be a serious illness which, instead of raising the temperature, lowers it, as in sudden pneumonia, and this usually means that the outlook is grave. It can also happen after a heart attack, after using certain drugs, and during strokes. But a very old person sitting quite still in a chair for several hours is sometimes found to have severe hypothermia, as if the heat-regulating mechanisms in the body are suddenly thrown out of action totally without warning.

Symptoms of hypothermia

Hypothermia can cause deaths and is more dangerous than the fall in temperature would suggest. A small drop can be a danger sign in an old person. It is therefore imperative that anyone who deals with older people should know of it and be wary in suspicious circumstances. As a relative of an older person you should be aware of the signs: a cold room and lack of activity, slow and slurred speech, a slow pulse, a small amount of confusion but no shivering. A victim may be drowsy but he or she does not look cold. The face and hands may often look warm and red or purple-red, which tends to throw everyone off the scent. The extremities feel cold but so do the hands of many people in cold weather. A crucial point is that the places that are normally always warm, like the abdominal wall or the insides of the thighs, are as cold as marble.

An ordinary clinical thermometer will read as low as 35°C (90.5°F) at its lowest mark. It doesn't, however, give a reading

235

of the body temperature if it is less than this so it may give a false impression that there is no urgency. If you have an older person living in the house, or even for yourself, you should make sure that you have a thermometer covering the range of 24° to 40°C (75° to 104°F). The best way to check a low reading is to place a low-reading thermometer in the rectum for five minutes.

Emergency treatment for hypothermia is still not satisfactory. Rapid external warming is dangerous and can cause death. Warming should be carefully controlled at no more than 1°F rise an hour, simply by putting a few blankets on the victim and keeping the room warm but not applying any heat directly.

However, the real answer to hypothermia is practical. Firstly, we must do all we can to help older people keep warm by good housing, good clothes, enough money for fuel, plenty of hot food and, above all, by encouraging them, even bullying them, to move about and generate some of their own internal heat. Secondly, by always being on the alert for the condition, which comes on slowly and takes us unawares, and which is so very dangerous. Then it is possible that we might catch the temperature before it falls too low. If the temperature drops no lower than 32°C it may be possible to warm the person up at home, but ask your doctor's advice in any case. At any lower temperature the person should be taken into the hospital as quickly as possible where he or she can be treated by experts.

Preventing hypothermia
It's possible to become dangerously cold without realizing it — living environment should have a minimum temperature of 20°C (68°F). This wrap is ideal for long winter evenings.

Diabetes (diabetes mellitus)

Do-it-yourself tests
Twice a day you should test your urine for glucose levels. Drop a tablet into a sample of your urine and match it to the color chart.

There are two main forms of diabetes: one comes on at any stage and is due to a failure to produce insulin in the pancreas; the other is more common as we get older and is due to a "relative" lack of insulin (not a true deficiency) made worse by a high carbohydrate diet, obesity and increasing age. As with other glands in the body, the pancreas becomes less efficient as we age. The amount of insulin it produces, therefore, can become insufficient to cope with the amount of sugar in the blood and diabetes can result. This is especially likely to happen if you are overweight. There is a school of thought which believes that diabetes is the only disease related to excess weight. Heredity, too, plays an important part as nearly a third of diabetics over forty have a family history of the disease.

The symptoms of diabetes are increased thirst, passing large quantities of urine, loss of weight and weakness, but these are rarely present in the more elderly cases and occasionally diabetes is confused with some other conditions such as cholecystitis, kidney failure and heart failure.

Diabetes increases the risk of several other diseases if it is not treated properly and kept under good control. Kidney disease, coronary artery disease, cerebrovascular disease and narrowing of the blood vessels to the legs preventing walking for any distance are all commoner in diabetics than in the average population. So are damage to the retina of the eye, glaucoma and damage to nerves in the limbs and face, which cause blunting of sensation and weakening of muscle strength. Atherosclerosis develops twice as fast in diabetics as in the rest of the population; and coronary artery disease is twice as common in diabetic men and five times as common in diabetic women.

Not all diabetics need treatment with insulin. Diabetes that begins in middle or older age can often be controlled simply by weight reduction. For many others, diabetes can be controlled by taking tablets orally. If you are a diabetic always consult your doctor about cuts, abrasions and bruises on your extremities, and about any serious damage. You should visit the podiatrist regularly and have annual examinations (or more frequent checks if your eyesight is deteriorating) by an ophthalmologist.

If you are sensible you can expect to continue leading a full and healthy life. Do have regular medical check-ups to see that everything is fine and follow the timetable of meals and snacks that your doctor advises. Self-discipline is vital.

Hyperthyroidism and Hypothyroidism

These are the two commonest disorders of the thyroid gland: hyperthyroidism describes an overactive thyroid and hypothyroidism an underactive gland. Overproduction of thyroid hormones is commonest between the ages of twenty and fifty. It hardly ever occurs in those who are over seventy. Very often the disease goes undiagnosed because its symptoms may be different from normal with aging.

Symptoms in the elderly primarily affect the heart and give rise to things like palpitations and insufficient heart function. Mental symptoms such as depression and confusion are fairly common and so is weight loss. Sometimes the most outstanding symptom is a feeling of weakness and fatigue. Contrary to the way it affects younger people, the basal metabolic rate need not be raised.

Hypothyroidism may be less common than hyperthyroidism. Mild cases probably go unnoticed, as the sufferers and the people around them think the symptoms are the result of normal aging. The symptoms are the same in younger and older patients. Most victims suffer from feeling the cold; their voices become lower and croaky; their faces may appear puffy; they suffer from physical and mental sluggishness; they are often constipated.

One of the reasons why this condition is missed is that the full picture may take a very long time to develop and therefore gradual change is accepted. It is essential that you take vague symptoms that worry you to your doctor, and if he or she doesn't mention it, ask about the possibility of an underactive thyroid. Only in this way will you help to prevent serious complications developing.

Diverticulosis

This, the presence of diverticula, and diverticulitis, inflammation in the diverticula, are rare in young adults and tend to increase from age forty onwards. If you are prone to diverticular disease, the overall number may increase with age. Women are affected more often than men.

Diverticula are tiny balloons of intestinal lining that burst through the muscular wall of the intestine. They are usually about 1 or 2 centimeters long. Fecal material can collect either in or at the mouth of the tiny diverticulum and block it off. It may then become infected and ulcerate. The commonest symptoms are bouts of bleeding with constipation, diarrhea and left-sided lower abdominal pain in between. Most complications are rare.

To look after diverticular disease, you should go on a high residue diet and possibly obtain antibiotics from your doctor. You can bulk up your diet by using bran on food and in cooking, and eating some stringy vegetables like cabbage or parsnip each day. The skins of peas and beans are good too, and have some fresh fruit with the skin still on, say an apple or a pear, every day. This is exactly opposite to the kind of diet recommended when I was a student, but it's absolutely correct.

Ulcers

Duodenal and gastric ulcers reach their peak in middle age. In younger people pain can be the predominating symptom, but as we get older there may be no symptoms at all, or they may be unexpected, like weight loss, anemia and painless vomiting. The first symptoms of an ulcer, at say sixty, may result from chronic ulcer developed at forty. If an ulcer appears for the first time when you are sixty, the outlook for a complete cure is very good. Very often the symptoms of an ulcer are very mild, such as a loss of appetite, a general feeling of malaise and some slight discomfort at the lower end of the breastbone. The temptation is to treat yourself with antacids, which can lead to a dangerous delay in an accurate diagnosis.

The most serious complication of a long-standing peptic ulcer is hemorrhage. If you have a peptic ulcer you should watch more and more carefully as you grow older for a black, tarry stool, which almost certainly means that you had a bleed from your stomach. If you ever vomit blood, be it bright red or very dark red, you should contact your doctor immediately. Very small hemorrhages over the long term can lead to quite a severe iron deficiency anemia (see page 233). If you are becoming anemic, a peptic ulcer is slightly different in older patients than in younger people. Bed-rest and a special "gastric diet" have been shown to be fairly ineffective in older people. In the long term, smoking should be avoided; antacids can be used to relieve the pain, but not freely – only in the quantities prescribed.

Nowadays there are some newer treatments which promote

healing. One highly effective medication is called *cimetidine*. This treatment is only available on prescription and when you are on it you should be carefully monitored by your doctor with regular check-ups.

Hiatus hernia

This becomes more common as we get older because the tissues inside our bodies become slack. When the opening in the diaphragm, which lets the gullet (esophagus) pass through from the chest into the abdomen, becomes slightly enlarged, it is possible for a small part of the stomach to slide up through into the chest. This encourages reflux of the acid contents of the stomach, which in turn may cause some soreness, inflammation and ulceration at the end of the gullet. However, the majority of hiatus hernias present no symptoms and are of no medical consequence.

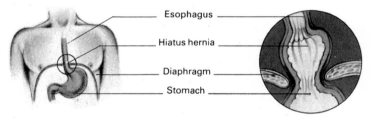

Esophagus

Hiatus hernia

Diaphragm

Stomach

Hiatus hernia occurs when the abdominal portion of the esophagus protrudes upwards through the hiatus into the chest-cavity.

It's quite common as we get older, especially if we are overweight. The main symptom is usually heartburn or perhaps regurgitation of acid fluid.

If you suffer with symptoms such as heartburn associated with the hiatus hernia, you should sleep with the head of your bed raised and avoid stooping. Reduce the size of your meals, especially those you eat late in the evening. If you are overweight you should diet. Other than these things, you can get drug treatment from your doctor, cimetidine, which is also used for the treatment of peptic ulceration. You should take antacids prescribed by your doctor four times a day after meals. This will relieve many of the symptoms due to a reflux of esophagus. In the rare cases when symptoms persist your doctor may advise surgery to repair it. This involves a relatively simple operation after which you will be able to continue with normal activities within a few days.

Mouth disorders

It is not uncommon for older people to complain of a sore tongue or mouth ulcers. These may be due to trauma from sharp or irregular broken teeth as well as other causes such as a vitamin deficiency, anemia and possibly other blood diseases, as well as plain ordinary aphthous ulceration and infection. Any sore or ulcer that persists should be evaluated by your doctor.

Aphthous ulceration, which can be quite extensive as we get older, will respond to pellets containing hydrocortisone, which can be sucked. These are very effective in relieving pain.

Sometimes a sore tongue is due to drug therapy or to an infection in the mouth. The commonest infection by far is monilia (candida albicans), which is known to most people as thrush. It is quite common if antibiotics have been taken for long periods by mouth. If you can see white patches on your tongue, throat or on the inside of your cheeks, it should make you suspicious. Ask your doctor to confirm the diagnosis and he or she will take small specimens for culture from the mouth and throat and give you *nystatin* as pills, lozenges or mouth wash.

Jaundice

Not an affliction found particularly in older people, jaundice is a fairly common sign of liver disease. It can be part of an inflammation of the liver such as occurs with infectious hepatitis; it can be due to the effect of toxic drugs, or cirrhosis, among other things. Jaundice is not necessarily a sinister sign. More than half of its sufferers will recover completely from their liver compaints.

Jaundice can often be due to a gall stone blocking the exit from the gall bladder. An older person who has one or more attacks of jaundice due to this cause, confirmed by special X-ray tests, should be considered for surgery to remove the blockage. A new method of treatment is to try to dissolve gall stones of the cholesterol type by giving medication in the form of bile salts. Treatment is continued for about six months.

Cirrhosis

This is the terminal state of liver injury and decay. The liver becomes very small, hard and lumpy, and is unable to function properly. It is irreversible. Alcoholism (see page 61) with its

241

long-term dietary deficiencies is far and away the most important and serious cause of cirrhosis. The liver can be rested and further damage sometimes halted by giving up drinking. Continued assault to the liver will inevitably lead to liver failure, coma and death.

Gall stones

Gall stones are responsible for about a quarter of all attacks of abdominal pain. In the fifties and sixties gall stones are more common in women than in men, but after seventy there is no difference in the sexes.

The most common symptoms of gall stones are nausea, indigestion, a feeling of queasiness after eating fatty meals, vomitting and pain. Gall stone pain usually occurs just below the edge of the rib cage on the right-hand side and it may go up to the point of the right shoulder.

Gall stones can be removed by surgery, but for some patients over the age of sixty doctors may prefer a more conservative approach. If you are overweight you will be asked to lose weight. Then you should avoid all fatty foods and you should take antacids. You can eat carbohydrates and a lot of protein, however. Surgical removal of the gall bladder, with the gall stones is considered to end frequent mild attacks or when the condition is acute, very severe or life-threatening.

Antacids Antacids neutralize acid in the stomach and so relieve indigestion and heartburn. They also control the pain from a duodenal ulcer.
● Read the constituents on the packet before purchasing. Avoid anything that contains more the 115 milligrams of sodium in the maximum daily dose.
● Don't take anything that contains aspirin, phenacetin, or caffeine as these may irritate the stomach; phenacetin can damage the kidneys when taken in the long term.
● Antacids that contain calcium carbonate can cause constipation and raise the calcium levels too high. They can also promote production of acid in the stomach.
● The two safest antacids are aluminum hydroxide and magnesium hydroxide. Aluminum hydroxide has no limits on dosage and it is slow in its action, but it usually gives prolonged relief. Its major undesirable effect is constipation. Magnesium hydroxide is efficient and it is safe but it does cause diarrhea.
● Anyone with a kidney problem should only use antacids under the care of a doctor.

Constipation

This can be a common accompanient of aging, but it doesn't have to be. The causes are many and varied: an unbalanced diet with lack of fiber and bulk; lack of exercise; overusing aperients and ignoring the emptying reflex. Another problem is the psychological attitude of many people today that a daily bowel movement is essential for health. This, of course, is not true, but as people become older and more self-absorbed in their bodies, this preoccupation with constipation increases so it seems that nearly every elderly person complains about it.

No laxative, aperient or cathartic is perfect or harmless, and it is generally thought that their regular use can do little good and a lot of harm. One of the dangerous effects of laxatives is to prevent absorption of important vitamins from the diet. The body's mineral balance can also be seriously affected by laxatives. Most over-the-counter preparations containing kaolin and pectin should be left on the shelf because their effectiveness is questionable. They could be said to be a waste of money because they do very little good.

Occasionally, constipation in older people results in fecal impaction. The feces become hard and relatively immobile due to the slow passage of bowel contents and the excessive absorption of fluids in the large bowel. Then the hardened feces become molded by the movements of the bowel and stay firmly in one place. As we get older we become less aware of the bowel reflex when the rectum becomes full. Sometimes the feces become round and pebble-like so that they may even resemble gall stones. In almost 100 percent of cases the feces impact in the rectum.

Treatment for constipation

As far as managing your long-term constipation is concerned you should be reassured that a regular bowel action can be achieved with the appropriate treatment. First of all you must drink quite a lot of fluid to keep the motions soft. You must add additional fiber to your daily diet if it primarily contains refined carbohydrates like bread, cake and chocolate biscuits. You can do this by simply adding bran to semi-liquid dishes such as porridge and cereal, and you might even try putting bran into your cake mixes. Alert your doctor that you have a tendency to be constipated as there are certain drugs which are known to make it worse and these should be avoided. Only very gentle laxatives should be used for the treatment of long-term constipation, but if the feces have become impacted it may be necessary to use suppositories or an enema, repeated if this is needed, to dislodge the hardened stool.

Hemorrhoids

These are present in the majority of people over the age of fifty. They can be internal, inside the anus, or external, projecting from the anus. Hemorrhoids are really varicose veins of the rectum and they are caused by prolonged over-use of laxatives or enemas, having to strain at stool, chronic coughing, or, in women, by pregnancy.

There are many preparations on the market which claim to treat itching, swollen tissues and promote healing. However, there is very little evidence that these products actually do what the advertisements say they do. Always get a specific treatment from your doctor prior to using over-the-counter preparation.

Treatment for hemorrhoids

This comes in two forms: suppositories and ointments. Nearly all suppositories contain local anaesthetics such as *lignocaine* or *benzocaine*. These should never be applied to the skin as they may cause an allergy. Chemicals that shrink the swollen tissue are also available – one such is *ephedrine* – and there are also antiseptics. Suppositories frequently move up the rectum after they have been inserted, and therefore move away from the area they are supposed to be treating.

One of the best ways to treat hemorrhoids is to get at the root cause, for instance a chronic chest cough, and at chronic constipation or laziness of the bowel by bulking and softening the stool. Doing this is far more effective. Surgical treatment can also be effective in several cases.

Cataracts

All of us, it has been said, would develop cataracts if we lived long enough. The stage beyond yellowing is the formation of opacities in the lens so that it is no longer transparent. This interferes with the passage of light to the back of the eye, the

A cataract is the progressive clouding up of the jelly-like substance which forms the lens of the eye. In severe cases, the total lens may be affected, making the pupil in front white. Effects on vision differ depending on the extent and location of the cataract but they can blur direct vision.

White pupil   **Normal eye**   Cataract in lens   Lens

retina. Depending on the number and severity of the opacities, a person will find his or her vision blurred and dim. From the age of forty onwards, nearly all of us find that we need a brighter and brighter light to read in.

Lens opacities cannot be dissolved away, but surgical treatment is extremely effective and safe. The lens with the cataract is removed. This is an operation normally performed under local anesthetic but fearful patients may require a general anesthetic. Such an eye becomes very far-sighted and lenses are required to correct the vision; these may be glasses, contact lenses or plastic lens implants.

As cataracts are eminently treatable and will not lead to blindness, there is no need for anyone to be needlessly frightened by the entirely false belief that cataracts will be severely disabling. Though your vision will not be completely restored to normal – cataract glasses have quite thick lenses so that objects appear magnified and seem closer than they really are – it is just a question of your adjusting.

Glaucoma

The second most common disorder of the eyes as we grow older is glaucoma. This is a condition of an abnormally high fluid pressure within the eye. It has nothing to do with cancer or high blood pressure and so it need not spell doom. Go immediately to your doctor when you suffer symptoms so that they are recognized and given proper care, attention and treatment. If you are alert to the first symptoms of glaucoma, even the smallest loss of vision can be prevented.

The symptoms of glaucoma include blurred vision, dull pain in the eye, watering of the eyes, nausea and headache. Another early warning sign is the appearance of "haloes" around electric lights. Glaucoma usually starts after forty, and leads

When the eye is normal (right) fluid, aqueous humor circulates in order to drain it via a drainage channel. If the channel becomes blocked (center) there is a build-up of fluid. An iridectomy can be performed on the eye to produce an artificial channel (far right) through which the fluid can drain.

Drainage channel

Obstruction

Artificial channel

to the gradual loss of peripheral vision if it goes untreated. This means that we find ourselves bumping into things or not seeing things on either side of us; not seeing a passing car is a common complaint. All this results in "tunnel vision". If glaucoma is left untreated, the peripheral vision dwindles until we can only see what is directly in front of us. This can eventually lead to total blindness.

Acute (angle-closure) glaucoma is treated by surgery that removes part of the iris to allow pressure to be equalized; chronic (wide-angle) glaucoma is treated medically with eye-drops or tablets that reduce the secretion into the eye.

Since glaucoma is easily detected, it is very important that from our forties onward we have annual eye examinations to check the angle between the iris and the cornea and the internal position of the eye.

Varicose veins

This condition is not restricted to a particular age group, but it is quite common in older women who have borne children. Varicose veins are aggravated by occupations that involve a lot of standing. Such veins are raised and twisted and stand out from the back of the leg between the knee and ankle. They have very thin walls and contain a large volume of blood so that they can be easily damaged and may cause hemorrhaging.

If you have varicose veins, you should wear elastic stockings or support hose, especially if you are doing a lot of standing. Take them off when you go to bed or sit down with your feet up, or when you go out for a walk. These stockings help to keep blood from pooling in the legs. Elevating the legs whenever possible is also helpful.

Varicose veins can be treated with injections containing irritating solutions that produce inflammation. The body responds to such inflammation by creating scar tissue, which stops the high-pressure backflow of blood through the vein and reduces swelling. The first treatment for seriously overweight patients is weight reduction. Those with extensive varicose veins or ones which extend to the groin may need to be treated surgically. Two procedures – stripping and tying off – are available. Stripping involves passing a wire along the length of the vein, and tying off involves cutting out the vein.

Irritating dry brown patches may appear on the lower part of the leg, which can form into an ulcer. These ulcers must be treated immediately by a medically qualified person before they develop into something more dangerous.

PUTTING ON SUPPORT STOCKINGS

It is important that you see your doctor before using elastic stockings or support hose because in some instances they can be dangerous. They should have open toes – to allow your toes to breathe comfortably.

Then, slowly draw the rest of the stocking over your leg, smoothing out all the creases as you go. This is a good deal easier if you wear pimply rubber gloves.

Apply a little talcum powder to your leg and then turn the stocking inside-out down to its foot and pull the foot portion over your toes.

A thigh-length elastic stocking with a waist attachment for a man.

Shingles

Shingles, caused by herpes zoster, can bring real disability as we get older. It is an infection of the nerve roots by a virus that is linked to childhood chickenpox. It is remarkably common among late middle-aged and older people and it can make them quite ill over a long period.

It causes intense pain in the area that has been affected. This is then followed by a severely blistered rash, which takes 10 to 14 days to disappear. The rash is distributed in a sharply marked band over the area of the affected nerve.

In the elderly the head and face, including the eye (if your eye is affected, seek expert advice from an ophthalmologist urgently), are quite often affected and the pain can be intense. Worse still, the pain or acute tenderness may persist for many months or even years after the rash has gone. To make things still worse, treatment of this post-herpetic pain is notoriously difficult.

One of the things which can be done is to make sure you avoid going near small children suffering from chickenpox – even your grandchildren. If your eye is affected by shingles, seek expert advice from an ophthalmologist urgently.

Falls or drop attacks

Falls become more common as we get older. The following are some of the causes:
- Accidents (about a third of all falls);
- Insufficient bloodflow to the brain;
- Drop attacks;
- Heart and blood vessel disorders (such as high blood pressure, irregular heart beats, coronary thrombosis);
- Dehydration;
- Anemia;
- Osteoarthosis;
- Any disorder that makes the gait shuffling and stumbling (e.g. Parkinsonism);
- Seizures.

Accidental falls

Cervical neck collar
This is comfortable to wear and it will prevent any sudden neck movement.

These may be caused by minor paralysis or stiff joints, but more often they are due to poor home conditions such as worn-out floor coverings, trailing wires, and insecure stair carpets and rods. All these, coupled with failing vision and poor lighting, increase the risk of our falling, especially if we are inclined to wander. As we get older, our control of swaying gets less, and this means that we find it more difficult to correct a false movement once we have committed ourselves to it.

Insufficient blood supply to the brain can occur as the result of an osteoarthritic change in the vertebral bones of the neck. The blood vessels supplying the part of the brain that controls many of our movements are filled from an artery that runs through a canal between the bones. Osteoarthritis in the neck vertebrae can cause narrowing of the bony canal. Classically, it causes a sudden loss of balance directly following rapid neck movements, and one of the ways of controlling attacks is to limit the amount of movement of the head and neck. If your doctor recommends it, you can wear a full cervical collar during the day and at night substitute it for a soft collar.

Drop attacks

These can occur in anyone, including the young, but the kind experienced by people as they get older is a specific entity. First of all the falls are often sudden. Some older people will simply say that they found themselves on the ground, and they may have had considerable difficulty in getting up although they seem to be able to move all their limbs perfectly well. Once they are standing, however, they can walk away as if nothing had happened. Doctors think that this kind of drop attack is most often caused by temporary loss of the mechanism that regulates the flow of blood and oxygen to the brain. It appears to be precipitated by prolonged standing and can usually be prevented by periodic movements of the legs, such as a shifting of weight. The reflexes can be restored fairly rapidly if we can press the soles of our feet against a wall.

One of the most serious side-effects of a drop attack is that it destroys confidence and prevents going out, even locally to the store. Occasionally, following a drop attack, a person is unable to get back onto his or her feet. This is risky if a person lives alone, so he or she should know how to get up from the floor without help.

Trigeminal neuralgia

This excessively painful condition is almost unknown under the age of fifty. It is a condition causing severe "lightning" flashes of pain in parts of the face supplied by the trigeminal nerve, namely the cheeks, nose and mouth. Attacks are typically brought on by cold, wind, movement, eating and touching the trigger area during shaving, etc. Quite often a victim feels in real dread at the possibility of firing off an attack. He or she may even not wash his or face, or eat, lest it start off the pain.

This is a difficult condition to treat but one new drug, *carbamazepine*, is sometimes helpful. If the pain is unremitting, it is possible, under general anesthesia, to inject a small amount of an anesthetic into the nerve root, which may keep the person completely free of pain for about two years. Then the injection has to be repeated.

Headaches

Any kind of new headache must be carefully investigated. It is not always true, as some people say, that migraine sufferers improve and have fewer attacks as they grow older. A headache could be symptomatic of several things: that a stroke is about to occur; or depression which needs treatment; or renal failure; or as a side effect of certain drugs. Most important of all, a persistent headache in the forehead or temples raises the possibility of an inflammation of the blood vessel that runs up the side of the face and often looks a bity lumpy and tortuous as we get older. This can be treated very effectively with new drugs, so help from the doctors should be sought. The most common is still the tension headache.

249

Special hazards and unexpected happenings

One of the things that happens to our bodies as we get older is an inability to cope with change and debility. So a severe fall that puts us to bed may be complicated by a chest infection if we get a minor cold. In our younger days our lungs would have been capable of putting up a stronger defense.

Leg vein thrombosis

Clotting of the blood in the deep veins of the legs is a well-known risk of general and gynecological surgery, but recent research has shown that it occurs so often as to be frightening and it is worthwhile doing anything we can to prevent it from happening in the first place.

Basically, thrombosis (clotting) is caused by a lessening of the pumping action of the leg muscles which normally send the venous blood back to the heart. The blood becomes static. This is more likely to happen as we get older because we may lie quite still for a long time. In addition, existing heart disease may have reduced our blood circulation – a contributing cause of a leg vein thrombosis.

Such a condition is bad in itself, but one of its worst complications is that the clot may become detached from the leg, so that it passes to the heart, and thence immediately to the lungs where it will cause failure of the blood supply there. This condition, *pulmonary embolus*, will cause a sudden urgent attack of breathlessness, blueness of the skin and chest pain. These attacks can be fatal in people of any age, but the older we are, the greater the danger.

The warning signs that a thrombosis may be occurring in one of our legs is that there will be swelling and the legs will be of disparate sizes. There may be a blue discoloration of the skin, and coldness. Another common symptom is pain in the calf and along the inner side of the thigh. You should know what to look for and to pick up early signs and keep a watch out for them. To prevent clots, you can keep your legs moving – bending and straightening your knees for say, ten to fifteen times every hour, though only a little exercise can be enough. You can also do leg and foot movements of all kinds while you are in bed and leg swinging over the edge of the bed. A bed cradle will help because your legs will then not be restricted, but pillows should not be put under your knees or thighs. Breathing exercises and taking plenty of fluids also help.

A bed cradle will prevent your bedclothes pressing on any painful areas on your legs.

Superficial thrombo-phlebitis This is quite a different condition. It is an inflammation of the veins near the surface of the skin, and such an area becomes swollen, tender, red and warm. It does not carry the risk of embolism and for this reason is much less serious.

Pneumonia

Older people who lie down for any length of time are susceptible to pneumonia. This is due to a combination of pooling of the secretions in the lung, the possibility of infection, and poor ventilation because of shallow breathing. It is a very good reason for trying to keep older people out of the hospital because it can spread around a ward of frail people like an infectious disease. Smoking lowers lung defenses against infection.

Pneumonia can occur quite severely in a matter of hours and your doctor may advise that you go into hospital for a while but he or she will certainly advise cough medicines and antibiotics. The flu vaccine, by helping protect against the flu, can reduce the risk of pneumonia.

Dehydration

This is one of the diseases of deprivation. It is also one of the hazards of being ill. We have seen already that the older we get the smaller the reserves in our kidneys, and they need ample water to work. Many older people get into a habit of drinking very little, especially women. Some people with a tendency to be incontinent imagine that they will lessen the problem by drinking less. In fact, the reverse is true. If there is very little urine flushing out the bladder, there is a tendency for it to become infected and for cystitis to develop.

Older people who go to bed feeling ill may not feel like getting up to make themselves a drink. The danger of dehydration is much worse if there is diarrhea and vomiting. In an older person, dehydration will come on all the more quickly and there may be a very serious deficiency of water and salt. Both invalids, and those who care for them, often do not understand the need for fluids. Fears and instincts about incontinence may suggest cutting down fluid intake. When you are ill you may have a constant battle with yourself to drink enough but both you and the people who look after you must win it.

Epileptic attacks

It's a good idea if you are an epileptic to wear a bracelet with the condition printed on the back. This will alert people if you have a sudden attack.

Most people suffering from epilepsy live normal lives with the attacks well controlled by medications. However, fits can come for the first time as we get older, and they must be fully investigated. Many appear to have no known cause, but certain things have to be ruled out. One must always be on the alert for a stroke or a heart attack that first appears as a fit.

The epilepsy may take two forms: *grand mal* and *petit mal*. The major epileptic attacks usually start with sudden unconsciousness, rigid muscles, breath holding and a bluish-gray color of the skin, and then jerking movements which gradually subside. It is essential to keep the airways clear. Minor epilepsy is momentary. The person may stop what he or she is doing, look vacant and then carry on. This kind of epilepsy is not very common in older people but when it does occur the absences can last much longer than in younger people.

Hysterical fits

These are quite different in cause but may be difficult to distinguish from epilepsy. Sometimes they may be a way for an older person to register a protest against something that displeases him or her, but it is not put on just for show. An hysterical person does not consciously understand the reasons behind the attack. He or she is quite likely to be noisy, dramatic, make strange movements or writhe on the floor. However, the person usually never hurts him or herself.

Simple fainting

Fainting happens quite commonly in older people as a result of pain, oppressive heat, psychological stress, severe anemia or unexpected internal bleeding. If none of these conditions is at the root of the problem, recovery is usually quick, though not as quick as in younger people. Fainting should never be dismissed lightly in later life, because it usually has a specific reason and treatment may be needed, so you should ask your doctor's advice as soon as you possibly can.

Little strokes

People with narrowing of the arteries of the brain are sometimes liable to have attacks where they may feel a weakness of a limb or loss of vision, lose their speech, or perhaps feel giddy and faint, but the attack passes away very quickly. They are alarming for everyone and they may be an early sign of a more serious and lasting stroke. Anyone who has such an attack should get medical attention promptly.

Abnormal hypoglycemic attacks

These attacks are due to a *serious* fall in blood sugar and when they occur the victim feels cold, sweats and becomes unconscious very rapidly. Attacks occur in diabetics (see page 237) who have been given too much insulin or who are not eating the full diet that has been described for them. Hypoglycemic attacks can, of course, occur in diabetics of any age, but they are of special importance in later life because often heart attacks and strokes come on at the same time. Hypoglycemia must be carefully avoided and it is better for older diabetics to show just a little sugar when their urine is tested to stay on the safe side.

It has become fashionable to claim to suffer a hypoglycemic attack whenever one feels dizzy, lightheaded and weak. Physiological hypoglycemia, that is when we are hungry, needs no treatment. It is self-correcting and should not be interfered with. Medically correctable hypoglycemia is very rare, and should only be treated by a physician.

Vertigo

Vertigo is one of the most common of all our symptoms as we get older and very often the feelings are difficult to describe. The older we are, the greater the chance of our experiencing vertigo. Women are more likely affected by this condition than men.

There are many possible causes and often we never get to the root of the matter. Wax in the ears, ear disease, high and low blood pressure and also certain drugs are among the commonest, and there are links between vertigo and deafness, and one particular type called *Ménière's disease*, which has a preponderancy in people, particularly men, over the age of

253

about forty-five or fifty. Ménière's disease is an acute and violent type of giddiness in which the patient has a sensation of spinning and vomiting and every movement is a nightmare. It is due to disease in the balancing organ of the inner ear, and can be treated successfully with certain new drugs from your doctor.

Accidents

Statistics show that as we get older, we are more susceptible to accidents. And for the older population especially, accidents can have serious consequences, sometimes causing disability and even death. In fact, accidents are among the top ten leading causes of death for people aged sixty-five to seventy-five. Those common accidents with potentially fatal consequences include falls, death by fire and pedestrian deaths caused by motor vehicles.

However, there is a silver lining to these statistics; the death rate from accidents among those in the sixty-five-and-over age group has fallen dramatically in the last two decades. This may be due, at least in part, to the growing public awareness of the need to stay fit, mobile and alert as we grow older. With proper precautions, many accidents can indeed be prevented. Most fatal accidents in this age group, for example, occur in the home. By anticipating our changing needs realistically, we can install safety conditions in the home thereby preventing many common accidents.

What specifically causes the rise in accidents in older people?

Deteriorating vision, hearing and balance, combined with dizziness, the possibility of drop attacks, unsteady gait, less mobile joints and stiff muscles, all contribute to accidents. Drugs, of course, may also disturb our balance, bring on symptoms of Parkinsonism, affect our hearing and make us unsteady on our feet. Some medications have been blamed for causing accidents.

Accidents involving older people seem to occur at a particular time of day — most of them between 6 a.m. and 12 noon. This corresponds to getting up and out of bed, dressing, and the period of greatest activity for most people. Accidents then decrease during the afternoon hours when many of us will be taking a rest, and there is a moderate increase between 5 and 9 p.m., which corresponds to dinner and going to bed. Very few accidents are reported between 9 p.m. and 6 a.m., when we are probably in bed. Of those that do occur during the night, about

30 percent are due to falls when the person tries to get out of bed. Of these, 15 percent are when the person reaches for an object on the bedside table and more than half while the person is walking in the room or to the bathroom.

This emphasizes the importance of vigilantly taking precautions to prevent accidents.

Burns and scalds

Burns and scalds are so frequent in older people living at home that everyone should be taught about preventive measures, including the installation of smoke alarms.
- Smoking in bed or in an easy chair, especially after drinking alcohol, may cause fire and death;
- Forgetting to turn off the hot water or a gas jet;
- Fire spreading rapidly from the kitchen to the bedroom of a split-level house;
- Casement windows, which are often too small for escape if there is an emergency;
- Ovens in wall units without adjacent counter space for hot and heavy utensils;
- Loose clothing may be caught in the flames of a gas jet;
- Hot kettles may be touched or dropped;
- A modern stove with complex dials and controls may be confusing to many people (see *Adapting your environment*).

Fractures

These are markedly different in older people. Usually it takes a considerable amount of violence and a direct injury to break the bone of a younger person. In contrast, fractures in the elderly can result from minimum or moderate violence and the site of the fracture is usually right next to a joint rather than the shaft of a bone. Fractures of this kind are more likely in women than in men, especially fractures of the hip, the lower end of the forearm and the vertebrae in the spine.

Research has shown that fracture of the neck of the femur (the thighbone) is dependent on the amount of bone present in it. It can decrease below a critical level with osteoporosis (see page 232). In addition, 20 percent of women and about 40 percent of men who fracture the neck of the femur are also suffering from osteomalacia (see page 232). This, in turn, varies with the season of the year, being highest in February to April and lowest in October to December in the Northen hemisphere. The obvious conclusion is that the variation in the hours of sunshine is responsible for the seasonal change, and this makes vitamin D deficiency a very important factor. As we get older, we need vitamin D and calcium, both of which can be prescribed for us by a doctor, to keep our bones healthy.

Fractures of the wrist are affected by age and sex; they are common in young boys and girls but uncommon in adults. There is then a steep rise in women as they get older, but this is not the case with men. This is thought to be due to a hormone deficiency syndrome related to the menopause and it can be corrected with hormone supplements (see *Specialist help*). In older age, crush fractures of the vertebrae become more and more common. This fracture causes a compression of the softened spinal bones and most authorities believe the primary cause is osteoporosis.

Surgical treatment

It's not surprising that most of us are afraid of surgery; after all, most of us are squeamish at the sight of blood. There are always risks with surgery, but they are getting lower and lower for everyone. Surgery in older people is a matter of balancing risks, and yet many older people themselves are convinced that surgery has a doubtful chance of success, and feel that operations will be dangerous "at any age." Of course, no one can operate on a patient without consent, and no one should try to put pressure on a person to accept surgery if he or she is against it. It is important to realize what surgery can and cannot do and not be unduly afraid of it. In fact, nearly 1 in 10 older people who enter the hospital benefit from surgical treatment.

Our aim is to arrive at the age of retirement in the best possible health, and it is true that some surgical correction is better done in our forties and fifties when problems are much smaller, rather than our having something done much later in life as an emergency. Examples might include abnormalities of the feet, hernias or arthritis of the hip. Of course, we have to have the courage and foresight when younger to appreciate what the disability might mean in later life.

There has been a tendency in the past for many doctors to be conservative in their treatment of older patients. A major operation was thought inadvisable except if there was a real emergency and surgery was the only answer. Even now we do not advise operations for trivial conditions, and very rarely simply for cosmetic purposes. Nevertheless there have been notable advances in anesthetics, in surgical techniques and especially in the pre-operative preparation of patients and their post-operative care. The hazards are, therefore, much less serious than they were. Now, it often happens that a new operation is devised and used for younger, resilient patients successfully, after which its use is extended to help older people.

The aims of surgery for older people are not quite the same as for people who are younger, nor for that matter are the aims of rehabilitation. A young person wants a total cure so that he or she can appear normal and as inconspicuous as possible. On the other hand, many an older patient's main purpose is to have restored to him or her as much capability and comfort as possible in the circumstances, and the result may be a long way from perfection. It must not be despised for all that. Doctors who have a broad, humane outlook give countless benefits to older people, but the surgeons who are perfectionists look upon an older body as already past being able to benefit from their skills. These doctors are not of much use to the elderly.

Fractures and surgical wounds

These heal very well in older people if the circumstances are right; the main one is having a well-nourished body. Anesthetics these days have much smaller risks than they did even a couple of decades ago. As an older person is most at risk if he or she is inactive and confined to bed, it is important to get the person into an upright position as soon as possible.

The patient's viewpoint

This, our viewpoint, should be considered at all times. It is not surprising that we are very cautious about radical treatments. When we were younger the risks of surgery were very much higher than they are today, and many of the operations that we now consider to be simple did not even exist. Often we cannot be expected to judge these chances and we have to be advised. We have a right to know how great the risks of an operation are, and it is only fair that we know. In an emergency state, the sort of thing we need to be told is "the risks are so-and-so, but if the operation is not done the likelihood is such and such." It is also necessary to be told what will happen after the operation, and as some doctors neglect to do this, it is as well to have another, maybe a younger person, to go with us to see doctors, so that he or she can insist that we be given information that is our right. There is nothing more annoying and worrying that not knowing what is going on around us.

257

Here are some reasons why operations are performed for older patients:

- Real emergencies where immediate life-saving is the object.
- An operation to save life but which does not necessarily have to happen immediately – it could be delayed and a good moment chosen for us to have it.
- An operation that might cure the condition and also might not – and only time will show.
- An operation that will not cure, but that would help with the very severe symptoms, e.g. pain.
- An operation that might make a patient more mobile, speed up recovery or reduce the risk of complications.
- Planned operation simply for comfort.

What surgery can do for older people

It used to be that people beyond a certain age were virtually disqualified from having surgery. With improvements in anesthetics and surgical procedures this is no longer so. At any age being able to have surgery is more dependent on your fitness than anything else. So keep fit, don't deny yourself surgery.

Abdominal surgery

Almost any known catastophe in the abdomen can strike as we get older. Emergency operations are quite common and quite serious when they are performed on unhealthy people.

Some conditions are quite common, like the perforation of a diverticulum in a patient suffering from diverticulitis (see page 238), or twisting of the bowel so that the blood supply is cut off. As I have already mentioned, many of the classical signs of these illnesses and conditions, like perforation of the stomach from a peptic ulcer, or acute appendicitis, or strangulation of a hernia, are often not present and the diagnosis can be misled. This means that it is very important for you to take all complaints about abdominal pain seriously, and have a medical opinion.

Many of the abdominal operations can be planned ahead and carried out with safety and success. These include operations for gastric ulcers, for narrowing the outlet of the stomach, for removal of the gall bladder due to repeated attacks of infections or gall stones, and operations for slow-growing tumors in the colon or rectum. Colostomy is feasible for an obstruction of the lower bowel (see page 259) and it also helps in the treatment of diverticulitis, after which a diet with bran is advisable.

COLOSTOMY

A colostomy is a surgical opening made in the front of the abdominal wall. Through this, material from the colon, or large intestine, is passed.

One performed on the left side of the colon, shown here, passes solid material, because more liquid has been absorbed from the food during digestion. A colostomy on the right side of the abdomen discharges liquid feces which is passed through the stoma into a bag.

Colon

Stoma

Colostomy bag

Belt for support

In the area of gynecology

Apart from dealing with cancer of the uterus and ovarian cysts, surgeons are often asked to help women with less serious conditions such as stress incontinence. This is the trickling loss of urine that happens only with coughing or straining. Because of increased pressure in the abdomen, there may be complete prolapse of the uterus, which is distressing and also comparatively common (see page 170). As women get older, elaborate repair operations are often not feasible, but there are very simple procedures that can give complete relief from a uterine prolapse to make a woman more comfortable.

One small and simple operation involves inserting a silver wire into the wall of the rectum to prevent a prolapse that "comes down" repeatedly. This symptom causes a great deal of distress, particularly to the frail, older woman, who is the most likely victim. Such a simple operation entirely cures a rectal prolapse when she would otherwise have to stay in a hospital, and perhaps even in bed, because sitting up caused the prolapse always to be "down" and therefore uncomfortable.

Hysterectomy

Hysterectomy involves surgical removal of the uterus. In some forms of hysterectomy other reproductive organs may be removed at the same time, such as the cervix and the fallopian tubes. When a complete hysterectomy is performed the ovaries are removed too, an important fact for you to know before you have your operation because it means that your monthly cycle of female hormones will stop forever. This means that you may need replacements of those hormones, hormone replacement therapy.

About 25 percent of all women fifty and over have had hysterectomies in the USA. Quite often, and particularly in the USA, hysterectomy is performed for comparatively trivial reasons such as the removal of small fibroids. There are even some doctors who advocate routine hysterectomy once child bearing is over and may recommend prophylactic hysterectomy to prevent a cancer developing. I see no reason for this last operation unless there is clear medical indication that this is necessary such as very heavy and frequent periods or suspected cancer. Removal of the uterus is one of the greatest losses that a woman can suffer both physically and more importantly, psychologically.

Reasons for hysterectomy

There are several reasons why hysterectomy may be advocated by your gynecologist: to remove cancer in the vagina, cervix, uterus, fallopian tubes and ovary; or to treat severe and uncontrollable pelvic infections. Under some circumstances a hysterectomy has to be performed to stop severe and uncontrolled bleeding. These are the kinds of life-threatening diseases where hysterectomy is absolutely necessary.

There are some other pelvic conditions that affect women where a hysterectomy is one of the treatments to be considered. These would be extensive and very painful endometrioses, large or multiple fibroid tumors, injuries to the pelvic musculature at childbirth that are severe enough to interfere with bowel or bladder function, recurrent and severe attacks of pelvic infection and vaginal bleeding which is so heavy that anemia results. These cannot be controlled with hormone treatment so your doctor may recommend hysterectomy.

HYSTERECTOMY OPERATIONS

Ovaries
Fallopian tubes
Uterus
Cervix
Vagina

Total abdominal hysterectomy and vaginal hysterectomy
This is removal of the uterus and the cervix through a horizontal incision in the lower abdomen. Alternatively, an incision is made in the vagina.

Complete hysterectomy
This involves removal of the uterus, cervix, fallopian tubes and ovaries through a transverse incision in the lower abdomen.

Sub-total hysterectomy
This operation is not done very often because the cervix on its own has no essential function. The uterus is removed but not the cervix, ovaries or fallopian tubes.

TIMETABLE OF RECOVERY AFTER HYSTERECTOMY

WEEK 1

You'll be encouraged to get out of bed in one or two days. You may have pain and discomfort from wound. You may find urination difficult (tell the nursing staff), you may need an I.V. drip for 24/36 hours until you take solid food, then minor wind pains.

WEEK 2

Home at 7 to 10 days. Don't stay in bed but take it easy. No moderate activity, e.g. walking ½ mile for three more weeks. Can walk upstairs, sit in garden. Don't carry any weights or lift anything heavy.

WEEKS 3-4

Gradually increase activities and take rest periods rather than rest most of the time and being active occasionally. Go to bed early. Try slowly making the bed to see if you can stretch a little (STOP IF ANY PAIN).

WEEK 5

Start moderate activity – going to the store and doing light shopping, do light housework, walk the dog. Go to the hairdressers. Do gentle exercises. Stop if you feel tired.

WEEK 6

Do mobility exercises every day plus some strengthening exercises. You may still feel tired at end of day so rest with feet up for 15-20 minutes. Start bending gently but not to floor.

WEEK 7

You should be back to full normal activity. Continue exercises. Sexual intercourse safe and possible. Rest once a day with feet up.

WEEK 8

You can go back to work if it's sedentary. The rest of your life should be entirely normal. Don't bend to floor. Don't lift.

WEEKS 9-10

You can safely bend fully and lift.

You should talk to a gynecologist in some detail about the need for your hysterectomy and ensure that you are satisfied in your own mind that it is absolutely necessary, that you want to have it done and that your partner agrees with you. Never forget that hysterectomy is an irrevocable step. Once it is done you are sterile. If ovaries are removed you will have an artificial menopause after the operation and you may well suffer menopausal symptoms. Some women fear that they may put on weight after hysterectomy but this is absolutely untrue. You will only put on weight if you eat too many of the wrong things; a diet rich in protein, fresh vegetables and fruit will help you to recover and give you sufficient energy to undertake exercises.

Sex after hysterectomy

Quite a few women are concerned about their sex drive and how much enjoyment they will derive from sex. Research has shown that neither need be impaired if the operation is done well and if a woman deals positively with changes that do occur. Just as many women experience an increased sexual drive as experience a lessening. If you find after a hysterectomy that anatomically you are not able to have intercourse, you should consult your gynecologist immediately and ask for rectification. Another effect that women are concerned about is depression. Hormonal changes can affect emotions and a sense of loss may be a normal response, but both will usually pass with time and the increased freedom allowed by the correction of the condition that necessitated the operation.

261

Orthopedic surgery

This branch of surgery offers great possibilities because it can correct deformities, relieve pain, and improve a person's chance of walking. Successful replacement of diseased hip joints has been done for twenty-five years or more, and now artificial replacements of the knee joints are becoming more and more feasible. They are likely to be suggested for older people who are crippled by a type of osteoarthritis that causes great deformity, pain and a limitation on activity. Broken hip bones – a very common injury, especially in women as they get older – can either be "fixed" with nails and plates, or replaced entirely so that the patient can be walking again in a fraction of the time it took formerly. The old days of full-scale hospital nursing for broken legs extending over many weeks, patients strung up with a network of suspension and traction apparatus, risking innumerable life-threatening complications, are virtually over.

Other helpful orthopedic operations include corrections of foot faults of all kinds. There is help for patients whose limbs are crippled and distorted from rheumatoid arthritis. Usually, contractures and tendons are severed to correct foot drop and to allow permanently bent legs to be straightened, so that a fresh start in walking can be made.

Neurosurgery

As we get older we may be prone to tumors and other abnormalities within the brain or spinal column that need surgical treatment. Most of these tumors are *not* malignant, but nearly all of them require detailed investigation. Other important areas in which neurosurgery can help older people are the treatment of the severe pain of trigeminal neuralgia (see page 248) and the cure of blood clots (see page 234), which grow larger and may be fatal if they are not surgically removed and in Parkinson's disease using sterolactic techniques.

Genito-urinary surgery

Even in quite old people it is possible, indeed it might be essential, to remove a kidney that has been destroyed by stones or riddled with infection. After all, it may have ceased to be an effective kidney some time ago, so the remaining kidney is presumably keeping pace with the extra load, and its capacity is really quite easy to test. Surgery is possible, too, for bladder abnormalities and cancer. Otherwise it is the prostate gland that offers the surgeon a full field for action.

Surgery of the blood vessels

This part of surgical work is making great strides forward and opportunities are opening up for older people, in whom artery disease is widespread. It is possible to replace parts of diseased blood vessels with artificial grafts. Large arteries like those of the leg can have grafts or by-pass operations done at low risk.

Surgery has a lot to contribute to preventive medicine in the older patient. For instance, certain sorts of strokes can be treated with grafts or by-pass operations, thereby preventing further strokes. If special X-ray techniques show that there is obstruction to the arteries in just one place, the obstruction can be removed by opening the vessel and "coring it out" just as one might core out an apple.

Plastic surgery
No doubt older people consult plastic surgeons in order to give themselves an appearance of youth (see *Specialist help*). Apart from this use of surgery, there are many other ways in which plastic surgeons will save lives and correct gross deformities for instance, by treating serious burns, by removing skin tumors, by correcting eyelid deformities, which become commoner as we grow older, and by removing obviously disfiguring or painful blemishes like sebaceous cysts or fatty tumors. Plastic surgeons are often needed to help in treating some varicose leg ulcers or for providing covering skin grafts for large pressure sores.

Pain relief
Research into pain pathways and the setting up of pain clinics have resulted in a number of effective treatments for relieving intractable pain, especially in older people. Some older patients can benefit from these advances and the possibility should always be kept in mind.

In the past, surgeons cut pain-conducting tracts in the spinal cord. Now it is quite common for injections of alcohol or other drugs to be made into the spinal cord so that immediate and, we hope, permanent pain relief can be given. These techniques are most often studied and perfected by anesthetists.

Amputation
Most of us would see the necessity to have a part or a whole of a limb amputated as being the end of the world, but there are many examples to show that this is not the case. A large number of patients who have suffered the misfortune of an amputation walk again with help, thanks to a good artificial limb and plenty of encouragement. Even double amputation need not be a total disaster. There was a case reported of a splendid lady who, at the age of ninety-one, had her two legs amputated, and was taught to walk again on two full-length artificial limbs with no one supporting her.

Everyone deserves the chance to adjust psychologically and emotionally to the prospect of losing a part or all of a limb, and to build up a positive approach to post-operative rehabilitation. Therefore, I feel that every person should be given sound psychiatric counseling so that he or she can get used to the idea.

Living with long-term ailments

When you, or someone close to you, is chronically sick or disabled you have to adapt your lifestyle to cope with it. This can be difficult. We all have to learn to live with our bodies when they are no longer as young as they were; only unhappiness can result from unrealistic expectations and placing heavier burdens on our physical and mental resources than they can bear. On the other hand, there is no reason why you shouldn't look ahead positively; there are ways to prevent a chronic ailment from completely dominating your life – no ailment need do this if you take care of it thoughtfully.

Chronic ailments not only affect the person involved, they also have a significant effect on offspring – often themselves middle-aged adults, who may be suddenly confronted with financial, emotional and moral problems. Deciding whether to keep, and then look after, an older person in our own home, or to try and support the person in his or hers or in an institution, is difficult. Institutionalization is stressful for both the person and the relatives. Grandchildren can be affected by stressed parents, and by reduced family finances. An incapacitated, sometimes disoriented, incontinent and crotchety grandparent in the home, instead of a loving and generous one, is particularly disturbing for children.

Fifty onward is a significant stage in all our lives and our states of health can vary widely. You may or may not be quite fit and healthy; you may have a partner or parent to care for who is less than fit; you may want to find out how to cope better with a chronic ailment should it occur. Therefore, where appropriate, I have addressed myself directly to the reader as the concerned party. However, where I feel the information is more likely to be of use to you as a "caretaker" of others, I have worded it more generally.

Chronic heart disease

Heart attacks　If you are recovering from a heart attack you will need to rest and possibly reorganize your usual activities until your heart muscle is healed. Several weeks of strict rest may be ordered. However, many physicians now mobilize heart patients sooner than was customary in the past. Your doctor may order chair rest if you need long periods of relaxation; while you cannot be more active in a chair than in bed, sometimes the upright position is more comfortable. It allows for easier breathing, it prevents pooling of blood in the lungs and it may improve the efficiency of your breathing. These measures will considerably ease the workload on the heart.

Although rest is important for a person who has had a heart attack, you should never allow yourself to be labeled as an invalid. You should be encouraged to join in physical and social activity as soon as recuperation is complete, even though it may be somewhat limited. The degree of mobility you have will be an important way of measuring your improvement, both to you and your family, doctors and nurses. Prolonged bed rest is dangerous in that you may begin to feel hopeless, and more importantly, it can lead to complications such as weakness of the muscles, the formation of blood clots, particularly in the legs and lungs, and bed sores.

After the acute phase of a coronary thrombosis you will probably be looked after at home unless home care is impossible. You and your family should be told clearly that you have had a heart attack, and be reassured that home care is best. In this instance, your family doctor and the local visiting nurse association or other home care programs have an important role to play in keeping up your morale. If you must stay in the hospital then the most comfortable place is a ward of a small community hospital where you will find the pace slower, and where routines are geared to the needs of others of your age. In a busy general hospital you may get a bit depressed and even frightened at all the activity going on twenty-four hours a day. We all feel vulnerable when we are unwell.

Whether you are at home or in the hospital you should be encouraged to become mobile as soon as possible. From the beginning you should sit up in a chair and use a commode. Doctors now feel that early mobilization decreases, rather than increases, complications after a coronary thrombosis. For instance, if you pass a stool into a bed pan you put a great strain on your heart; thus you should not be allowed to use one unless you will find that is is absolutely necessary.

If, after your heart attack, you are suffering from a recalcitrantly slow heart rate and it doesn't respond to drug therapy, then the treatment of choice for you may be an electronic pacemaker. Most doctors agree that age and ill health are not contra-indications to having one fitted, and you should only be denied a pacemaker if your general mental and physical health is so poor that you would not enjoy the benefits of having one. Your doctor will advise you on this.

PACEMAKERS

Pacemaker operations are relatively common these days. In Britain each year, one person in every 20,000 has one implanted and in the USA, one person in every 4,000, so if your doctor recommends one it is no cause for alarm.

A pacemaker is a device that sends a stimulating current to electrodes in contact with the heart muscle. It has a small generating unit powered by a battery that lasts three to four years, though nuclear-powered pacemakers are now being tested which will last a great deal longer.

If it is not intended for long-term use then the generating unit can be attached to a belt. Alternatively, it can be implanted under the large muscle on the left of the chest.

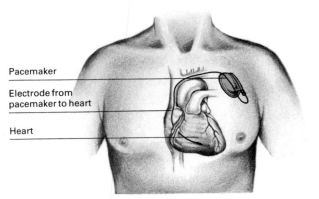

Pacemaker

Electrode from pacemaker to heart

Heart

Angina

Angina pectoris, or chest pain associated with heart disease, may become less of a problem as we grow older. Some people who are troubled with angina in their fifties lose it as they age further. It is unusual for people who get chest pain to feel incapacitated, probably because they take little exercise. The symptoms can be controlled, and to a certain extent pre-empted, by putting a tablet of glyceryl trinitrate under your tongue whenever you feel the angina coming on or if you intend to do something strenuous in about a half-hour's time. This occasionally may reduce your blood pressure and you may feel a bit dizzy. Certain new drugs called *beta-blocking agents* will reduce the workload on your heart but they may also cause dizziness. Rely on sensible advice and support from your family, doctors and nurses concerning the amount of activity you should undertake with the help of medication.

Hypotension

Sometimes, as we get older, we become hesitant, rather confused and shaky when we stand up even though we are bright and co-operative and alert when sitting in a chair. The reason is that blood pressure is normal when we are sitting down and falls as soon as we stand up. This is called postural hypotension. There are several practical things which can be done to prevent this fall in blood pressure: you can lessen the risk by getting up very slowly from a chair or bed; your doctor or physiotherapist can give you a set of exercises that will help you to prevent your blood pressure falling suddenly; elastic stockings and corsets will prevent pooling of blood in the lower legs or abdomen, and your doctor may consider salt-retaining drugs, which are sometimes helpful. The condition can also be brought on by many drugs; check this possibility with your doctor.

Hypertension   Treatment for hypertension must relate to your own problems and the effect that high blood pressure has on you. There is no blanket solution. Treatment has to be tailor-made for you, and any drugs should be carefully and slowly adjusted according to *your* particular response. There are a variety of drugs that can be used with the aim of keeping your blood pressure down, and not causing side effects. One of the commonest is a diuretic agent that makes you pass quite a lot of fluid. Bear in mind, however, the possibility that you may have some pre-existing urinary incontinence (see pages 291-293). A diuretic may make this worse and your doctor should take this into consideration. There is very little point in treating one condition if it is going to make another any worse.

Treatment   All patients with chronic heart disease will have to cope with
régimes   three main types of treatment.

Drugs
If you suffer from such conditions as hypertension and angina pectoris you will be on long-term drugs; you will probably have to live with them for the rest of your life. If you are suffering from angina pectoris, for instance, you will have to carry around with you a supply of glyceryl trinitrate. The other drugs most commonly prescribed are nitrates, beta blockers, and calcium blockers.

Diet
If you have heart disease, you will probably be put on some form of diet, one that mainly restricts foods containing cholesterol (cheese, eggs, smoked salmon, etc.), animal fats, and the amount of salt you take. You will have to live with this diet for the rest of your life. It is not so bad, you can still have treats, through stopping cigarette smoking in one fell swoop can do more to ensure that you don't have another coronary thrombosis than any other single thing. Alcohol, on the other hand, in moderate quantities, can be good for you. You may well live longer for taking a glass or two of wine a day rather than remaining abstemious.

Exercise

The modern approach to treating heart disease is, in consultation with your doctor, to make sure that your body has plenty of exercise – exercise that raises the pulse rate to 120 beats per minute for two minutes a day (or whatever your doctor recommends) and puts all your joints through their full range of movements. Being over-protective about youself, considering yourself an invalid and moving only short distances slowly will do you more harm than good. Don't be over-cautious as long as your doctor knows and approves.

Strokes

A person having a stroke is nearly always insecure and therefore it is vital to adopt positive attitudes to counteract natural fears. Hospital admission will depend on the severity of the stroke and the availability of help and rehabilitation in the home or at a nearby hospital outpatients' department.

The people who have looked after the victim in the hospital should be in close touch with all those who will care for him or her at home. There should be a medical assessment of the person in your home. Help with any structural adaptations to the home (see *Adapting your environment*) can be requested from your local social services or health department. To be of maximum benefit, adaptations must be carried out quickly, ideally before the patient goes home, and of course with his or her agreement. You shold make certain that any health visitors and therapists continue visiting all stroke patients returning home. Problems can then be highlighted at an early stage, and measures taken. Some people may be unable to take care of themselves, and accommodation in residential homes or continuing care hospitals may be necessary for their own security and peace of mind.

Recovering from a stroke

Almost two-thirds of people who have had a stroke will recover spontaneously: half within the first week or two and the remainder somewhat later, but still to a point where they are capable of independent self-care and returning home. It is worth having a very positive attitude in looking after a patient with a stroke, encouraging him or her to have an optimistic outlook, to be determined and to exercise – both physically and intellectually – as often as possible. Even a proportion of those people who seem severely disabled can progress to self-care and

269

a degree of independence.

It is important that someone who's had a stroke is set realistic goals; these should be reviewed frequently to make sure that they are being achieved. If they are not, the situation may be reassessed. A simple grading system may be used, but it is probably better to describe goals in terms of what activities can be done, such as turning over in bed, sitting up alone, standing up with help, etc. A stroke victim must be encouraged to do things for him or herself rather than to have them done for him or her. Try to resist the temptation to help. It's better to encourage a person to achieve a goal – which may be to feed him or herself – even though this may be a rather messy and protracted procedure.

Initially, movements are developed in bed, followed by exercises out of bed aimed at retraining lost balance and function of the body. When these are developed, the person should be able to stand unaided and then progress to walking. Once the person is able to walk it is important that he or she should walk to the lavatory. This small achievement confers disproportionate self-confidence.

People who are suffering great difficulty with their speech and pronunciation should have an assessment by a speech therapist as soon as possible, and speech therapy should be started. It is quite important that we test to see whether a person can communicate by writing or using a typewriter as this is a separate skill, though closely related to reading and speaking.

Some stroke victims appear to be uncooperative and a bit awkward. This may be only apparent to us, not intentional. It is the understandable result of someone's inability to hear and coordinate movements. A common defect after a stroke is loss of position sense, so while the person may have remarkable muscle power in, say, making a punching movement into your open hand, this is of little help if he or she doesn't know how to use it and control it. Also, the brain can receive false messages so that a paralyzed limb does not appear paralyzed to the person who has had a stroke, and he or she is unable to recognize the paralysis without being told. Another strange situation is when a person with a stroke can only receive information on the side that is not paralyzed. If you wish to speak you have to walk from the affected side to the unaffected side, as though you had gone through a door to get to the person's consciousness in order to be understood.

Exercise therapy At first, occupational therapy may have to be confined to, say, only the good arm, but as some activity starts to reappear in the other hand and arm, effort has to be concentrated on encouraging their activities, however small they may be. The weak hand, in particular, should work at squeezing a soft rubber ball, a roll of plastic foam, or a piece of plastic putty. Only at a later stage, supposing hand/arm recovery is proven to be unlikely, should occupational therapy be concentrated on making it possible for a person to live, dress, cook and manage generally with the remaining normal hand. At an early stage the person should be fully dressed in his or her own clothes and good shoes. He or she can now do no end of bed drills by placing the feet against a board and pulling him or herself up and down from a chair, by using the bed rail or a specially raised T bar. This is one of the first steps to independence and it is vitally important for morale. Even more important are the first steps in walking after doing trunk and leg extension exercises on the bed to strengthen those "lazy" muscles.

Patients with strokes can benefit from, and enjoy, organized class work. They can take part in competitive activity, perform group exercises, play indoor ball games and indulge in other activities that encourage particular muscle movements in a cheerful, competitive team spirit. Nursing staff, relatives and family, and possibly even neighbors, should be involved in this activity, encouraging, congratulating, showing sympathy but remaining equally optimistic, and seeing that the types of activities that patients are taught are continued in the ward, in the bathroom, at the wash basin and, of course, when the patient is rehabilitated at home.

A specially-raised T-bar permits exercise in bed.

Once at home, the patient should be helped through a range of normal daily activities with the physiotherapist and the occupational therapist, so that performance can be recorded. If any aids such as sticks or gadgets are necessary, they should be provided. There is a great variety of aids for eating, cleaning teeth, putting on clothes, stockings and shoes, lifting, cutting bread, reaching for distant objects, and generally making independent life possible for people whose recovery may only be partial, a selection of which can be seen on page 272.

Any remaining needs that are required in the home, and gadgets that the patient may require in order to lead a semi-active life at home, may be supplied by your local health, social service agency or through private service organizations.

Each person has to capitalize on existing abilities so that useful movements can be developed. Being satisfied with impaired function of "what's left" must be rejected.

AIDS FOR THE STROKE SUFFERER

This is a small selection of some of the aids that can be bought easily to help day-to-day living or perhaps adapted from existing things you already own.

Tray
A handle on a tray will prevent spillage.

Rolling pin
A one-handed rolling pin can be easily adapted from one more conventional.

Cards
An inverted kitchen brush allows all playing cards to be visible at a glance.

Cutlery
A deep bowl or a plate guard prevents food from sliding off the plate and it should be used with either a combined knife and fork or a pusher-spoon.

Breadboard
A spiked board is useful for cutting and buttering bread and for peeling potatoes. It should have a non-slip base.

Telephone arm
This clamps on to the edge of the table (right) to hold the receiver.

Bookmark
This will keep the pages flat for reading.

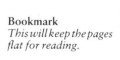

Helping with recovery

Anyone who's had a stroke, even if he or she has made a good recovery, is still "at risk" from accidents, further strokes, and other problems associated with hardening of the arteries such as hypothermia (see page 235). Regular follow-ups and visits will be essential. As a relative you should consider short-term or intermittent hospital admission as a method of management, not only to relieve yourself of excessive burdens of care, but also to ensure that optimum performance is being achieved.

The treatment of stroke illness in the elderly is one of the most demanding and challenging aspects of medical care, both by the professions and families and friends. The attitudes to the disease by the patient, his or her relatives and therapists, play a vital part in recovery. Greater success will be achieved if everyone shows realistic optimism. Complete recovery for a stroke is not instantaneous — full rehabilitation is usually only achieved after a period of two or three months or even longer. For this reason, the admission of a stroke patient to an acute medical ward with a rapid tempo is often inappropriate. Some hospitals have special units specifically designed for the management of strokes. With the concentration of everyone's skills, the results have been most encouraging. With the development of new aids the future looks more promising.

TIPS TO HELP SOMEONE RECOVERING FROM A STROKE

- Adopt an encouraging, positive approach, but avoid artificial praise. If you are relaxed and unhurried this, in turn, will reduce the person's apprehension and tension considerably.
- Keep your own speech simple and slow, but never childish. Unless the person was deaf before his or her stroke, there is no need to raise your voice.
- Encourage the person to talk and give plenty of time for response. Do not put words into the person's mouth.
- Let the person know when attempts at speech are successful and encourage the person to continue. Minimize correction and criticism at all times.
- Difficulty with speech does not mean that the stroke sufferer has lost any basic intelligence. If speech is difficult, try showing objects and pictures and encourage the person to point to the things that are wanted.

- Place clothing where patients can easily see it. Later, if there is a partial loss of vision, you may try to help them learn to compensate by moving the clothes slightly out of their range of vision and getting them to turn their head.
- Start dressing on the bed and progress to the sitting position on the side of the bed or chair. Be sure that the person has plenty of support.
- Put a full-length mirror in the person's room so that he or she has an opportunity to observe mistakes made in dressing and to note improvements.
- Try to get patients to dress themselves so that they are satisfied with their appearance.
- Keep background music to a minimum, for instance, from the television or radio. Watch out for minor distractions that preoccupy the stroke sufferer.

CLOTHING AIDS

Selecting clothing is a very personal process and there is no reason why this should change for somebody who is suffering from a stroke.

Clothing aids encourage a person to accept much independence.

Velcro can be used to adapt buttons, cuffs and, as shown here, ties. Remember to choose clothes in light-weight and stretch fabrics.

Make sure that shoes support your feet well. Elastic shoe laces may be bought or the one-handed method learned.

Use suspenders to pull up trousers or put loops on to underwear. This is often the most difficult stage of dressing.

Cancer

It seems presumptuous to suggest how a person might cope with the task of facing life with incurable cancer and come to terms with the possibility of imminent death. Living with cancer is surely more about living with oneself than anything else. Doctors are often of help in spiritual matters but not, I think, in illnesses of this kind. You can find much strength from religious and spiritual counselors, who have had experience in helping people to come to terms with such a situation.

If one considers practicalities, I would refer to page 282 where I suggest quite a lot on making confinement to bed as comfortable as possible. Another alternative may be the growing hospice movement, which can bring great comfort to patients and families on either a live-in or home-visitor basis.

There are several other ways that we can provide assistance to a person who is dying from cancer.

● Never pretend the patient isn't dying. Always make conversations open and honest. Try to share the responsibility if the patient sees dying as a crisis.

● Always make sure the patient has contact with other people. Concentrate on making these times as rewarding and as fulfilling as you possibly can under the circumstances.

● Help the patient to suffer grief at the loss of family and friends but make sure good relationships are retained with a clear idea of what the days hold.

● Encourage the person to accept the situation with dignity and integrity in this immensely difficult time, something that will become increasingly difficult as time goes by.

● Try not to let negative views creep in. Keep up the person's self-respect. Try to avoid personal shame and deprecation. The important thing is to help a person toward death as he or she would wish. Everyone's death will be different, but it can be appropriate to the person, and this should be borne in mind at all times.

It is important, however, that the patient understand the truth about his or her condition and its implications. Though there will be worries about the pain and discomfort that lie in the future the person can be reassured that much can be done.

Chronic arthritis

How well you learn to live with chronic arthritis and get the best out of life has as much to do with your attitude of mind as anything else. The same amount of joint disease can cause complete disablement in one person and hardly any in another. We all know people with chronic arthritis who are agile and sprightly, do their own shopping, ride bicycles, and do all their own housework. The people who succumb to arthritis and let it rule their lives are self-pitying, are using their condition to appear helpless and to gain sympathy from others, and feel negative toward themselves, the arthritis and the world around them. If you try to be the other kind of person you will feel that life improves almost immediately, and you are capable of doing a great deal more than you ever thought.

Some of us can lead quite normal lives without having to make any alterations to our homes. Sometimes, simple things like making use of quilts or electric blankets, instead of heavy comforters, can make a great deal of difference. There are also many specially designed gadgets available (see page 276).

AIDS FOR THE ARTHRITIC

It is quite possible to lead a normal life no matter how chronic our arthritis.

Below is a selection of some of the many specially designed gadgets.

Cutlery
This is just one of the many existing aids to eating available. There are many other designs for thick-handled cutlery.

Dress-making scissors
These electric scissors will make it easy to continue sewing and dressmaking.

Can opener
A hand-held electric can opener is often easier to use than one mounted on the wall.

b

c

d

e

f

Writing
Increasing the diameter of a pencil or pen aids writing so use the following: **a**, *rubber band;* **b**, *rubber sleeve;* **c**, *pimple rubber sleeve;* **d**, *adhesive tape;* **e**, *plastic ball; or* **f**, *sponge.*

Scissors
Self-opening scissors with extra wide loops are made to accommodate swollen fingers.

Dressing aid
A dressing stick made from an old wooden coat-hanger will pull straps over the shoulder by the V-notch.

Cutting bread
Hold the bread down with a flat hand and cut across. This way there is less strain on the fingers and wrists.

Keys
A toggle device attached to a key helps a weak grip as well as arthritis.

TIPS FOR LIVING WITH OSTEOARTHROSIS

These guidelines will help you to live with osteoarthrosis.

- Do not make any wrenching, heaving movements on rigid door knobs and tight screw-topped jars. Use the whole of your hand to lift any heavy objects from below, certainly not with first finger and thumb.
- Exercise and walking are fine, but beware of standing and walking on hard surfaces for prolonged periods.
- Sitting in cramped seats becomes painful after half an hour or so. When this happens it is helpful if you stand up, walk around or massage your knees.
- Sitting with your legs crossed (like Buddha) is not good for your knees.
- Hips stiffen quickly if not exercised. Sitting like Buddha, though bad for your knees, is good for your hips. An important exercise is for you to flex your knees to a right angle.
- Backs stiffen with age so it's a good thing if you exercise your spine after a hot bath or shower. Swimming is also good.
- Necks stiffen if not exercised, so regular relaxation exercises keep your neck supple.
- Sensible footwear is essential. Don't wear pointed shoes because they push your big toe out of line.
- When lifting heavy objects bend your knees and straighten your spine.
- Stay trim. Extra weight means less exercise and immobile joints.

TIPS FOR LIVING WITH RHEUMATOID ARTHRITIS

These guidelines will help you to live with rheumatoid arthritis.

- Energy is important so make certain you preserve it.
- Full range of movement exercises are necessary. Keep supple; exercise after a bath or shower. Not doing enough will lead to stiffness; doing too much will increase pain and swelling in the joints.
- Eat like any other healthy person. Diet does not influence rheumatoid arthritis.
- Alcohol can be good in moderation.
- Maintain hobbies and interests. Lead as full a life as you are able. A good general rule to follow is if any exertion makes you ache badly for more than two hours afterward or makes you feel bad next day,, then you have taken too much.
- Take drugs as prescribed; if any medicines cause symptoms then tell your doctor about them.
- Don't expect any miracle cure. Great tolerance and patience are most needed.

Pain relievers Hot baths or showers are often helpful in easing pains, as are hot water bottles and heating pads and lamps. However don't overdo the latter and burn your skin.

Your doctor can supply you with painkillers and other drugs to ease your condition but often keeping yourself busy and active can be the best medicine. Anxiety and depression, coupled with uncertainty and fears of the future, definitely aggravate pain. A positive and hopeful approach to life and enjoyment of hobbies and other interests can make life full and interesting and increase your pain threshold. You should get out of the house as much as possible and try keeping a job – even a part-time one – and develop interests.

EXERCISES FOR ARTHRITIS

You should make certain you put all your joints through a full range of motion every day – though don't over-exercise.

Shoulders and arms
Hold your arms straight down but across your body, then lift them upwards and outwards uncrossing them as you go. With your arms in this position, clasp your hands behind your head.

Feet
Push your toes and feet down and then pull them up towards you. Move your toes and ankles round in a large circle.

Hips and knees
Lie down, preferably on the floor, and exercise one leg at a time. In turn, bend each leg up on to your chest toward the opposite shoulder.

The movements below will help you to keep up muscle strength and joints moving properly (5-20 times daily).

Wrists
Rest your arms on a table or arm of a chair without supporting your hand. Bend your hand down toward the floor and then lift it up.

Next, move your hand to the left and then to the right. When you are doing this make sure your hand rests in the mid-position and is in line with your forearm and does not fall downwards.

Hands and fingers
Bend your fingers and grip tightly, then stretch and spread your fingers. Touch the tip of each finger in turn with your thumb.

Quadriceps exercises can be done by just tightening the thigh muscles and pulling the knee-cap up. Some people find it easier to pull the foot up from the ankle while lying down, and this tightens the thigh muscles; others let their legs dangle over a chair, then bring their knee up straight and hold it there for ten seconds before letting it go down slowly.

Brain failure

In many senses brain failure is like failure of any other organ in the body, such as the heart or the kidneys, simply a gradual decline. Most doctors would agree that brain failure has occurred in a person where there is failing mental capacity and an inability to cope with everyday life unless he or she gets help and support. Furthermore, the person may be a danger to him or herself and to others, by behaving in an inappropriate way.

There are drugs that claim to cure brain failure. Of course, they don't. This has given them a bad name and has spread the belief that nothing can be done. This is not true – there is a good deal that *can* be done. Drugs can alter moods, reduce depression and paranoia; mild sleeping pills can prevent wandering and embarrassing behavior at night. Sometimes older people have inverted sleep rhythms and mild sleeping pills will give a good night's sleep and cut out the nocturnal noise and activity that is common.

Both family and neighbors are often concerned about the danger when such a person wanders around, leaves the gas unlit, or uses matches and lighters, etc. But many of these problems are easy to overcome; for example, you can fit a lock to the front and back doors to keep an affected person inside a supervised house; the local gas company can fit fail-safe gas taps.

Many of the accompaniments of brain failure such as incontinence (see pages 291-3) may not be due to brain failure *per se* and should always be thoroughly investigated.

There are social aspects to the care of a demented patient that are very important, and if you are concerned in this kind of situation you need support and help, too.

The role of partners in brain failure

The majority of people suffering from brain failure live at home either with a partner or child, or with some kind of regular supervision. Probably the happiest situation is when there is a loving partner of long standing. Such couples have lived through life sharing a great deal, and will go on to share and cope with one of them having brain failure. Many people are strengthened by having shared a world war; they remember hunger marches; they remember times before the motor car, air travel and space travel. Even if they have had a marriage that is tinged with "hatred," long-standing familiarity goes hand in hand with a preparedness to care for a partner in distress. Such a partner may find it fairly easy to cope with the escalating demands of the other. The "queer turns" and "dizzy spells" may worsen so slowly that the partner is given time to adjust. Furthermore, the calm and tranquility of long and

279

complementary pairing makes anxiety, depression or paranoid thoughts and attitudes very much less likely to happen.

There is no question that the "husband and wife team" has many ingredients for success. Other caring groups have to develop the same trick, while providing help without invading self-sufficiency. This conflict, of what a person needs to live a normal life and what he or she actually wants, can be a source of great unhappiness and contribute to the development of paranoia and depression. It makes dementia appear worse than it really is.

Other family members can be similarly good. Sisters and brothers often come together again in later life and opposite or same sex siblings provide care for each other that is usually very impressive, even though it may fall short of the quality and quantity of care that exists between married partners. The most frequent support system is daughter/parent or daughter/parent-in-law.

Help with care People who are suffering from brain failure need to be visited regularly so that you can anticipate problems and look for solutions. Many people feel a lot better if they attend a day center or a luncheon club, or receive voluntary visiting. If you can arrange this regularly then it will provide great relief for you and others in your family. Health visitors, social workers and psychiatric nurses can be consulted to reassure you and make you feel that you are not alone. Most communities have a service by which they arrange for periods of relief with holiday admissions to an appropriate residential home or hospital to give you and your family a rest. One of the most important aspects of the continuing care of a person with brain failure is that there has to be an atmosphere of trust between everyone who is concerned. When there is a crisis, relief should be immediately available and no one should have to wait until tomorrow, even worse next week. Agreements and contracts must be honored, so that you as a family must see, as well as feel, that you are being supported.

In many cases the family can be augmented by nurses, visitors and workers in order to be able to help an older person to have a well-supported life at home. There are medicines, walking-sticks, nursing expertise, modifications to the house, home help, and meals-on-wheels.

Inevitably, some patients will require institutional care when attempts to maintain them in the community fail. Entry into a special residential home should be planned well ahead. If possible, strict custodial care should be replaced by methods that encourage independence, raising the morale of patients.

TIPS FOR ENVIRONMENT AND MEDICATION

Drugs help your internal environment, but possibly more important is the help that you can get in adjusting to your external environment – the world about you. The following will act as guidelines for both.

● You should try to keep up a close liaison with your doctor, social worker and physiotherapist.

● To live an active, mobile life you are going to have to encourage yourself to *get* dressed rather than *be* dressed, go to the lavatory rather than use a bed pan or a commode, and spend as much time as you possibly can practicing walking whether with a walking aid or without.

● With active exercises physiotherapists can increase the range of movement of both your joints and limbs and give you greater mobility.

● You can also increase your mobility by using a variety of walking aids.

● If you are unable to walk at all you will almost certainly still be capable of leading an independent life in a wheelchair.

● You may find that you are not quite capable of overcoming obstacles such as the steps and stairs in your home, but you can ask the physiotherapist to visit your home to make a first-hand assessment of the sort of obstacles that may interfere with everyday living, and improve them.

● An occupational therapist can have a vital role to play in helping you to get back to normal activities. The occupational therapist working with the physiotherapist will ensure that you are able to get in and out of bed, to get dressed and undressed, to walk, and to use the lavatory. If you can do all of these things without help then there is absolutely no need for you to stay in the hospital a moment longer.

● Doctors and social workers consider skills such as cooking, housekeeping and shopping as luxuries that should never prevent your discharge from the hospital, since you can get help from meals-on-wheels, a home help, a laundry service, or through your local social-services agency.

● Drugs prescribed by your doctor will help to make your body well and they will be an aid in carrying out the acts of everyday life. Below are some basic guidelines and principles you need to know before taking drugs.

● As we get older our reaction to drugs can change. We may become more sensitive to them and therefore need a smaller dose than before, or become insensitive to them and require more than before. It is therefore necessary for doctors to treat every patient individually, and adjust the dose of a drug according to your response. Doses of drugs should be increased or decreased by very small amounts, slowly.

● Many drugs hitherto harmless may not remain so. A good working rule is that all drugs should be considered potentially risky as you grow older. If your doctor has decided that a drug is essential then it is his or her duty to monitor the effects of the drug very carefully.

● The drugs you are taking must be kept constantly under review. Older people frequently have more than one condition and this may mean that you have to take more than one drug. Doctors have also to be aware of how many drugs you are taking (including aspirin or antacid) and you yourself should be on the lookout for possible interactions between the drugs.

● For younger people and children, doctors sometimes give a large *loading* to start off a treatment with rapid response. In older people this is very rarely necessary and the maintenance dose is often lower than in younger people.

● Always be suspicious of routine repeat prescriptions for a long-term complaint. They should never be given to the older patient for longer than a period of two to three months, depending on the complaint.

Confinement to chairs and beds

Choosing chairs

Inevitably, as we get older we spend a good deal of time sitting, and chairs become perhaps the most important part of our furniture. Few of us give any thought to chairs. The worst ones for older people are the modern, low, sloping-backed chairs with thick upholstery and broad arms. We need chairs in which we can sit up well with our backs straight, hips and knees at an angle of 90°, or certainly as near to this as possible (see page 38).

It is important for us to keep our backs straight even while sitting and to distribute our weight evenly over our buttocks and thighs. Chairs should have arms because these help us to get in and out, but the arms should be slender at their ends so that they can be grasped by hands that may be weak or arthritic. Most people agree that a partly upholstered wooden arm is best. The really critical measurement is the height of the seat to the floor, which should be the same measurement as the sole of the foot to the knee. It is much better to have a chair too high than too low.

Different chairs may be needed during the course of an illness. Firm, high armchairs with wings and built-in trays and foot rests are good if the person is very frail and disabled, but light, modern, dining-style chairs will do if he or she is convalescent or usually spends time fairly actively in day rooms. It is possible to get specially-designed chairs that have extra long legs. Not all people need high-backed chairs. Some less able ones will hold a better sitting position and keep more alert if they have lower backs to their chairs.

Aging relatives may fall forward out of very high chairs. However, the modern geriatric chair in its various versions can correct this. Its swiveling but fastenable tray table will lessen the risk (though some people will manage to slide down even this). Otherwise it is possible to place a person in the chair facing toward the side of the bed so that the risks of falling forward are very much less.

Getting out of and into a chair

Getting out of chairs is very difficult when one knee is stiff. With two stiff or straight-splinted knees, the chair might even have to be made twenty-six or more inches from the floor. Yet even this can be done. There could be no better example of how necessary it is to match furniture to people and their physical problems to make life comfortable.

The design of a chair is very important. It should be stable and strong because we put all our weight on one side when we get up and we may fall back heavily when we sit down. This latter is inadvisable and should be avoided (see opposite). Padding at the front of the seat allows circulation in the legs.

GETTING OUT OF AND INTO A CHAIR

Unfortunately, few people understand how to get off a chair safely. You might find it necessary to demonstrate the correct technique time and time again for a forgetful relative. This, however, will be well worth the effort.

When getting out of a chair, your feet should be brought back underneath with your hands placed forward on the arms of the chair.

Lean forward until the point of overbalancing and thrust forward and upward with your arms and thigh muscles.

Still holding the arms of the chair wait until you are perfectly balanced. Sitting down should always involve the reverse process.

The correct bed　Your bed should be suitable in height; nursing in low beds is impossible, and trying to get out of beds that are too high is dangerous. Bed heights, like chair heights, are critical for elderly people who are learning to be independent. A good back rest and an overbed chain and handle are necessary, as are castors on the bed; these must be of the locking type.

Safety sides should be used, not to restrain but to prevent ill or restless people rolling out of bed. Modern, telescopic, temporary safety sides are clamped down onto the frame. They are silent in action, safe, and fold down unobtrusively to bed level when not in use. They remain below mattress level so that it is simple to make the bed. Vertical spaces are not wide enough for a confused person to get his or her head stuck.

Bed cradles, which hold bedclothes off the legs, ankles and feet, should be a rule of nursing an older person. They are usually made of tubular steel and are of the cantilevered type. They should be obligatory for any person who could possibly develop a foot drop; all stroke cases; and anyone who is immobilized, as they can help in the prevention of pressure sores. Having the correct bed is an investment.

Exercising in bed People who are confined to bed also need regular exercise sessions so that muscles are not allowed to become disused, joints don't become stiff and mobility and strength are retained. Exercises can be devised where the therapist resists pushing or pulling arm movements and kicking or leg-raising movements while the person is attempting to make them.

It is possible to exercise the arms, shoulders and hip girdle by pulling on weights and pulleys, punching at suspended punch balls and exercising in suspension. Suspension means that the effect of gravity is counteracted. The limb is held from an overhead frame with ropes, slings and springs so that little muscle power can produce large ranges of movement; these special suspension techniques help a lot of people. It is possible to make muscle groups work harder and harder by working against more and more powerful springs. Home nurses with the help of relatives who are 'handymen' can often set up simple suspension exercises by attaching pulleys and hooks to ring bolts in the ceiling.

Problems of movement

As we get older our walking slows down. Many older people can walk very well, but seldom very fast. We walk more and more deliberately as if concentrating on what always has been a complex activity. Failure to concentrate may lead to disaster. If we begin to stand with our bodies bent and stooped, the way we walk soon suffers and we tend to lean forward, sliding our feet without swinging our arms. Arm swinging helps greatly in keeping our balance, and it is well worth encouraging. Most of us could take longer paces if we swung our arms and lifted our feet higher. Some of us who walk very badly on the flat can still walk upstairs quite well. If we walk poorly without having any abnormality, it is mainly because of bad habits and our not making demands on ourselves. However, if we have painful feet or don't possess shoes with a good enough support or wear our bedroom slippers (which give no support or firm basis for walking) all day, we can make walking more difficult than it need be, which makes life uncomfortable.

Overweight people characteristically waddle in an attempt to distribute their weight safely, but waddling can also indicate a joint disease like arthritis (see page 275).

Aids to walking

As we get older, we become especially afraid of falling over backward, so it helps to push something in front like a stable walking aid. (This can also be a help if we are frightened of having a walking stick, or a giddy stick.) When frightened, we instinctively lean forward and any stick is held far out in front. If we've lost all confidence or have been lying in bed for a long time we tend to totter forward with tiny steps and look absolutely terrified. This kind of walking represents a great fear of falling and it is difficult to overcome. Sometimes we have to be put on an inclined board to help us get a more normal balance. Or we may start to walk normally as long as there is someone there to help us, but revert to our faltering steps as soon as the support is gone.

Some of us need sticks but will not use them because we think it is a sign of decrepitude. This is a bad mistake. We should ignore what other people might think and use this simple tool, which could make the difference between activity and being confined to a chair. The stick is surely a sight of seniority – not a hint of one foot in the grave. All sticks should be rubber tipped, stout enough to bear our weight and long enough so that when we hold them by our sides our elbows are just bent.

If we are learning to walk again we should try to look up – not at our feet. Some of us may have lost the sense of knowing where our feet are, but this is rare. When starting out, the way should be quite free of obstacles and we should have a target to watch at eye level. Sometimes it's a good idea to stamp our feet down and practice stepping over things. Slippery floors, or those that appear slippery because of reflections, are frightening, so it's best trying to walk on carpets or on floors that are patterned with colored tiles to split up the appearance of uniform polished surfaces. It is regrettable that there will never be enough physiotherapists to help us all; therefore we should ask for help from everyone we can. More people want to help than you may think. These include our relatives, social workers, home-helps, and neighbors.

Walking frames are stable and rubber tips prevent sliding.

Despite severe disabilities most of us retain a tenacious desire to remain mobile and would rather slide downstairs in the morning. If you hang on to this determination and gather up your courage you will never stay confined. It does take a lot of strength and effort to be this positive but it can be done.

Taking care of feet

Many older feet are deformed and painful and this is bound to interfere with comfortable walking and mobility generally. If we want to keep moving, regular foot attention is a most crucial matter. Orthopedic abnormalities such as bunions should be put right, nails should be cut and other faults like corns should be dealt with by a podiatrist *every four to eight weeks.*

If you are a diabetic, special risks are involved (see *Special medical problems*). You should never attempt to cut your nails or corns. You must wear good, stout shoes with no rough parts inside and be careful to avoid any kind of injury, however slight, to your feet. Wash your feet regularly in warm water, dry them and powder them carefully. These are good rules, too, for any older or not-so-old feet whose owners want them to be healthy for long-life use. Ask your doctor and podiatrist for more tips to keep your feet healthy and comfortable.

Wash your feet regularly in warm water to minimize the risk of fungal infection.

Dry your feet carefully, paying special attention to the spaces between your toes.

Powder them carefully to dry out those wrinkly areas that are difficult to get to with a towel.

Nursing an older person

The nursing of older people can be problematical. Here are some practical tips that may help you if you are a relative or even if you are the older patient.

Practical nursing

To make a good approach to a person you are nursing, you should do so face-to-face at the right height. The best position for doing this if the person is in a bed or chair is to kneel on one knee. This position is hard on the stockings and trousers, not to say the knees, but is, by far, the best for making real contact. Speak clearly but not necessarily loudly, and look into his or her eyes. Give the person time to consider the answer he or she wishes to make. Use plain, adult language with a touch of humor, adding the reassuring pressure of your hand when things are difficult. Talking down to elderly people as if they were children is deplorable. Tying up an older woman's hair in girlish ribbons is equally unacceptable. The key is to be kind and sympathetic always, and always to allow the person to do what he or she is able without any help. This will require self-discipline on your part.

If you are nursing an older person you should introduce yourself by name and do as much as possible to help the person orient him or herself. When people are confused you may have to introduce yourself several times until all the information sinks in. Older people do not naturally pick up simple ideas about where they are, what time lunch is, even which way the lavatory is, as younger people do.

When you approach a blind person, you should also introduce yourself clearly to prevent any anxiety or alarm: "Hello, Mother, it's Mary." If you approach a deaf person, you should be clearly in the line of vision when it is straight ahead, and you must make every effort to communicate with the deaf person by careful articulation of words, not shouting, offering the chance to lip read and writing words down and making signs. This will make communication a great deal easier.

Here is a list of the sort of things you should be on the lookout for if you are a patient or if you are nursing one.

Raised toilet seat

- It is far safer for the person to be up than confined to bed. The rule should be, every patient up unless the doctor says otherwise.
- For beds, see page 283.
- Tables are best if they are of the cantilevered type that can go over the bed or chair and still better if they will tilt back as a book rest or writing desk.
- For chairs, see page 282.
- Commodes are much better than bed pans if the person is confined to bed. Almost anything is better than a bed pan.
- A sanitary chair is one with a toilet seat in which a frail person can be taken from his or her bed to the toilet itself and is clearly better than anything except making the actual journey, walking. These chairs require that the doorways and bathrooms should be large enough to accommodate them.
- Toilets should be of the ordinary height, but some should have raised seats for special patients. It is helpful if the toilet is constructed with rails to assist the person to get up and down,

Commode

287

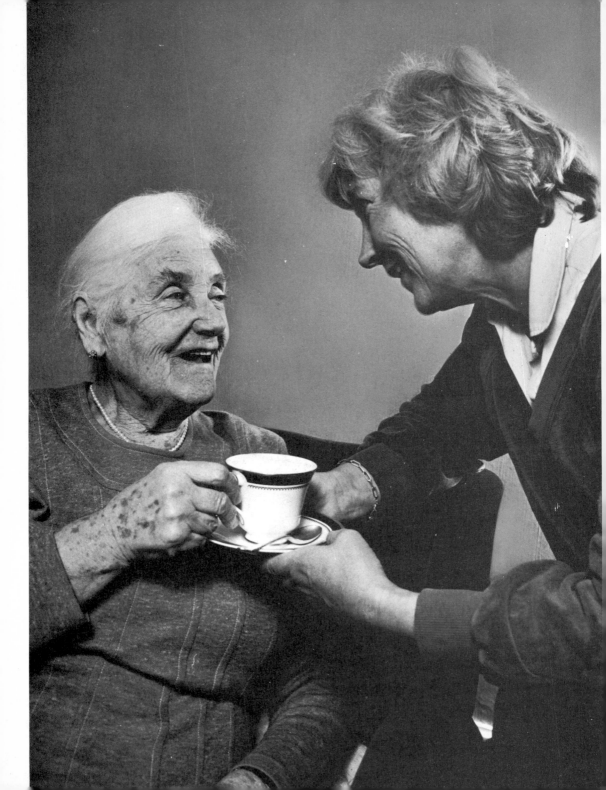

and these rails must allow a sanitary chair to go over the toilet. The toilet, if possible, should be off-center in the room so that a helper can comfortably get around to one side to help with clothing.

● For practical purposes, baths should be accessible on all sides, and contain aids like the widely used bath seat, bath board, hand rail or upright pole. There should be a non-slip mat of special material, and a non-slip surface in each bath. Many people are frightened of drowning in an ordinary long bath and prefer a sitting type bath. There are many kinds of sitting-type baths.

● To most people a shower bath suggests something under which they stand controlling the taps themselves. Many older patients can be *given* a shower and enjoy it. They can sit in a shower sink or on a waterproof stool holding onto a grab handle while they are bathed by another person who holds a flexible shower pipe and sponge.

● Devices such as hoists for lifting patients are very useful, especially if they are obese or frightened of being handled. There are many types of hoist – hydraulic, wall-mounted and electric; the latter being mounted on a gantry so that an intelligent but very disabled person could take him or herself from the bath to toilet to wheelchair.

It is helpful to make a list, such as the one below, to remind yourself of the stages of progress that are being made.

CHECKLIST FOR DAILY LIVING

Using this checklist you will be able to assess the every-day improvement that your "patient" makes.

Feeding
Self
With help
Adaptive equipment
Use of knife, fork, spoon, cup

Ambulation
Weight bearing
With help
Use of cane, crutch, brace
Wheelchair

Exercise
Passive
Active
Passive resistant
Active resistant

Dressing and hygiene
Self
With help
Adaptive equipment
Teeth, hair, shaving etc.

Transfer activities
Bed to wheelchair
Wheelchair to bed
Commode
Lock wheelchair
Use of chair

Bath
Self
With help
Adaptive equipment
Tub shower room

Positioning
Bed
In wheelchair
In chair
Dependent

Writing, reading etc.
Self
With help
Adaptive equipment

A word about privacy

One of the difficult parts of getting older is that we may find it necessary, though no less difficult, to surrender the privacy of our homes and lives because home helpers, meals-on-wheels, health visitors and nurses may become necessary to live a normal life. Even if we are only indirectly concerned, for instance when caring for an older relative, we should be aware that the loss of privacy and independence can be a shocking and shameful experience. Self-reliance is one of the few sources of pride left to a person as he or she grows older.

Privacy is one of the aspects of living that most of us jealously guard and take great care to protect. In a social sense, there are times when it seems acceptable to let strangers in: if, for instance, we are ill and need the care of a doctor; if we are in legal trouble and have to allow the lawyers to share our secrets. But when you think about it, we do most of the important things in our lives away from the eyes of the world. Even if we do share with someone, it is usually a partner or a person who is very close to us through family links. At any rate, most of us decide when, and with whom, we share our lives. Any violation of this right to privacy can make us fight fiercely to cling to any last vestiges of it. This fight can become violent as we grow older because privacy becomes more important.

People who are self-possessed can find it crushing to realize that they are unable to look after themselves and give care to others. For such people, words, medicine and medical investigations seem futile and irrelevant. What is needed is time and old-fashioned care by creative people in the proper surroundings. However, these are nearly always scarce, expensive and undervalued.

Coping with sexual feelings The sexual feelings of people who are learning to live with long-term complaints are often ignored; worse, they are judged by moralistic doctors, nurses, and even family. Many studies have shown that sexual behavior continues into old age (see *A lifetime of loving*).

Nursing experience and long-term facilities have shown that the frail older person, although not able to participate in overt sexual behavior, will still demonstrate that he or she has sexual feelings and needs. An example would be the seventy-year-old man, who, despite being frail and suffering from Parkinsonism, suddenly makes a suggestive remark or pinches a nurse. Another example might be the older woman who insists on holding the doctor's hand at each visit for a long period of time. It is not uncommon for visitors to encounter masturbation or exposure behavior in long-term care patients.

The elderly person should be provided the opportunity to pursue sexual outlets that have been his or her right throughout the years prior to that time. It is not the place of relatives or health professionals to judge what is normal and what is abnormal.

Families may need help and counseling concerning the sexuality of parents, grandparents and other relatives. Many family members have great difficulty accepting that their parents were, and still are, sexual human beings. Also all of us must appreciate the effect of the mass media on the image of the older person as perceived by others and by the older generation themselves. Older people in many cases have internalized the attitude that they are not attractive to others and that they are sexually diminished.

In addition to the fact that sex continues to be an important part of the lives of most older people, other factors such as closeness, a feeling of being valued, intimacy and the psychological effects of touch are very important. Research has shown that older people are helped a great deal simply by warm human gestures such as touching or holding hands, and maintaining direct eye contact face to face. This appears not only to be true in patients who have had strokes, but in older people in general. The person does better and communication appears to be tremendously improved by touching and keeping good visual contact whenever this is possible.

Incontinence

Incontinence is something we meet more and more often as we grow older — from the stress incontinence that is quite often experienced by women in their late forties and fifties, generally due to disturbance of the pelvic floor muscles during delivery, to the frank urinary incontinence and fecal incontinence that may be experienced by people in their late sixties and seventies. This affects approximately 40 percent of people in the very old age group. It may be due to restriction in bed or a change from familiar surroundings. Incontinence that starts during any acute illness usually disappears when the illness is cured.

Easing the problem

Incontinence may be made worse or even brought on when a person has to face ill-health and a strange environment like a hospital or home. Mobility is extremely important. Many older people have difficulty in going to the toilet quickly enough.

291

INCONTINENCE AIDS

There are several factors to be considered when choosing aids to help incontinent people; individual needs are of prime importance. Age and condition, both physical and mental, should be taken into account.

Urinal
This is valuable when a person cannot move.

Female urinal
This is small and light, easy to use in bed.

Feminal
This is a polythene bag inserted in a plastic holder.

Fitted pants
These are made of soft material with a waterproof outside pouch.

Stretch pants
These are light, open-stretch pants designed to fit any person.

French knickers
These have a wide leg opening for convenience.

Dress
The flaps at the back can be moved of this wrap-over back.

Kylie bed sheet
This combines a drawsheet with an underpad.

This is particularly significant after a stroke, where disability is complicated by over-activity of the bladder. Drugs that increase the output of urine (diuretics) also make incontinence worse. The design and layout of accommodation and the amount of supporting care have a direct bearing on the extent to which these factors create problems for older people.

Where immobility is a problem, care must be taken to ensure that the patient has ready access to a toilet. This may mean getting a commode at home. Wherever possible, however, attempts should be made to adapt the lavatory to the person's needs. If it is inaccessible you may even have to think about moving it to a more suitable situation.

Toilet training plays an important part in helping to care for an incontinent person. It is particularly important when the capacity of the bladder is kept low by irritability in the walls or weakness of the sphincter. In this case people should be encouraged to visit the toilet once every two hours. You may have to wake the person during the course of the night. This is less distressing than for him or her to awake in a urine-soaked bed in the middle of the night or the morning.

Bed pans should be avoided because they make emptying the bladder and the bowel physiologically and psychologically difficult. They also cause increased dependence on other people. Commodes have a limited value in the management of severely disabled people at home. In most other situations, they should be avoided, because patients begin to consider themselves permanent invalids and this discourages them from trying to be mobile and independent.

Whenever severe and embarrassing incontinence is due to prostatic enlargement, surgery should be considered now that prostatectomy can be performed by an internal cutting knife which is passed up a very fine tube inside the urethra (see page 217). Surgical repair should also be considered when stress incontinence in a woman is due to a relaxed pelvic floor.

For an incontinent woman, nothing of a practical nature has been developed, except more water-absorbent materials, which can be used as incontinence pads. The simplest form of pad is a sheet of water-absorbent paper with a waterproof backing. Although this pad only absorbs a limited quantity of urine, it can be of value in reducing the amount of laundry necessary for bedfast patients with relatively mild incontinence.

Loss of bowel control

Fecal incontinence or loss of bowel control is much less common than that of bladder control. Some of the causes would include hard, stone-like feces, diarrhea, leakage of liquid paraffin, damage to the pelvic floor, and loss of the inhibition reflex, which stops the bowel from emptying itself all the time.

Fecal incontinence due to hardening of feces in the rectum and large bowel is really the result of leakage of liquid feces from the anus. The large intestine secretes excess mucus in response to the presence of hard feces. It can usually be treated by using an enema. Once the colon has been emptied of feces, it is essential that regular bowel movements be maintained. This can be helped by choosing the right diet.

Pressure sores

Pressure, or bed sores are better prevented than treated. A.N. Exton-Smith, a professor of geriatrics at University College Hospital, London, has shown that it is possible to predict which people will be most endangered by giving them a score related to certain of their abilities.

PRONE TO PRESSURE SORES?

The scoring is best done in the first place by a doctor, but a rough score can be achieved by an observant relative. It will vary according to progress and so it needs to be repeated.

General Condition	Score
Good	0
Fair	1
Poor	2
Bad	3

Mental State	Score
Alert	0
Confused	1
Apathetic	2
Stuporose	3

Activity	Score
Ambulant	0
Walks with help	1
Chairfast	2
In bed all day	3

Mobility in Bed	Score
Full	0
Slight limitation	1
Very limited	2
Immobile	3

Incontinence	Score
Continent	0
Occasional incontinence	1
Usually incontinent of urine	2
Doubly incontinent	3

Total =

The interpretation of the test is as follows:
I. The higher the score the greater the risk of pressure sores. The best score is O, the worst I5.

2. Scores of 7 and upward indicate a severe risk. Preventive measures should be concentrated most on patients with high scores.

Causes of bed sores

Bed sores are due to pressure, causing loss of blood flow, death of cells, then ulceration of the part that is being pressed. The most commonly injured place is the lower part of the back and buttocks when the patient is lying down on the back, and on the hip prominence when the person is lying on the side. Other commonly injured areas will be the heels (especially the backs), the ankles, the knees, the backs of the elbows, and the ribs as illustrated below.

In the sitting position, half of our body weight is supported on eight percent of the sitting surface and pressures can exceed 300 millimeters of mercury. The inevitable result of sitting or lying immobile for any length of time will be the development of pressure sores over the bony prominences.

In a well person, sitting or lying still will be uncomfortable and we automatically shift our weight. However, in the older person with diminished sensation, debilitation or disablement, shifting of weight may not happen and ulceration will result. In order for the wound to heal, pressure must be eliminated, and anything that prevents the wound healing should be minimized. These factors would be anemia, dehydration, any chronic illness and some medications such as steroids.

The tinted areas indicate the areas of the body most vulnerable to pressure in somebody lying or sitting for long periods of time.

It is important to avoid those other factors which irritate the condition, namely moisture next to the skin, friction, or even crumbs in the bed.

Treatment of bed sores

The main part of treatment is frequent changes in position at least every two hours to minimize the development of ulcers in other areas. Proper skin care is important, and the area should be washed three times a day with a very mild soap and then a thin layer of ointment should be applied to lubricate the skin. Only if the ulcer is becoming infected should anti-bacterial ointments be used on the sore itself.

Artificial sheepskin bootees relieve pressure on the heel.

Gentle massage of the area is beneficial on the basis that it stimulates blood circulation and increases blood flow there. Other treatment can be aimed at preventing pressure ulcers elsewhere – the elbows, knees and heels should be padded. A water mattress and sponge rubber or gel-filled cushions are also helpful in distributing the pressure more easily when in a sitting position. All areas that are commonly affected by pressure sores should be checked at frequent intervals so that they can be looked after immediately if a sore develops.

Adapting your environment

First and foremost a home provides shelter and comfort, but it's also a private place where you can find self-expression and independence. As we grow older it is important that a home should be a place where we feel safe and secure, so be security conscious. If you are a particularly nervous person have a burglar alarm and smoke alarm fitted throughout your house, put a spy-hole in your front door and perhaps even install an intercom. Feeling at ease means being able to relax.

Plan ahead so that you can make changes to your house gradually, over a period of several years, so that everything is in place and ready for use when most needed. Start by putting all electric sockets about 3ft (1m) from the floor so that they can be easily found and reached. Always have two sets of lighting in every room, to provide better light, and a spare light source in case you blow a fuse. Always get an expert to do any gas and electricity repairs.

Have plenty of comfortable places around the house where you can take a break from daily chores. If necessary, lengthen or shorten chair and table legs and fit them with plastic or rubber tips to make them non slip. Hunt around for good chair designs; it's well worth investing in an electrically operated elevating seat that helps you to sit down and get up.

Many accidents happen in our homes as we get older because our senses of smell become blunted as we age. Without a strong sense of smell, you may fail to detect leaking gas for long periods and this is a serious hazard. If you have the opportunity to plan well ahead, or if you are intending to purchase a retirement home, opt for the safety of electricity and all-electric appliances throughout your property.

Be on the look-out for whatever other labor-saving devices there are apart from those mentioned in this chapter. Planning your resources carefully means that you need not carry heavy cleaning equipment backward and forward. If you can afford it, keep two sets, one upstairs and one down.

PLANNING A KITCHEN

Preparing a kitchen for the time when you have stiffer joints and weaker muscles needs careful consideration. Everything used frequently should be close at hand, along two adjacent walls of the kitchen.

Work surfaces will be much more comfortable if they are lower than standard. A knee-hole under the sink will make life easier because you can sit while washing up or preparing vegetables. A refrigerator and stove should be at a height you can reach easily. Standard stoves with ovens and broilers below can be difficult to manage so have a small, table-top toaster, oven or grill.

Kitchen aids

Cutlery and plates
Specially made cutlery and kitchen tools are available with thick, grooved handles that are easy to hold.

Mincer
This is useful to chop, shred or mix small amounts of food.

Serving cart
A solidly built serving cart serves a dual purpose; it saves walking to and fro unnecessarily and it can be a useful walking aid.

Eye-level oven

Transparent saucepans

Pull-out drawer for storing pans

Pan stabilizer

Reacher so that you don't have to stretch

Pull-out work surface

Combined washing machine/spin dryer

Long cord on the shade to avoid stretching

Spring-based, wall-mounted can opener

Safety lock

Long-handled lever taps that do not need twisting

Light, pull-out plastic drawers make everything visible at a glance

Long-levered door handle

Carousel. If you need to sit at the sink leave space for a knee-hole

Special unbreakable glass

Non-slip floor

Long-handled dustpan and brush

Light-weight iron and flex

Ironing board in a sit-down position

PLANNING A BATHROOM

I remember well the bathroom of my childhood: spartan and cold, freezing ice on the window. Now I prefer it to be warm and inviting.

A bidet is no longer a luxury. It's very comfortable, quick and easy to use. Don't use rugs; even rubber-backed ones slip and wrinkle at the edges. Fitted carpets are a good investment. When filling the bath put the cold water in first and then fill with hot water until you reach a comfortable temperature.

Bathroom safety aids

Shower aids
We all enjoy long soaks in the bath but often prefer a quick shower. It is worth investing in a shower unit with a thermostatic control or an anti-scald device. There are various types of permanent folding or removable shower seats available to suit individual needs and it's important to have a safety rail if you have to step over a threshold, into a bath for instance. A shelf with toiletries should be inside the unit to avoid unnecessary stretching.

Bath seat
There are many types of bath seat on the market but one that fits inside the bath is usually stronger and much more secure than one suspended from the bath's rim.

Bath mat
Non-slip or suction mats or adhesive-backed, rubber-silicone treads in your bath or shower are a vital precaution against slipping.

Side grab bar
for leverage

Large shelf for adjustable
shaving/make-up mirror
and toiletries

Side grab bars for
safety and support

Don't keep any pills
that are no longer
required

A secure seat
that fits inside
the bath

Non-slip floor

Padded
bath seat

Keep a stable seat
here to help you dress

Long-levered taps for
the basin and bath

A bidet is no longer a
luxury but a necessity

Thermostatically controlled
adjustable shower

PLANNING A BEDROOM

As I get older I tend more and more to use my bedroom as a sitting room. This is where I keep a book case of interesting books and magazines.

Now is the time to get that electric blanket that you have been promising yourself. Do follow all of the manufacturer's instructions and have it checked in the autumn ready for use through the winter.

Choosing the right bed is important. It must be easy to get in and out of and it might be useful to have a solid piece of furniture next to it for leverage.

Daily living aids

Dealing with shoes
A long-handled shoe-horn (left) saves bending down, as does this device (above) when it comes to taking shoes off.

Front-fastening brassiere
This makes dressing simpler for weak and arthritic hands.

Extend-a-hand
Such an aid can be adjusted to reach any length as though it were tailor-made.

Bed rest
This is useful when reading or watching T.V. It's the same shape as the back and sides of a comfortable armchair.

Zipper pulls
These make zippers easier to open and close. Wide loops can be made from spare material.

Always remember to switch off an electric blanket before you go to sleep

Only put things that you seldom use on high shelves

A two-way light switch near the bed

T.V. remote control to save you getting up

Transparent pull-out drawers make clothes visible at a glance

A shelf will stop your accidentally resting against a hot radiator

Keep a flashlight by the bed

Have a T.V. on wheels for when you feel like an early night or a lie-in

Deep pile, fitted carpets will keep the room warm

Comfortable chair

This bed table can be adjusted to an angle suitable for reading or for meals in bed

PLANNING A LIVING ROOM

This is a room that is going to be used more and more so it's worth taking the time and trouble to make it as comfortable as possible. Rooms facing west and south catch the sun, so they make ideal living rooms.

Everything used regularly needs to be close at hand: T.V. control, stereo, knitting, telephone and reading lamp. Make sure that there are no trailing wires to trip over and also that there are no sharp edges on the furniture. If you have an open fire make sure that the guard has a fine, spark-proof mesh. Finally, draft proof doors and windows.

Chairlifts

Most of us find climbing stairs a problem at some point in our lives but this needn't necessarily mean confinement to one floor.

Stairlifts are available that can be fitted unobtrusively to most shapes of staircases. The motor and control mechanisms are compactly housed under the seat so that they don't take up too great an area and don't hinder other stair users.

Two-way light switch

A half-step is useful, if you have restricted leg movement

Put an extra rail along the staircase

Long-levered door handles

Hallways

These should be well-lit and have two-way switches at the top and bottom of the stairs. If your hallway is narrow leave it clutter free; chairs and small tables are unnecessary.

Wooden extensions to chair arms provide support

Lightweight carpet sweeper

Security locks on all doors

A kitchen hatch will save carrying to and fro

Make sure you have sufficient lighting for reading

Have easy-to-manage indoor plants.

Carpet must be well fastened

A comfortable, supportive cushion on a favorite chair

Comfortable rocking chair for a mid-afternoon snooze

Non-slip mat

Have a volume control fitted to the telephone earpiece

PLANNING A GARDEN

Gardening is a very relaxing and creative hobby. If a garden is small enough to be manageable there will always be a corner that needs attention when you have some spare time. Some thought on the design of the garden, choosing the right tools and selecting flowers and plants that need little attention, all mean less effort in the long term. Flower beds should not be too wide, so that they can be tended from the path, and lawns without flower beds or shrubs in the middle are easier to mow.

Staking plants and flowers can be difficult because it involves a lot of bending down and a good deal of balancing, so have self-supporting plants.

Light-weight tools with extra-thick handles are easy to hold with a weak grip and there are many plastic pots and trays and even light, peat-based compost available in gardening shops. Don't stay in one position for too long if it's uncomfortable; do a little at a time and do stop before getting tired!

Gardening aids

Bulb planter Pivoting spade Fork handle grip

Look out for dual-purpose tools because they can save money, and space in the tool shed.

Kneeler/stool

Have a seat somewhere on the raised flower bed

This is a tool for lifting leaves without bending

A well-balanced light-weight wheelbarrow is easy to pull and tip

Flower beds should be well edged so that any trailing, slippery plants do not obstruct the path

Window boxes can be tended from indoors

A small, well-drained lawn is easy to maintain

Front and back doors, as well as windows, should have strong locks. A spy hole is a good idea

Pathways should be wide and made of non-slip slabs

OTHER USEFUL HOUSEHOLD AIDS

Shopping cart with a seat
Here is something useful in several ways: it has a built-in seat; it is a useful walking aid when being pushed along; and it has ample storage space.

Furniture blocks
If tables, chairs and beds are not at the most convenient height they can be raised by fitting wooden blocks to the legs. These need to be hollow to a third down so that they securely support the legs.

Jar opener
Fixed underneath a shelf, a jar can be opened by twisting with one hand.

Dolly
Such a labor-saving device means less carrying. It's useful for a pail or a vacuum cleaner and can be pushed along the floor by a foot or a cane.

Leg support
This needs to be securely fastened before it can provide adequate support.

Plugs
If you have handles fitted to plugs they immediately become easier to pull from their sockets.

Tap turner
This can be readily bought, made in plastic or wood, to suit any tap in the house.

Suitcase on wheels
When you go on vacation, wheels and a towing handle make life easier.

Security chain
This, with a spy-hole, means that you can check who your visitors are before opening the door.

Entry phone
This is not only useful for security, it saves walking flights of stairs to let visitors in.

SAFETY TIPS

More accidents, most of which could have been prevented, occur in the home than anywhere else, and it is now especially important to take adequate safety precautions. Here is a list of useful household safety tips:

● Don't lean over the front two burners of the stove to get to pans cooking on the back two;

● When cooking in an open frying pan, keep a lid the same size nearby in case the fat catches fire. Cutting off the oxygen by putting the lid over the flames quickly extinguishes them. Don't forget to turn off the source of the heat immediately;

● Keep a fire extinguisher in the kitchen, but never attempt to tackle any fire that might get out of hand. Go for assistance immediately;

● Cook vegetables in a steamer to avoid having to drain boiling water;

● Use oven gloves rather than pot holders when taking hot dishes out of the oven because they provide a much better grip;

● Use a ladle when transferring hot sauces from one pan to another to avoid spillage;

● A long barbecue utensil is ideal for turning food in the oven without having to get too close to the heat;

● Don't have deep shelves that make it necessary to stack utensils, and fit narrow rims along the edges so that nothing can slip off accidentally;

● Don't overload electrical circuits;

● Make sure that no electrical cords are lying where they may be tripped over;

● Only use good quality plugs;

● Make sure all plugs are wired correctly;

● Check flexes and fittings regularly;

● Have your wiring circuit tested every five years;

● If you have a time-switched heater make sure it is well clear of curtains and furnishings;

● Switch off the television and stereo when not using them and remove the plugs from their sockets;

● Have all your household appliances serviced regularly by an expert;

● Be sure that all carpeting is well fixed to the floor, and especially to stairs;

● Tack down all loose rugs;

● Have a telephone extension in every room if you possibly can, and emergency numbers on pads nearby;

● If you live alone arrange for a neighbor to stop by at least once a day.

Useful addresses

This section of useful addresses is relevant to the various chapters in the book. If you feel that you need advice and guidance on a specific problem, one of these organizations will be able to help you, or at least, put you in touch with one that can.

Also, a useful list of the 662 area agencies on aging established under the Older Americans Act is available from the United States Government Printing Office, Washington, D.C. 20402, for $6.50 (stock number 052-070-05816-1).

GROWING THROUGH LIFE

Gray Panthers
3635 Chestnut St.
Philadelphia, PA 19104

National Alliance of Senior Citizens
101 Park Washington Court
Suite 125
Falls Church, VA 22046

National Association of Mature People
Box 26792
Oklahoma City, OK 73126

National Council of Senior Citizens
925 15th St., N.W.
Washington, D.C. 20036

National Institute of Aging
900 Rockville Pike
Bethesda, MD 20205

KEEPING PHYSICALLY FIT

Al-Anon Family Group Hq.
P.O. Box 182
Madison Sq. Station
New York, N.Y. 10159

Alcohol and Drug Problems Association
of North America
1101 15th St., N.W., Ste. 204
Washington, D.C. 20005

Alcoholics Anonymous
General Service Office
P.O. Box 459
Grand Central Station
New York, N.Y. 10163

American Heart Association
7320 Greenville Ave.
Dallas, TX 75231

National Council on Alcoholism, Inc.
733 Third Avenue
New York, N.Y. 10017

National Institute on Drug Abuse and
Alcoholism
Parklawn Building
5600 Fishers Lane
Rockville, MD 20852

National Institute on Drug Abuse
5600 Fishers Lane
Rockville, MD 20852

KEEPING A TRANQUIL MIND

Family Service America
44 East 23 St.
New York, N.Y. 10010

Federation of Protestant Welfare
Agencies
281 Park Ave. S.
New York, N.Y. 10010

Jewish Information and Referral Service
130 E. 59 St.
New York, N.Y. 10022

National Conference of Catholic
Charities
1346 Connecticut Ave., N.W.
Washington, D.C. 20036

RETIREMENT

ACTION
806 Connecticut Ave., N.W.
Washington, D.C 20525
(Federal agency administering senior
volunteer programs)

American Association of Retired Persons
1909 K St., N.W.
Washington, D.C. 20049

Older Women's League
1325 G St., N.W.
Lower Level B
Washington, D.C. 20005

Service Corps of Retired Executives
Small Business Administration
1441 L St., N.W.
Washington, D.C. 20416

LIVING WITH LONG-TERM AILMENTS

The following companies distribute aids
to living.
(Check your telephone yellow pages
under Hospital or Surgical Supplies also.)

The Able Child
154 Chambers Street
New York N.Y. 10007
(Cutlery and the Maddok Aids catalog.)

Bailey Manufacturing Co.
118 Lee Street
Lodi, OH 44254

Cleo Living Aids
3957 Mayfield Rd.
Mayfield, OH 44121

Fashionable Aids for the
Eldery and Handicapped
Rocky Hill, N.J. 08553

Seniorama, Ltd. USA
P.O. Box 282
Snug Harbor, MA 02332

All addresses were correct at the time of
printing.

Index

Acknowledgments

Dorling Kindersley would like to thank the following for their help and assistance: Warren Mitchell and Gordon Dungate for their hard work on the typesetting and make-up; Jonathan Dean; Choice magazine for pre-retirement; Disabled Living Foundation; Les Greenyer; The Harrow Health Care Centre; Michael Sobell Day Centre; Pearl Posner; Rita Roberts; Saga Holidays plc; Dr John Schetrumpf; and all those who took the time and trouble to be models for reference shots and photographs. Hair by James of Vidal Sassoon for jacket photograph of Dr Stoppard.

Illustrators
David Baird
Andrew Farmer
Elaine Keenan
Edwina Keene
Patricia Ludlow
Coral Mula

Photographers
Maria Bartha
Geoff Dann
Nancy Durrell-McKenna
Peter Fisher
Paul Fletcher
Andrew de Lory

Picture Agencies
John Watney
Zefa UK Ltd

About the Author

The author of DAY BY DAY BABY CARE and DR. MIRIAM STOPPARD'S PREGNANCY AND BIRTH BOOK, Dr. Miriam Stoppard is a health educator, doctor, mother, businesswoman, journalist, and television personality. She lives in England with her playwright-husband Tom Stoppard.